NO PLACE FOR A WOMAN

INTERPRETING THE CIVIL WAR
Texts and Contexts

EDITOR
Angela M. Zombek
University of North Carolina, Wilmington

Aaron Astor
Maryville College

Wiliam B. Kurtz
University of Virginia

Joseph M. Beilein Jr.
Pennsylvania State University

Brian Craig Miller
Mission College

Douglas R. Egerton
Le Moyne College

Jennifer M. Murray
Oklahoma State University

J. Matthew Gallman
University of Florida

Jonathan W. White
Christopher Newport University

Hilary N. Green
University of Alabama

Timothy Williams
University of Oregon

The **Interpreting the Civil War** series focuses on America's long Civil War era, from the rise of antebellum sectional tensions through Reconstruction.

These studies, which include both critical monographs and edited compilations, bring new social, political, economic, or cultural perspectives to our understanding of sectional tensions, the war years, Reconstruction, and memory. Studies reflect a broad, national perspective; the vantage point of local history; or the direct experiences of individuals through annotated primary source collections.

No Place for a Woman

Harriet Dame's Civil War

To Hans and Chris,

Mike Pride

Mike Pride

The Kent State University Press

Kent, Ohio

ISBN 978-1-60635-451-3

Manufactured in the United States of America

Cataloging information for this title is available at the Library of Congress.

26 25 24 23 22   5 4 3 2 1

To Monique Pride,
my keeper

Contents

Maps

By Charlotte Thibault

Foreword

"I want something to do." With these words, declared in the voice of young Tribulation Periwinkle, Louisa May Alcott began her 1863 autobiographical novella, *Hospital Sketches*. Tribulation's mother, father, and three siblings all offered suggestions, befitting the skills and options of a young, white, middle-class woman living in Concord, Massachusetts. Finally, Tribulation's young brother suggested that she become a military nurse. So she signed up and her journey began.

I have often wondered what we should make of Tribulation's original announcement. Was she in search of an outlet for her ardent patriotism? Was she anxious to contribute to the Union's war effort? Or was she a bit bored and in search of something to do? I have suspected that it was really the last. Alcott journeyed to Washington, D.C., where she threw herself into nursing at a Georgetown hospital. She stayed only a few months before she was felled by illness, but in her time on the hospital wards Alcott—writing as Tribulation—created the best account we have of life in a Civil War hospital.

More than a year before Alcott left home in search of adventures, Harriet Dame of Concord, New Hampshire, stepped forward to serve as a matron with the newly formed Second New Hampshire Volunteer Infantry Regiment. It was barely two weeks after the fall of Fort Sumter. Dame would spend the full four years of the Civil War serving the New Hampshire volunteers and the Union cause on a host of battlefields, encampments, and hospitals. Nearly thirty years after the war ended, Dame—still serving the nation and her state—penned a reflective five-thousand-word letter explaining her long career service. "When the war first broke out, or was talked of, even," she wrote, "I began to look about me to see what a woman could do."[1] That short passage captures Harriet Dame's public life from 1861 through 1865. She went off to war in search of things that she could do. Once she had ventured from home, Dame persistently found ways both large and small to contribute to the lives of those around her. She nursed; she sewed; she cooked; she gathered donations; she sacrificed her own comforts for those around her.

Mike Pride is the ideal author to tell Harriet Dame's story. A retired editor of New Hampshire's *Concord Monitor,* he knows his way around exhaustive research and New Hampshire history. And he knows how to tell a fascinating story. As a historian of the Civil War era, Pride is a steady guide through this marvelous life. In truth, *No Place for a Woman* combines several tales, stitched together so seamlessly that the reader is unlikely to fully grasp Pride's expertise. Dame's life story is, of course, at the center of things. Throughout the war and into the decades beyond, she maintained a dedication to the Second New Hampshire and other troops from her state, often knowing the regiment's men by name.

Dame traveled and camped with the men of the Second, nursing them back to health, sewing when needed, cooking, and lending her leadership in times of strife. But there were times when she was not with the regiment. She spent much of early 1863 helping to organize and direct the rooms of the New Hampshire Soldiers' Aid Association in Washington. There she visited soldiers in hospitals, aided visitors from the state in search of loved ones, and ran a large voluntary enterprise collecting and distributing goods to hospitalized men from the Granite State. Dame left the regiment to travel down the East Coast to South Carolina and into Florida to inspect medical facilities in Union war hospitals and assess future needs. By war's end, she had taken charge of the nursing staff and the kitchen at a major Union hospital in Virginia. She was, in short, perpetually in search of how she might be useful.

Even in those months when Dame was not personally with the Second, Pride tells us the regiment's story, providing an elegant history of New Hampshire's longest-serving Civil War regiment. As with many other fighting regiments, the striking thing is how much history these men made and witnessed. They fought at the First Battle of Bull Run and then headed south to the Virginia Peninsula in 1862, taking heavy casualties at Williamsburg and fighting during the Seven Days battles. They were at the Second Battle of Bull Run and Fredericksburg before fighting valiantly at Gettysburg's Peach Orchard. In 1864, after Ulysses S. Grant took command of Union forces, the Second suffered through the Union disaster at Cold Harbor. The Second's story also offers a microhistory of the Union's diverse volunteer regiments. The original recruits served for three years, and many reenlisted as the regiment reformed. In 1863 they took an extended furlough home to vote in a crucial gubernatorial election. Throughout their service, often with the aid of Harriet Dame, the men maintained a steady contact with the home front, accepting all manner of voluntary assistance both during and after the war.

In piecing together the Second's history, Pride turns to a wealth of evidence, from letters, diaries, regimental histories, newspapers, personal recollections, and all manner of invaluable documents. The result is a story of a regiment and of several individual New Hampshire men, many of whom knew Harriet Dame well. She nursed more than a few in their dying days. Others survived the war and attended annual gatherings commemorating their service. Dame became an integral part of that rich postwar life, remaining an honored member of the regiment and its commemorations.

Until the regiment left the service in December 1865, nine months after the war ended, Harriet Dame had remained faithful to the Second. She made herself part of its history by perpetually asking, and then carrying out, whatever "a woman could do." For the historian, or for the reader of history, Dame's public career is highly distinctive while also illustrative of myriad wartime themes involving activist women. This is one woman's story, but also a story that reveals glimpses of the wartime lives of thousands of women, in pieces large and small.

When Louisa May Alcott, alias Tribulation Periwinkle, set off to Washington in 1862, she joined a host of women—in the North and in the South—who responded to the war's challenges by embarking on a new voluntaristic path, bending society's cultural rules in large and small ways. Quite a few in the Northern states pioneered the career of professional nursing for women. It is easy to imagine that these women followed gender-encoded, maternalistic instincts to the needs of the sick and wounded. But in truth the business of military nursing, particularly in a professional sense, was quite new for women during the Civil War. Nurses who worked with doctors on hospital wards or in makeshift battlefield tents were overwhelmingly men, not women. (Meanwhile, African American women in substantial numbers found employment in these hospitals, but without the title or compensation of official "nurses.") The creation of a Civil War cohort of professional female nurses owed everything to the considerable efforts of Superintendent of Nursing Dorothea Dix, who established rigorous professional and personal guidelines for her recruits. Women like Alcott and Dame carved out roles for themselves, working with wounded men in various guises outside of Dix's official rubric.

Alcott and hundreds of other female nurses entered formal hospital structures on the home front or nearer the fighting with a hierarchy of trained nurses. They worked with, and were subordinate to, male doctors. Some of their letters and diaries describe both tensions among nurses and clashes with male doctors who both resented working with women and grew jealous of their authority.

Although properly recalled as a Civil War nurse, Harriet Dame's war was quite different from these other women. As "matron" of the Second New Hampshire, she threw herself into whatever task needed to be done. She tended to wounded men on battlefields and in emergency hospitals. She nursed men stricken with the war's many infectious diseases. As Pride explains, she also sewed, cooked, counseled the men, and raised money on their behalf. Perhaps most striking, Dame spent long stretches as the only woman in the vicinity. Sometimes she shared space and responsibilities with another woman, for better or worse, but for much of her war she enjoyed autonomy. She also encountered and got to know some of the celebrated women of the war, including Dix, Clara Barton, and Sophronia Bucklin. Dame befriended and worked with various men, including doctors, ministers, military officers, and enlistees down to the lowliest private. Many left behind accounts of her labors and their friendships with her. For all these relationships, Dame constantly found her own space and seemed most content when she controlled her own actions without excessive direction from others.

Harriet Dame's story is a marvelous window into how Civil War voluntarism really worked. Although the war saw the creation of various large voluntary societies, particularly in the North, the machinery of wartime voluntarism really depended on energetic individuals—usually women—working with local or perhaps statewide bodies. Dame consistently turned to New Hampshire contacts to collect money and materials to supply her men. When she ran the New Hampshire Soldiers' Aid Association in Washington, the overarching voluntary structure depended on statewide efforts rather than a federal system. It was New Hampshire's governor who employed Dame to travel to South Carolina, Florida, and other points to check on the treatment of that state's soldiers in various military hospitals.

After the Civil War, Harriet Dame earned deserved recognition from the citizens of New Hampshire for her labors in aid of the war effort and her ongoing public work for the New Hampshire Volunteers. Dame's story is not unknown today. Her name appears in various works on New Hampshire during the Civil War. But she is hardly a household name, even among those of us who study the Civil War home front and the role of women.

Immediately after the Civil War, several publishing houses in the North produced large volumes celebrating the wartime contributions of Northern women. In 1866, noted author Frank Moore published *Women of the War*, including extended biographies of about forty notable nurses and volunteers. The following year Linus P. Brockett and Mary C. Vaughan released *Woman's Work in the Civil War: A Record of Heroism, Patriotism, and Patience*. This hefty volume, which ran to nearly eight hundred pages, considered an array of topical chapters and a huge number of women who served as nurses, organizers, philanthropists, spies, and all manner of female patriots.[2] As a historian who has worked at the cusp of home-front history and women's history for many decades, I always liked to think of these two books—and a few similar ones—as an outstanding historic marker. They recorded what Northern women had done during the war, and their publications perhaps attested to some modest shift in how Northerners thought about women in public life. With the war safely won, savvy publishers produced these hefty tomes celebrating the wartime work of Northern women, seemingly speaking to a ready market of readers anxious to see those stories.

But then there is Harriet Dame's wonderful wartime story. Frank Moore devoted not a page to her service among the forty or so women he profiled. Brockett and Vaughan's much more encyclopedic volume included a detailed index. It included a Harriet Dame on one page of text, in a long list of heroic women. But that list said that this Harriet Dame was from Wisconsin.[3] Somehow Harriet Dame, who worked so nobly with the Second New Hampshire and for her state, failed to receive her due in these postwar tomes.

It is right and fitting that Mike Pride has brought her story to life for a new and appreciative audience.

J. Matthew Gallman
Professor Emeritus
University of Florida

Introduction

The woman lost her identity in the nurse
—HARRIET PATIENCE DAME,
1893 Boston Journal interview

As spectators arrived on the lawn of the New Hampshire State House one fair summer day in 1892, they beheld a large statue wrapped in an enormous American flag. For the moment, Old Glory covered the bronze likeness of John Parker Hale, the state's antislavery senator and orator, extending his arm to address the future. One chair on the platform for the speakers who would dedicate the statue awaited seventy-five-year-old Frederick Douglass, a living symbol of slavery and an icon of its abolition.[1] Anyone who chanced to look up at the right moment to the second floor of the State House would have seen a celebrity even more ancient than Douglass making her way to a choice vantage point on the balcony of the portico. Her name was Harriet Patience Dame.

A Concord writer spotted Dame and decided to interview her. "Among the interested spectators who viewed the scene from the state house balcony," Frances Abbott observed, "stood a woman whose army service has probably no equal in the country."[2] Although Dame's bones and balance had begun to fail her, Abbott detected in her a vigor that belied her age. "No one looking at her upright figure, bright, dark eyes and strong, kindly features, the cheerful self-reliance, would imagine that Miss Dame could be in her 78th year," she wrote.

Thirty-one years earlier, after more than half a lifetime fending for herself and giving to others, Dame had abruptly abandoned her boardinghouse a few blocks north of the State House to accompany the Second New Hampshire Volunteers to Washington.[3] She joined the regiment, a unit of a thousand men, as a "matron." In her case, this term proved to be a catchall. She cooked, sewed, befriended, mothered, and scrounged, but most important of all, she

1

Harriet Dame in 1893 ("Harriet P. Dame," MOLLUS-Mass Civil War Photograph Collection Volume 83, U.S. Army Heritage and Education Center, Carlisle, PA)

nursed the sick and wounded. Not until eight months after the war ended and the regiment mustered out did she return to civilian life. During those four and a half years, she never took a furlough. She left her duties just once, when her brother died.

The United States Treasury Department hired Dame as a clerk in 1867, and she was still on the job when the Hale statue was dedicated. She spent time in New Hampshire each summer, staying in Concord with her blind sister, who was eighty-two in 1892. "I suppose I am growing old now, and every year I go back I think I will take it easy, just as so many of the clerks do," Dame told Frances Abbott. "But then, it's no use. First I know, I get mad at myself and go to work harder than ever."[4]

These summer sojourns also afforded Dame the chance to meet with the gray and graying men she still called "my boys." In a hillside village looking out over Weirs Beach on Lake Winnipesaukee, the New Hampshire Veterans Association held annual reunions. The old soldiers of the state's regiments had built stately Victorian- and Queen Anne–style houses where they congregated for the meetings. Dame had paid for the Second New Hampshire's house. Many of the veterans were also members of the Grand Army of the Republic, a powerful national fraternal organization formed shortly after the war.

A few weeks after the Hale statue dedication, a group of veterans of the Second would escort Dame from the lakeside railroad station up to the house, where "the most attractive apartment has been set aside for her use for life."[5] She would carry a vintage parasol bearing a card that identified it as "Harriet P. Dame's only weapon in the Army of the Potomac, from 1861 to 1865." She had nursed the wounded in the chaotic aftermaths of the battles of Williamsburg, Oak Grove, Second Bull Run, Gettysburg, and Cold Harbor. Veterans of all the New Hampshire regiments, not just her own, knew and revered her. Dame had lived as they lived, traveled the roads they traveled, survived artillery fire, capture, defeat, and retreat. She had led a forlorn party of sick men across the Virginia Peninsula to keep them out of enemy hands. From a landing on the James River, she had accompanied sick and wounded soldiers to hospitals in the North. Late in the war, she had cared for men of many regiments in the hospitals of Washington, DC, and at a large military hospital a few miles from General Grant's headquarters at City Point, Virginia. She had journeyed as far south as St. Augustine, Florida, to report to the governor on the medical care of New Hampshire regiments. Throughout the war she had written to the loved ones of soldiers with good news and bad. When necessary, as it too often was, she had arranged for their bodies to be shipped home to their families.

Many veterans regarded the unveiling of the Hale statue at the State House as one more opportunity to revisit their glory days. Whether or not they had agreed with John Parker Hale's opposition to slavery before the war, they were now soldiers of freedom in the pageant of the day. Hale was about to become only the third New Hampshire figure to stand guard over the State House yard, and his enshrinement cast the liberation of enslaved people as the chief accomplishment of the war. The statue had been the brainstorm of Sen. William E. Chandler, a state Republican leader for forty years.[6] Chandler also happened to be Hale's son-in-law, and his seven-year-old son, John Parker Hale Chandler, would have the honor of tugging the rope that lifted the flag from his late grandfather's image. Senator Chandler had paid for the statue, shepherded its creation by a foundry in Munich, and donated it to the state. "Of heroic size," the bronze likeness stood eight feet four inches tall atop an even taller pedestal of Concord granite. The legend on one side quoted Hale from 1845, when the rush to annex Texas as a slave state had converted him to steadfast abolitionism: "The measure of my ambition will be full if when my wife and children shall repair to my grave to drop the tear of affection to my memory they may read on my tombstone, he who lies beneath surrendered office, place and power rather than bow down and worship slavery."

Just before noon, as Dame and the rest of the crowd settled in, the dedication speakers marched to their seats on the platform near the statue. Once young Chandler had unveiled Hale's visage to admiring eyes and several speakers had recounted the story of his life, the chairman introduced the principal speaker.[7] A longtime friend of Hale's and the current commander of the Grand Army of the Republic, Col. Daniel Hall was renowned as "a ripe scholar" and "a polished orator."[8] In a tart mixed metaphor, a dissenter to this view declared Hall "the longest wind in N. H. [who] like the brook runs on forever."[9] On this day he unleashed a stem-winder that would fill eighty pages in a printed transcript of the ceremony. It was by far the longest stretch of a speechifying marathon that lasted four hours. Before Hall could finish his oration, he collapsed, fell mute, and had to be helped from the platform.

Although the record is silent on whether Harriet Dame was sitting or standing on the portico, surely someone had provided her with a chair before then. What she thought of Frederick Douglass's speech, which came soon after Hall's, is likewise unknown, but her experiences during the war provide a few clues. While her letters suggest that she paid little attention to politics, she lived in slave country for nearly her entire time in the field. She encountered many formerly enslaved people, seemed sympathetic to their plight, and called them "negroes," the politest term for Black people in her day. At one post in Maryland, a hint of pride crept into her assertion that local farmers in search of their missing slaves steered clear of the Second New Hampshire's camp and sought more fruitful ground. It delighted her when a runaway told her that many other enslaved people had escaped with him.[10] Later, as the matron of a large hospital near the front, she went out of her way to get food to a dying Black sergeant.[11]

The unveiling was not Frederick Douglass's debut in New Hampshire. Almost exactly fifty years earlier, while working for the abolition leader William Lloyd Garrison, he had made the first of several visits to the state on the antislavery circuit to speak at a church in Pittsfield.[12] Things had gone poorly. His hosts, who had not fed him after his long journey by coach, rode off to the event without offering him the empty seat in their carriage. He walked two miles to the church, where the congregation shunned him. When he asked a hotel owner for a room afterward, the man turned him down because of his race. Douglass stopped at the church cemetery to rest and collect his thoughts. As the rain came down, a local foe of abolition noticed him there and finally offered him a bed for the night.

The chairman at the dedication of the Hale statue introduced Douglass as "a distinguished citizen" who had now returned as the state's guest after New Hampshire residents of a half century ago denied him "the welcome due his manhood." Douglass charmed the crowd, opening with a joke he probably used often with white audiences. Rather than give a speech, he said, he wished he had been "allowed to sit here and only give color to this occasion." He fondly recalled his travels with Hale to antislavery events before the war and "the thrilling sentiments [Hale] was accustomed to utter in connection with the great cause of liberty." He reminded his listeners that it had taken courage for Hale to break with the Democratic Party on the slavery question. Douglass knew his history, mentioning an antebellum incident in which "the honest farmers of the state of New Hampshire thought themselves justified in yoking up ninety oxen to drag away a negro schoolhouse." This had happened at the Noyes Academy in Canaan, where a third of the forty-two students were Black. After removing the schoolhouse, the mob hunted down the students and attacked the houses in which they lodged. Douglass reminded his audience that, on the stump as an abolitionist, "John P. Hale had something to meet in the state of New Hampshire as well as in the state of South Carolina."[13]

Although Dame had known Hale, too, and no doubt appreciated Douglass's stirring words, another face in the crowd that day brought back a sharper memory. At the opening of the ceremony, a young man held Nathaniel Berry by the arm and guided him to his front-row seat. Berry was ninety-five years old. An up-from-poverty tanner and saddle-maker in his working days, he had become New Hampshire's governor eight weeks after the Civil War began. "Venerable man, you have come down to us from another generation," the chairman of the ceremony said in recognizing him.[14] Dame would never forget the late spring day in 1861 when Berry rejected her request for a pass to go to the front with the Second New Hampshire. She had worked around his opposition, but at the unveiling thirty-one years later, she ribbed him about his refusal. "Do you remember, Governor, that when I wanted to go to the front at the beginning of the war, you would not give me a pass because you said it was no place for a woman?" she asked.[15] Wise enough in his dotage to concede the point, Berry answered, "I do, but you knew better than I. The Lord had called you."

In the halls of Congress years earlier, the New Hampshire senator leading the effort to win a military pension for Dame summed up the testimony of many in describing her service. "Miss Dame was a fighting nurse on the field of battle, and under fire in many of the most deadly battles of the war," said Henry Blair. "Her story is one of wonderful heroism, rivaling anything ever told of woman, and surpassing the achievements of the bravest of men. She was the *mother* of the regiment, and no officer or soldier of the historic Second New Hampshire or of any other regiment has a record of which the state is so proud."[16] Blair believed that any future historian who told her full story "would perpetuate an example worthy of emulation to the latest times." Gilman Marston, the first colonel of her regiment, called her "the bravest woman I ever knew. I have seen her face a battery without flinching, while a man took refuge behind her to avoid the flying fragments of bursting shells. Of all the men and women who volunteered to serve their country during the late war, not one is more deserving of reward than Harriet P. Dame."[17] Some Northern newspapers used even saintlier prose in support of a pension for her. A Vermont editor wrote: "Her history is written in scars held under her ministering hands, in hearts to whom she by her presence and deeds brought hope and comfort amid the sufferings of war, and in the memories of stricken suffering ones, both blue and gray, for whom she cared."[18]

During the pension debate, Dame reluctantly complied with a request to provide a narrative account of her service for Congress's consideration. She wrote from Pineland, a rehabilitation home in Concord where she was looking after her sister, who had broken her arm in a fall. "Newspaper men and women, book writers, and many of my dear friends have *many* times asked the same thing of me, but my answer has always been if my army life would be properly written it would make a *big* book."[19]

This is not a big book, and certainly not the one Dame might have written, but it is one I have longed to write for years. I became fascinated with the Harriet Patience Dame story after coming to Concord forty-four years ago to edit the local newspaper. The city's Blossom Hill Cemetery was on one of my wife's and my walking routes for years, and we often paused at Dame's stately tombstone, with the diamond symbol of the Union Army's Third Corps as its crown. A few years ago, I wrote *Our War*, an attempt to tell New Hampshire's Civil War history by stringing together fifty human stories of eventful days from 1861 through 1865. I was sure when I began collecting these stories that Dame would be the central character in one of them. She made a cameo appearance in the book, but without letters, a wartime diary, or detailed narrative accounts from the period, I could not find enough material to tell a good story about her.

Then, in 2017, Scott Preston Hardy, a Concord history enthusiast, contacted me to say he had located a cache of wartime letters written by Dame. The owner was a dealer in historical items. Hardy kept in touch with me as he researched on his own and quizzed the dealer, who lived in Michigan, for further information. Once I was sure the find was authentic, I contacted the New Hampshire Historical Society. Wesley G. Balla, the society's director of collections and exhibitions, arranged to meet with the dealer at a Massachusetts flea market and examine the letters. Wes liked what he saw, and the society soon purchased them.

The collection includes about twenty letters and fragments of letters that Dame wrote to Anna Dwight Berry, a distant relative who lived across the street from her in Concord in 1861. They had both lost their fathers recently, which is perhaps why Dame befriended the teenaged Berry, who was thirty years her junior. The letters cover the first year of the war, and many of them are long, personal, and descriptive. Berry bound them into a letter-book either as she received them or after the war. The correspondence seems to have ended in the summer of 1862, but for years after Berry married a Boston businessman and moved to Massachusetts, she pasted postwar articles about Dame from the Boston papers in the back of the letter-book. These included two oral histories written from extensive interviews with Dame.

Armed with this material, I began to dig for wartime and postwar encounters and further interviews with Dame. I turned up only a dozen or so more letters, but possibly because the internet has made research far easier than it used to be, I found much more than I expected. In interviews, Dame took pains to dispel the common misconception that she had been on battlefields during battles. "It is never quite true to say that a woman is in a battle," she told Frances Abbott. "She can do nothing there. Her place is to take care of the men as they are brought in from the field. But my tent was always pitched within the lines and often I have worked all night on the field, helping to carry off the sick and wounded, and burying the dead."[20] She never trod upon a battlefield until after the shooting stopped. "A woman's work begins where the pomp and circumstance of glorious war has its ardor dampened," she told another interviewer. "In the rear of the fight her enthusiasm finds vent. As the groaning and dying are brought to her, her hands are never empty." In another reflective moment, she said that women who went to war "had no thought of any personal glory accruing from their self-sacrifice. We had no visions of standing in the presence of high officials, of hearing our names associated with deeds of great valor, or of planning gigantic moves of armies that would crush the enemy. We expected to follow only in the desolation after the battle, when glory was drenched in blood and the bravest men . . . lay trodden under the mad footsteps of friend and foe alike." When a man died while being cared for, "we had to stifle the rising sob and turn to the next one who was to live under our help and offer himself again to the work of conquering his country's destroyers," Dame said. "Self was absorbed in loving labor. The woman lost her identity in the nurse."[21]

Many people other than the soldiers left glimpses into Dame's life and experience during the war. Other nurses, including Dorothea Dix and Clara Barton, encountered her at several points in her journey and helped me understand the prejudices and other trials faced by women nurses. A loose-knit but determined coalition of New Hampshire women and men enabled Dame to become a remarkable provider of food, clothing, and other goods in the direst of times. She was so well known as a friend of the soldiers that some people at home sent her cash to spend on the men as she saw fit. Women formed clubs in towns and cities throughout the state to help feed and clothe the men in the field, and Dame served as a principal conduit of the goods they made. Especially in the aftermath of battles, the governor dispatched men to carry large stores of food and supplies to military hospitals, and nearly all these men came to know and trust Dame.

At one point in my research, I came across this passage in an 1887 newspaper profile of Dame: "No writer who attempts to chronicle all her thrilling, trying experiences under deadly fire on the field of battle, exposed to the contending elements of heaven, or over wounded, sick and dying soldiers in the hospitals, need ever hope to be successful."[22] While I grant the premise, I treated this statement not as an admonition but as an inspiration.

The deeper I delved into Dame's wartime experience, the more exceptional it seemed. My research included reading the diaries, letters, memoirs, and biographies of many Civil War nurses, a few famous, most less so, all able, eager, and hardworking. Along with the task they undertook, they endured the harsh prejudices of most of the male surgeons with whom they worked. But unlike nearly all the rest, Dame went to the front with the soldiers at the start of the war and camped with them wherever the war took them. If she was otherwise occupied when they needed her after a major battle, she dropped everything and flew to their aid. She was chosen again and again for big jobs: running a busy soldier-aid agency in Washington, making medical inspection tours for her state's governor, supervising the kitchen and the nurses at a huge field hospital near the front during the siege and the battles that won the war in the East. After Richmond fell and her regiment was assigned to occupy Virginia, she stayed to nurse these men until they mustered out in December 1865. A modest woman despite her strong opinions, Dame resisted frequent pleas to tell her own story after the war, and over time she slipped from the reach of history. The harder I struggled to find and restore her, the more I came to believe that the judgment of many who knew her well was true. A reporter who encountered her in 1882 said it best: "No other woman of the war did more, if as much."[23]

In writing Dame's story, I decided the best course was to blend her experiences with those of the soldiers she befriended and helped. Only by understanding their ordeals, defeats, and triumphs is it possible to comprehend hers. Dame's ceaseless determination to offer herself to the cause expanded her universe as the war ground on, but for her, as for most others, the war began close to home. Volunteer infantry regiments like the Second New Hampshire were formed by states. Especially during the first two years of the war, the companies within them consisted of men from the same cities or counties. Because Dame lived in Concord before the war, many of her closest acquaintances in the regiment came from that city and the towns around it. Among them were several members of the Goodwin Rifles, named in honor of Ichabod Goodwin, the governor when the war began, and in tribute to their marksmanship with the Sharpe's rifles they carried. These men served in the Second's Company B. Dame also spent much of her time with the regiment's staff officers, surgeons, and other medical personnel. In the pages ahead you will meet many of these men as they report on the camps, marches, and battles that shaped Dame's life with the regiment. Later in the war, when she cared for the sick and wounded of other regiments in field hospitals near battlefields and sieges, the civilians who delivered food and supplies to her recorded numerous firsthand accounts of Dame in action. In doing so, these men became valuable witnesses to her character and resolve.

To the veterans who gathered again at the State House dedication ceremony in 1892, the military victory represented by the Hale statue had once been anything but certain. Young men North and South rushed to volunteer in the spring of 1861 because they wanted to get in on the fight before it ended. Confidence that the war would be over in ninety days spread like a camp rumor. Instead, the war became the deadliest and most grueling in the nation's history. For many dark days, the Confederate Army held the upper hand. Because Harriet Dame was older than nearly all the men who joined the first wave of volunteers, she might also have been wiser about the likelihood of easy victory. Her motives differed from theirs, too. She knew many of the young men who were signing up and believed her skills and caring, her woman's touch, could help them and their comrades through the trying days ahead. She became so proficient and beloved in carrying out her mission that after she died, many of the old New Hampshire veterans believed she was worthy of a statue of her own.

Duty Calls

The little Fair Oaks railroad station sat less than ten miles from Richmond, the city through whose streets every man in the Second New Hampshire Volunteers expected to march any day now. On June 3, 1862, between the station and a stand of trees called Oak Grove, these men pitched their tents on ground where other regiments had fought a desperate battle just two days before. Harriet Dame was there, too, with her friends, the soldiers, within earshot of the enemy. "We camped right on the field, where neither men nor horses had yet been removed," she later wrote.[1] Heavy rain had exposed bodies in shallow graves, and the humid air held the dank odor of blood close to the ground. Ranker smells fouled the air, and green flies swarmed around the dead.[2] As Dame walked amid these human remains, she fought off her emotions. The scene turned her thoughts to what she might soon be called upon to do on this very field: feed the hungry, clean the wounds of the maimed, help lift the dead and prepare them for burial. She had joined the regiment with the conviction that a woman like her could make a difference in the aftermath of battle. Everything she had to offer—a kind word, a generous heart, skilled and willing hands—the wounded and dying men would need.

For all her resolve, Dame suffered pangs of despair as she walked this ground. Then she heard rebel soldiers singing in the distance, and their music broke the spell. As she moved amid the carnage, she tried to sing cheerful songs of her own.[3] That night, like the men of the Second who might soon face the enemy in battle, she retired to her tent and lay on the battlefield to sleep among the dead.

Many years later, her recollections of this time turned Dame's thinking to the pique she often felt toward some of the medical men who had worked at her side in the frenzy after the fighting. She understood the need for deference to authority in military life, but she could not abide biases rooted in gender and class. She often found herself "fighting the prejudices of surgeons and stewards. They quarreled with my 'methods,' as they termed my womanly humanity," she wrote.[4] To her, many of them were autocrats who regarded a gravely wounded man as little more than "a beautiful case."

Although there were medical men Dame admired, the common soldier who did his duty in the face of death stood first in her pantheon. She was forty-six years old at the start of the war, old enough to be the mother of most of them. She liked some officers, too, and even swooned a bit over the handsome ones. When any surgeon needed her, she was there for him, but she loathed self-important officers who acted as though their shoulder straps entitled them to lord over the men. At times, she also criticized other women who, in her view, faltered as war nurses. In the aftermath of battle, she exhausted herself day after day on behalf of privates and corporals, treating them as the sons she never had. "My boys," she came to call them. She cooked and sewed for them, stood in harm's way like them, and nursed and mourned them.[5] If she flinched at the sight of a ghastly wound, it was an inner flinch. She developed a keen eye for army humbug while also scorning shirkers and cowards in the ranks. She understood that no matter how well she did her job, young men must pay the price of the War of the Rebellion with their blood and their lives. She grasped from the start that her place during battle was as close to the battlefield as she could get without entering it during the fighting. Dame had decided at the beginning of the war that women were needed in the field because they could do necessary work that men would not. She left for the front as a matron in the Second New Hampshire before a single major battle had been fought. By the time she quit the army eight months after the war ended, the Second was just one of many regiments whose soldiers considered her a saint.

This was a remarkable transformation for a woman with no formal medical experience or training who, in the spring of 1861, had been the keeper of a boardinghouse in Concord, New Hampshire. The war came at a time when Dame was seeking a new direction. Her family obligations had diminished, freeing her to answer what she considered the call of duty. She dropped everything to go to a war that soon raged out of control, killed hundreds of thousands of Americans, and left the Union hanging by a thread.

She did not look like a woman who could withstand years of war. She was narrow in the shoulders and slight in stature. She parted her thin brown hair in the middle above her high forehead. Round cheeks and the curve of her

Harriet Dame in 1864 ("Harriet P. Dame [Army Nurse]," MOLLUS-Mass Civil War Photograph Collection Volume 79, U.S. Army Heritage and Education Center, Carlisle, PA)

chin lent her smooth face an oval shape. Her dark eyes could pierce. In a photograph taken during the war, her expression bore the serious look common to portraits of the time, but it was neither dour nor severe. When she mentioned certain men in her wartime letters, she sometimes sounded like a coquettish young girl. For all her friendships with men and the caring she would show the soldiers, there is no indication she had intimate relationships with anyone. In her day, she was probably considered a spinster.

Dame was born in 1815 in North Barnstead, New Hampshire, a village consisting of a church, a few stores, and a post office.[6] Her father James was a schoolmaster who also farmed and served his neighbors as a justice of the peace.[7] In addition to being well educated, Harriet was deft with a needle and thread. She moved to Boston in her late twenties and worked there for many years as a dressmaker.[8] This competitive position required great skill while offering talented women a chance to lead laborious but independent lives. By the time Dame settled in Concord in 1856, several members of her family had gathered in New Hampshire's capital. Her sister Mary Ellen Shackford, a capable woman despite her blindness, lived in the city with her husband, a millwright, and their many children. Their brother George owned and ran the Pavilion Hotel on the east side of North Main Street. He had started Concord's first omnibus to shuttle hotel guests to and from the train depot. Two other older brothers lived with their families in Michigan and Wisconsin. James Dame, Harriet's father, was nearly eighty years old when he and his wife Phebe moved into the Pavilion Hotel in around 1850. After Phebe died, Harriet returned to the family fold to help her father live out his life. She bought a boardinghouse a short walk down Main Street from the Pavilion, and James Dame moved in with her.[9] He died a few years later, leaving her with the house and a net worth of $1,200, a rare degree of financial security for a single woman.[10]

Women lacked the right to vote, but there was no way Dame could avoid or ignore the political turmoil that was driving the country to war. She lived right in the middle of it. At a time when the nation's foundation quaked and the debate over what to do about its fissures shaped political leadership at every level, her boardinghouse sat between the New Hampshire State House and Concord's new courthouse, where city hall shared space with the county court. One was a short walk along Main Street to the south, the other a short walk to the north. Partisan strife over slavery since the mid-1840s had culminated in Republican dominance of the city and the state. The Democracy, as the party of Andrew Jackson was called, had ruled the state for decades, but in the 1861 elections, not one Democrat won a seat on the city's governing body.

As the state capital, Concord enjoyed outsized political prominence. About eleven thousand people lived there at a time when New Hampshire still had far more farms than factories.[11] The city was home to both, but politics was its perpetual preoccupation. State elections were annual, and differences over national issues generated sharp divisions. Abraham Lincoln, who had recently lost a bid to unseat US Senator Stephen A. Douglas after a series of spirited debates, spoke at Phenix Hall on Main Street early one afternoon during the winter of 1860. The editor of the local New Hampshire Statesman was smitten with him. In an era when "compact" had a more capacious meaning than it does now, Asa McFarland began his account of the speech with these words: "Mr.

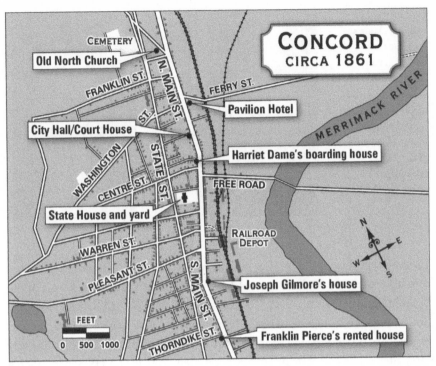

Concord, circa 1861

Lincoln addressed the people for an hour and a half in one of the most power-ful, logical, and compact speeches to which it was ever our good fortune to listen; an argument against the system of slavery, in defence of the position of the Republican party, from the deduction of which no reasonable man could possibly escape."[12] In a carriage drawn by four black horses, Lincoln rode to the courthouse for a tour. Both coming and going, the carriage passed Dame's boardinghouse.[13] After the party nominated Lincoln a few months later, Doug-las, his chief Democratic rival for the presidency, drew a crowd of five thousand people for a speech on the State House lawn.[14]

Some of the big local names in politics knew Dame's neighborhood well. John Rollins, the brother of her congressman, boarded at Dame's house. He had come to Concord to run the Rollins drugstore on Main Street after politics began to dominate his brother's life. Edward H. Rollins's journey mirrored the political turmoil of the 1850s. A Daniel Webster Whig at the start of the decade, he had become a Franklin Pierce Democrat, then a Know-Nothing, and, finally, a Republican. He had risen to Speaker of the New Hampshire House, headed the central committee of the new Republican Party, and led the delegation to

Left: Edward H. Rollins, Dame's neighbor and congressman (Library of Congress, LC-DIG-cwpbh-04851); *right:* Franklin Pierce (Courtesy of the New Hampshire Historical Society)

Chicago that started Lincoln on his way to the 1860 nomination.[15] Pierce, before his presidency, had lived on Montgomery Street a few houses west of the boardinghouse that Dame later owned. As president, he had befriended many Southern Democrats; one of them, Jefferson Davis of Mississippi, had been his secretary of war and would soon become president of the Confederacy. In early 1861, after Davis and four others resigned their seats in the US Senate, Pierce wrote to his pastor in Concord that they "were all sincere, union loving men and feel, with their constituents, that they have been driven out by long continued aggression and vituperative assault, on the part of those from whom they had a right to expect fair dealing, if not paternal regard." Pierce thought it would be "a great mistake to receive the fact that some of them retired in tears as evidence of weakness or selfish apprehension. Few men of truer patriotism, more varied learning or higher statesmanship have ever filled the vacated seats."[16] The former president and his wife Jane now rented a large house on South Main in Concord. A block or two nearer to downtown lived a political opposite, the railroad baron Joseph Gilmore, who would become a Republican wartime governor.[17] Between their houses and Dame's boardinghouse stood the headquarters of both major parties and the offices of five newspapers representing a spectrum of competing opinions, from pro-Southern ranters to righteous abolitionists.[18]

Dame's friend Henry McFarland, the twenty-nine-year-old son of the *Statesman* editor, owned a share of the paper, paid its bills, and handled the state printing contract. The *Statesman* occupied the basement and part of the first floor on the south side of the Phenix block. This gave McFarland a close-up view of state politics as the Union crumbled, although many people thought the national crisis would not come to that. McFarland detected this optimism in the muted local response to the alarming events of early 1861. "Secession had been threatened so long, that when the states proclaimed their withdrawal from the Union there was neither surprise nor excitement nor dismay," he later wrote. In February, the month the Confederacy ratified its constitution, Asa Fowler, a Republican judge in Concord whom Lincoln had met during his visit, served as a delegate to the Peace Convention in Washington. McFarland heard Fowler declare afterward that there would be no war. A prominent local Democrat predicted that all states, North and South, would eventually form a new union under the Confederate constitution. Realizing that this would mean a confederation "with slavery permitted in each state," McFarland was more inclined to believe Franklin Pierce, who considered a breakup of the Union inevitable. These speculations all occurred during what McFarland called a period of "weary waiting" between Lincoln's election and his inauguration in March.[19]

While Dame could not have missed the political churn and roil all around her, in the end the war came to her. Her boarders included several students of the Methodist Theological Seminary, a training center for ministers that had opened twelve years earlier in Concord's Old North Church. The building was a source of local pride. Within its walls in 1788, New Hampshire delegates had completed the job of forming the Union. Their vote to ratify the US Constitution gave the document the two-thirds majority it needed to begin improving upon the bonds that united the states. Now the students boarding at Dame's clashed over the rending of this national union. Some would soon leave Concord to take up arms for the North, some for the South. At least two Dartmouth College graduates also lived at Dame's. One would marry Dame's niece and enter the Union Army as a captain. The other, Ai Baker Thompson, enlisted during the Northern fury over the firing on Fort Sumter on April 12.[20] Little did either Thompson or Dame suspect that before three months had passed, the two of them would be sitting on opposite corners of her bunk outside an army tent in Washington, DC, each writing a letter to the same fifteen-year-old girl.

The girl was Anna Berry, a distant cousin of Dame's. She lived across the street from the boardinghouse with her widowed mother, her seventy-year-old grandfather, and an Irish servant.[21] The grandfather, Thomas Chadbourne, had been a Concord physician since 1814.[22] Harriet took a liking to Anna, an intellectually curious girl with charitable instincts who had just graduated from Concord High School.[23] Later, in corresponding with her from the war front, Dame would treat her as a mature young woman.

Word that President Lincoln had issued a call for seventy-five thousand volunteer troops clicked into the telegraph office on Main Street at eight o'clock on the morning of April 15, 1861. Friends who knew that Edward Sturtevant, the city's popular night police watchman, wanted to be the first man in the state to answer the call to war rushed to the Phenix Hotel to wake him. He ran three blocks to the State House and signed up at the adjutant general's office. Sturtevant then pitched a tent on the lawn outside and, with the help of Leonard Drown, a mechanic from neighboring Fisherville, recruited 226 men before the end of the month. Drown and many of the rest of them were known to Dame and would soon serve with her. By April 19, the "strange public stupor" that Henry McFarland described had vanished. At a lively meeting at city hall, Dame's boarder Ai Thompson and one of the Methodist students joined a long parade of speakers. The next day at the Eagle Hotel, the city's Democratic headquarters, Pierce addressed his neighbors, telling them he felt "the profoundest sadness when I see that those who have so often stood shoulder to shoulder in the face of foreign foes are now in imminent peril of standing face to face as the foes of each other." The former president did not consider armed aggression "a suitable or possible remedy for existing evils."[24] Despite the cheers after Pierce spoke, McFarland was not alone in detecting the absence of "battle smoke" in his words.[25]

Pierce's pessimism about the war had plenty of adherents. One of them was Robert Corning, a conductor on the Concord Railroad who heard the speech. He was no Democrat, having reveled in the ascent of the party of Lincoln and its sweep of the March state elections. "The old Democratic Party are down in these United States & the Republican Party is in power," he gushed in his diary.[26] The threat of war changed his mood. On April 19, the day after he received his commission as postmaster of Concord, he roved the city. "A grate excitement here," he wrote that night. "War—War, which I think is a dreadful thing." He prayed that Lincoln had the wisdom to resolve the issues at hand and keep the peace. Corning was even willing to give the Confederacy the new slave territory it wanted and to see the country divided. If the two sections failed to compromise, he believed, "there will be the greatest calamity come over the country that any man ever see. If war commences between the North & the South, I am satisfied that the South will concor and whip us out & have the cappital in spite of us." These views stood sharply against the wave of public confidence in the Union cause.

Concord quickly transformed into a wartime state capital, a task for which it was well suited. In addition to the Republicans' firm control at home, the party held all five New Hampshire seats in Congress, smoothing the way for cooperation with the new administration. Vacant land on the Dark Plains, a vast plateau across the Merrimack River from downtown, would provide training camps for several volunteer infantry regiments. The enlistment of railroad men, harness makers, blacksmiths, tanners, ornamental painters, hostlers, and shoemakers strained the local workforce, but opportunity also beckoned. Downtown haberdashers stocked up on officers' uniforms and shoulder straps, swords, and other military accessories. "Mourning Goods Always on Hand," Mrs. M. M. Smith assured potential customers of her milliner's shop on Main Street. Joseph Brown's nearby warehouse offered black walnut and chestnut coffins "of all shapes and sizes." Recruits from distant villages and towns lined up at the photographic studios of Richard Kimball and Benjamin Carr. There, stiff and unsmiling, they posed in their new uniforms for pictures for their mothers, wives, and girlfriends. The Abbot-Downing Company, the largest of Concord's three coach and wagon manufacturers, added ambulances, military wagons, and gun carriages to its inventory.[27]

After a study of the capital's economy shortly before the war, a researcher concluded, "An idle man or a gentleman of leisure is a curiosity in Concord." Indeed, jobs were plentiful in this manufacturing and government center. Three hundred and forty men manufactured wagons and carriages. Two hundred made shoes or boots. Three companies employed fifty-two men to produce melodeons and reed organs.[28] One merchant created, fitted, and sold theatrical wigs and beards along with "every article known to the Peruquean art."[29] Public employees staffed the state asylum, which included "a commodious building for unsafe and turbulent maniacs," and the two-acre, 120-cell state prison near Dame's boardinghouse. Tons of gray granite from the quarry on Rattlesnake Hill, some of it hammered into blocks by convicts, had been used to build the New Hampshire State House.[30] For the last two decades, Concord's fastest-growing enterprise had been the railroads, which employed three hundred local men. Car and engine houses, a machine shop, freight depots, and warehouses clustered near the passenger station. The web of tracks that radiated from the city's five-line hub soon began carrying volunteers from towns large and small to join their regiments in Concord. The station would also become the main departure point for regiments headed south and a destination for soldiers coming home on furlough or with their discharges.[31]

Two thousand men, twice as many as were needed, volunteered for the First New Hampshire Volunteers, a three-month regiment.[32] As the thousand men chosen to fill the First gathered at Camp Union across the river from downtown, their quartermaster ordered fifteen wagons and an ambulance from Abbot-Downing and harnesses for their teams from James Hill, whose company also made trunks. The quartermaster paid an average of $125 for each of the many horses the regiment needed to haul the wagons. The last members of the First mustered into the army on May 7, 1861, and the last of the equipment arrived a week later.[33] Volunteers not taken into this regiment were given a chance to join the Second New Hampshire Volunteers for a term of three years, not three months. Nearly five hundred men exercised this option, including Ai Thompson, Dame's boarder. Once the other half of the regiment had been filled, the Second settled into Fort Constitution on New Castle Island near Portsmouth to prepare for war.[34]

With Thompson and the Methodist seminarians gone, Dame suddenly had empty rooms at her boardinghouse and time on her hands. She knew many men in the First New Hampshire and began cooking and sewing for them and sending what she made across the Merrimack to Camp Union. When measles struck the regiment, she took in five recruits who had contracted the highly contagious virus. While usually mild in childhood, measles could be a serious disease in grown men. Its spread in the training camp was a harbinger of how even more dangerous diseases would imperil regiments filled by young men who came from farms and small towns where they had not been exposed to diseases. Another soldier arrived at the boardinghouse with rheumatic fever, soon to be a common malady among the troops.[35] "When the soldiers began to come into camp, I found plenty of work among the sick, and my house was at once a hospital," she later wrote.[36] Then Thompson came home from the New Hampshire seacoast with chills and fever. As he told Dame about the illnesses afflicting the ranks of the Second New Hampshire, he wondered aloud who would care for the regiment's sick and wounded in the field. Dame answered, "I will."[37]

As impulsive as this response might seem, it captured who Dame was and how well she understood herself. She was a resolute, self-confident, pragmatic Episcopalian who in recent weeks had found purpose in comforting the sick and shining a light of hope and kindness into their lives. To some degree, she reveled in the sense of adventure that animated most of the young men who rushed to join infantry regiments. "When the war first broke out, or was talked of, even, I began to look about me to see what a woman could do, should there ever be real fighting," she later recalled. Dame decided to go where she was most needed and could make the biggest difference. She had lived an independent life for decades and trusted her ability to deal with any hardship she might encounter. When the First New Hampshire marched down Main

Street to the train station on May 25, Dame was heartened to see that forty women accompanied the regiment, mostly soldiers' wives and mothers, some not. Although they had come simply to bid farewell to the men, their presence reinforced her idea that "there should be women willing to work and suffer—ever faithful and true to their country and their God—to go as nurses to take care of the soldiers when sick and wounded."[38]

Her hope of becoming such a woman faced obstacles and official obstinacy. The notion of women at the front appalled Nathaniel Berry, the incoming governor, who told Dame, "That is no place for a woman." He refused to issue her a pass to go with the Second New Hampshire on grounds that the federal government had not authorized women at the front. Gilman Marston, a US representative from Exeter, New Hampshire, and the colonel of the Second, also "looked with great disfavor on women entering the army."[39] They were both older men who held the common prejudices against women's participation in most fields of labor. Berry had been born in 1796, and Marston had been a lawyer for decades since graduating from Dartmouth and Harvard Law School.

If anything, military surgeons took an even harsher view. Georgeanna Woolsey Bacon, another early volunteer nurse, found doctors rude and dismissive, especially during the opening days of the war. They burdened women nurses with menial tasks day and night and offered them meager meals and lodging, hoping to make their lives "so unbearable that they should be forced in self-defence to leave."[40] Dorothea Dix, a prominent reformer in mental healthcare before the war, became the Union Army's superintendent of women nurses in Washington, hiring and supervising hundreds of them. Her strict qualifications required applicants to be at least thirty-five years old, clean, moral, and preferably homely. Regularly caught between her nurses and surgeons who disliked working with women, Dix often kowtowed to the surgeons. Some nursing recruits and high-ranking officials devised ways to avoid her. Jane Woolsey cheered her sister on when Georgeanna rebuffed Dix's efforts to prevent her from volunteering. "Outflank the Dix by any and every means in your power," she advised. Dix and Dame would work together and maintain cordial relations during the war and become allies later in life, but Dix would have been of little help to her when men in power tried to keep her from joining the Second New Hampshire in 1861. She did not believe women belonged with regiments in the field, and it cut against her nature to stand up for women who were challenged by men in authority.[41]

Dame had to find another way around the objections of Governor Berry and Colonel Marston. She turned to George Hubbard, the surgeon of the Second

New Hampshire, and Henry Parker, the pastor of Concord's South Congregational Church, who intended to become the regiment's chaplain. Hubbard bore
none of the animosity toward women nurses that most surgeons did. Whether
he or Parker spoke directly with Berry or Marston is unknown, but both supported Dame's ambition. Hubbard had already decided he wanted two capable
women to come with the regiment to help with the sick and wounded and per-
form other duties. He chose Dame and Mary Marden of Windham. They were
classified as matrons and hired at six dollars per month, less than half the wages
of an army private. Harriet Dame prepared to go to war.[42]

A few blocks away, Pastor Parker, a man she would soon characterize as the
regiment's best officer, did the same. He was a slight man of forty with a big
brain and exceptional courage. Mutton chops flared down his cheeks to his
jawbone, and a receding hairline capped his handsomely chiseled face. In one
of his last acts before joining his regiment, he spoke before a joint session of
the Legislature on Election Day. This fell on June 7, the day the two chambers
chose their leaders for the coming session and staged a parade and ceremony
to welcome Nathaniel Berry as the new governor.

In his speech, Parker wove Western history and Protestant philosophy into
a rational argument that the South's treason now threatened to destroy the
Union.[43] When he came to the cause of the national rupture, he spoke clearly
and firmly without ever uttering the word *slavery*. The United States and its
democratic ways had long been the envy of the world, he said, "with one sole
exception, in a single institution—the only thing the world could point to as
an inconsistency and a blot. We lamented it. We apologized for it at home,
and especially abroad. We cared to say but little about it, most of us. We rather
averted our eyes from it. . . . With this single exception, the aspect of our nation's life was without a blemish." It is unlikely Dame heard Parker's sermon,
but it would have moved her. She certainly agreed with him about the rebellion and the devotion of the young men who were volunteering by the thousands to put it down. Parker predicted in closing that freedom-loving Americans of future generations would not be disappointed when they looked back
on these men's efforts to save the Union.

The Second New Hampshire's top officers unanimously elected Parker
chaplain three days later.[44] Before he even had a chance to correct the proof of
the printed version of his speech, he left his wife and three children with the
family's Irish nanny and joined the regiment's journey south. The men had assembled and trained at Fort Constitution near Portsmouth, but people from
all around the state went to Boston to see the regiment off.[45] The men soon

pitched their tents at Camp Sullivan in Washington, just west of the Glenwood Cemetery and a mile or so north of the White House. Parker moved into his quarters there on June 25.

On that very day in Concord, a train pulled into the station bearing the body of Lt. Charles Webster Walker, descendant of a prominent local family and the first soldier of the Second New Hampshire from the city to die in the war. Walker had tumbled from a platform car as the regiment's train south lurched through New Jersey. The wheels crushed his right leg, and death quickly followed amputation at the hip. The memorial service on June

The funeral procession for Lieutenant Walker in downtown Concord. Dame attended his funeral. (Courtesy of the New Hampshire Historical Society)

26 was lavish, beginning with Walker's body lying in state at New Hampshire's capitol as an ornate, black-plumed hearse from the Abbot-Downing Company waited at the curb outside to carry him to his funeral. The procession accompanying the hearse included Governor Berry, most of the legislators, Concord's mayor, and several militias and delegations from fraternal organizations.[46] With the other mourners, Dame marched right past her boardinghouse toward the Old North Church. Twenty-eight years earlier at the Old North, the pastor who eulogized Walker had helped found the New Hampshire Anti-Slavery Society. After his sermon, Walker's fellow Masons laid him to rest at the nearby cemetery. Dame would long remember the sadness and solemnity of the day. "If I had time, I should like to write you my thoughts as I watched the great show," she would later tell Anna Berry.[47] Walker's funeral was a reminder of what lay ahead in the life she had chosen.

As she saw to the details of her departure, this somber event must have strengthened her resolve to go to war. Nevertheless, as the regimental historian would later write, "It is not probable that when she first opened her house for the reception of sick soldiers from the camp at Concord, she had any thought of the remarkable experience which lay before her."[48] Her decision to set out for untold dangers with a large group of young men fell far outside the social norms of her day. Despite one early encounter with a lecherous drunk, her caring ways and steady bearing would turn the soldiers around her into protective big brothers. George Dame, her actual brother, helped her find a renter for her boardinghouse and promised to keep an eye on it. Harriet was still brooding over the governor's opposition to her going, but she was not about to change her mind even though she had to pay part of her own train fare south.[49] For her, as for her country, it was a life-changing moment, and she was soon on her way. She would arrive in time for the war's first big battle, but, to her chagrin, she would witness it from a far greater distance than she had hoped.

"Oh, That I Were There"

By the time Harriet Dame settled into her tent at Camp Sullivan in early July 1861, the men of the Second New Hampshire expected to invade Virginia at any moment. While delivering a four-day supply of beef, bread, and coffee to the regimental kitchen, Pvt. Martin Haynes learned that the cooks had orders "to cook the meat, ready for a march."[1] A naïf and an optimist, he mused that the Second might depart at night to avoid the heat of day. The company captains put their men on alert. Cpl. Thomas Leaver, Dame's former neighbor and a sharpshooter in the Concord company, felt ill, but he assured his mother that when the call came, "I will shoulder my rifle and march as far as I can, which is all that I *can* do."[2] In Chaplain Henry Parker's idle hours, he toured the Capitol and met such luminaries as Sen. Andrew Johnson, who, as Tennessee's governor, had "stood up so nobly against secession."[3] Like many other new soldiers, Parker watched Congress open its special session on the Fourth of July. In calling for the legislators to meet, President Lincoln had asked them to express their will and to approve the means to put down the rebellion.[4] Parker, too, knew that the Second would soon march into Virginia.

Dame had been so sick the day she arrived that she spent a night at the National Hotel in downtown Washington before coming to her regiment's camp.[5] She and Mary Marden, the other matron, moved into a tent together beside the quarters of George Hubbard, the regimental surgeon. Camp Sullivan lay on a shady hill with panoramic views of the city, Arlington Heights, Georgetown, and, in the distance, Alexandria. The two women slept on a wide mattress and rolled it up each morning to give themselves more room inside the tent. With no routine in place, they had to create one, but Dame could not abide idle hands, especially her own. Prepared by her work as a dressmaker and a board-inghouse cook, she went looking for chores she could do better than the men. She sewed and mended. She made gruel, tea, and toast for sick soldiers. When Capt. Leonard Drown, a friend from home, gave her strawberries and Pvt. John Moore brought her milk, she distributed them among men in the ranks. It was a way of getting to know her comrades. Although Gilman Marston, the regi-ment's commander, had not yet approved the idea, she intended to accompany the soldiers when they marched to battle. She told one man she would go with them to Virginia or South Carolina or anywhere else they were ordered.

In these early days before its first campaign, her regiment must have been among the most literate in the army. One captain complained that "his men are too damned intelligent and really there is so much letter writing that it is a nuisance."[6] Chaplain Parker, who also served as the regiment's postmaster, found the job more taxing than expected. He was soon franking twenty-eight hundred to three thousand letters a week.[7]

Two of them were written simultaneously outside Dame's tent on Sunday, July 7.[8] She dragged her cot out into the shade of the oak and walnut trees and sat on one corner of it. A breeze soughed through the leaves as she began a let-ter to Anna Berry about her first days in camp. Dame wrote a fluid, though in-elegant, line that stretched out and flattened as she rushed on. She had hardly begun when Ai Thompson, her former boarder, happened by. He had recently been promoted to second lieutenant, but his new rank did not impress Dame. She ordered him to sit catty-corner from her on the cot and write Berry a let-ter, too. Like many others in camp, he expected to go to battle soon and had been using his rare days off to visit a friend and see the sights. He recounted these adventures to Berry, telling her how he had joined the throngs of soldiers who trooped to the Marshall House in Alexandria, where Elmer Ellsworth, the dashing colonel of the red-coated New York Zouaves, had been slain. On the day Virginia seceded from the Union, Ellsworth had cut down the large Con-federate flag mounted on the hotel's roof. As he descended the stairs with the flag, the hotel's owner shot him. Since that day in May, Thompson wrote Berry, the house had been "plundered from cellar to attic of all its furniture, the walls disfigured, the ceiling pulled down, the doors unhinged." Hardly a souvenir re-mained, but Thompson managed to extract one. He "cut a piece from the stair-way where Ellsworth stood when the fatal bullet pierced his heart." In the enve-lope with his letter to Berry, he enclosed a chip from the foot of the post at the head of the stairs. He also joked with her about Dame's voracious appetite: "She has eaten one small hard biscuit since she came to camp."

Originally, Gen. Irvin McDowell's army had been scheduled to march the day after Dame and Thompson wrote, but he had no choice but to postpone its departure. The army had two few supply wagons to carry what it needed for the campaign. Regiments and brigades were arriving late, making it difficult to organize the army. Meanwhile, the terms of some three-month regiments that had answered the first call to arms had nearly expired.[9]

While the delays irritated the soldiers, the women back home worried. Mary Parker, the chaplain's wife, believed her husband would face less danger than an infantry officer but fretted nonetheless over "how fierce the battle may be." Henry wrote her that he could not be certain when the regiment would march.[10] The next day, Martin Haynes informed his girlfriend in Manchester that the Second New Hampshire's marching orders had been rescinded. Before sealing the envelope, he scribbled a postscript announcing that new orders had just arrived. The regiment was to leave the next afternoon carrying three days' rations but "without camp equipage."[11] Wherever the men were going, they would be sleeping on the ground.

Harriet Dame would not accompany them on their first campaign after all. She was to remain at Camp Sullivan, her temper smoldering over this snub as the steamy days dragged by.[12] While her regiment finally readied for departure on July 16, she went hunting for Lieutenant Thompson to wish him well. It upset her to see him so joyful in the face of battle. Just as she returned to her tent, "our dear Mr. Parker" rode up, "looking so handsome" in the saddle. The very sight of him distressed her so much that she could not utter a word to him.[13] Even before these men left, she knew that worrying from afar would be worse than keeping busy behind the battle line.[14]

The regiment marched west that afternoon as part of the brigade commanded by Rhode Islander Ambrose Burnside. On horseback, in wagons, but mostly on foot, the men crossed the Long Bridge over the Potomac and bivouacked for the night on a hillside at Bailey's Crossroads. Since coming together in mid-May, they had dreamed of invading Virginia, and now here they were, bedding down under the stars on enemy soil. They stopped again at Fairfax Courthouse, where a Second New Hampshire captain yanked the Confederate flag from atop the courthouse and replaced it with the Stars and Stripes. Next, they went into camp near Centreville, seven miles east of Manassas Junction.[15] By Chaplain Parker's estimate, the Second and the rest of Colonel Burnside's brigade had joined a column totaling fifteen thousand soldiers shortly after leaving Washington. Along the way this force had fallen into line with a larger division, meaning the Union Army would enter battle with a strength of more than thirty thousand men.[16] Hours before dawn on July 21, as Burnside's brigade set out to meet the enemy at Bull Run, Pvt. Charles Jewett expressed the confidence of many men in the ranks about their chances against the rebels. "We have got them ahead of us and mean to keep them so," he assured his brother. "I have got a good gun and a seven-shooter besides and I mean to use them both. . . . We begin to see something like ware and that sutes me."[17]

Keeping Dame company back at Camp Sullivan was a class of men she had not recognized before her regiment marched away. She was so disgusted by the many shirkers among these men that, on the day of the battle, she poured out her anger to Anna Berry. "You probably never will experience what I have to day," she began. "You doubtless know that most of our reg't left here last Tuesday, some feeble and a few sick. Several cowards were left here. I don't rank with either class of the above thank God." Recent events had taught her a sad lesson. "There is no mistake we have some mean cowards in our reg't," she wrote. "One Lieut came home Friday night & pled sickness. This morning he's been at the City. . . . How he could leave & come here I can't understand."[18]

Adj. Samuel Langley also returned to Camp Sullivan, but he had come to assemble and deliver to the regiment anyone able to walk that far. He found sixty-five men who he believed could march and fight. They left camp the morning of the battle, too late to reach the Second New Hampshire in time to help. "We know there is a great battle going on in the vicinity of Manassas Junction & we know our folks are there and probably in the heat of battle," Dame wrote Berry. "In fact we have heard so. As I write [I] continually hear the distant cannon." The sound pricked her conscience. Even after Langley forced many men in camp to march off toward Manassas with him, Dame thought some of those left behind for a second time were healthy enough to fight. As for herself, she wondered why she had even joined the regiment if she would not be allowed to accompany the men when they needed her most. To the echoes of artillery fire, she lamented: "Here I am thirty miles from there doing nothing . . . and picturing some of my dear friends wounded, suffering & dying for care. Tomorrow if I am alive, I shall start for there if I have to walk." If she could get to the battle, she trusted the regiment's officers to protect her in the field and believed they would welcome her efforts to tend to the wounded. "I can do some good to some one if I can reach them," she wrote.[19]

For evidence to support this conviction, she only had to gaze over at the camp of the First Massachusetts Infantry, the regiment next door. These men guarded the Second's camp in the absence of her regiment. Three days earlier, some of them had undertaken an ill-fated reconnaissance mission at Blackburn's Ford on Bull Run. General McDowell, who commanded the force approaching Manassas Junction, sent them to find a position where he could deploy his army near the ford. When the Massachusetts men approached the enemy, two factors undid them: inexperience and the color of their uniforms. The uniforms were gray. When similarly clad soldiers appeared in a clearing before them, a Union captain wondered which side they were on. He moved forward from his company's line and asked the strangers in gray who they were. "Who are *you*?" one of them answered. "Massachusetts men," the captain replied. These were his last words. At Blackburn's Ford the First Massachusetts lost thirteen killed and twenty-five captured and wounded. After the survivors straggled back to their camp near Centreville, the heat of the day demanded immediate burial of the dead, but there was no wood for coffins. The bodies "were wrapped and covered with their own blankets and consigned to the earth." The regiment had many wounded, sunstruck, and sick men to transport back to Washington, but because McDowell's army was headed the other way, eastbound ambulances were hard to find. It was a challenge, but they made it.[20]

Dame sympathized with these men from her brigade. "They are our neighbors in New England, all Boston & Chelsea men, and they are taken care of by strangers and their fellow soldiers," she complained. In an age when women were all but forbidden in military camps, Dame witnessed the poor diet and clumsy treatment of the wounded Massachusetts soldiers. "I have seen enough of men nursing and preparing things for [the] sick to convince me that unless there are women to manage, sick people must suffer." As she wrote these lines, the cannon fire to the west grew louder and louder. "Either the battle has begun at a new place or our forces are being driven back," she surmised. "Oh that I were there."[21]

On July 21, the day Dame wrote to Berry, the men of the Second New Hampshire had risen at one o'clock in the morning and marched off an hour later. In the words of Dame's friend Lieutenant Thompson, they moved out "with their blankets on their shoulders, their haversacks full of hard bread, their canteens of water, with heavy muskets, and cartridge boxes full of ammunition, but with hearts as light as were their falling footsteps." The glow of the full moon made it seem to Thompson that "a phantom army was issuing forth from the mists of the night, armed with brightly burnished weapons of silver and gold." By the time the men reached the field of battle, they had little or no water to soothe their parched tongues. Worse, they soon realized that the rebels "had every advantage of us. They were under the cover of woods; we could not see them, only a few of their pickets. Their batteries were all around us, except in our rear, and commanded almost every position we could take to do them any injury." This placed the Second in the perfect spot "for the enemy to cut us in pieces."[22] Private Haynes described the regiment's rush to this discouraging position: "We were exposed to the concentrated fire of the entire rebel force then in action, and the sounds of their missiles, running through the whole scale of warlike music, from the savage rush of twelve pound shells to the spiteful 'pish' of the minié bullet, was ruinous to weak nerves."[23]

A sergeant noted the instinct of soldiers in their first battle to attempt to duck artillery shells. Most "would come and you would bow your head and they would pass over you," Hugh Richardson wrote to a friend back home. Others "would take off a leg, some an arm and some a head." Gov. William Sprague of Rhode Island had come to the battle as an aide to Colonel Burnside. Richardson described how a single shell beheaded Sprague's horse and killed Burnside's without wounding a man. In future battles, the tendency to duck would diminish, but at Bull Run, Richardson observed, "You never saw so much bowing in one day in your life."[24]

As men began to fall, Chaplain Parker ignored the danger with a selflessness that stunned all who saw him. "Among the wounded and the dying no presence was so welcome as his," Haynes wrote. "He would lead his horse with splendid courage where the bullets fell thickest and loading the animal with the wounded would carry them away to a place of safety only to return again and again on the same errand."[25] Pvt. John Rice, who was wounded so severely that his name would appear on lists of the dead, believed before the battle that his slight chaplain gave "little promise of usefulness in the rude field of war." Later, while lying on the ground shot through the lungs, Rice watched Parker ride through murderous fire to help move him to safer ground. Rice would survive to see many other heroic deeds, but nothing to equal "the calm courage with which this was done."[26] Yet another soldier described how Parker "worked like a day laborer to assist the men, and was so begrimed with sweat and dust, no one would have suspected he was a clergyman."[27]

Early in the battle, a ball struck Congressman Gilman Marston, the regiment's colonel, just below the shoulder. He pitched onto his face, and a soldier tried to tug him up by his wounded arm. "The air was burdened with choice selections from the old colonel's matchless vocabulary," a witness observed.[28] Parker rushed in with his own horse, helped boost the colonel into the saddle, and led him to an aid station. Union surgeons had gathered at Sudley Church, a farmhouse, and a barn.[29]

During a lull in the fighting, with the rebels retreating as their own line firmed up, the Union men thought they had carried the day. None other than General McDowell, the army's commander, told them so, riding along the line to their

Left: Chaplain Henry E. Parker was admired by the men of the Second, and by Harriet Dame. (Courtesy of the New Hampshire Historical Society); *right:* Gilman Marston, colonel and congressman (Library of Congress, LC-USZ62-96278)

cheers shouting, "Victory! Victory! The day is ours!"[30] A courier rushed back to pass this good news on to the Second's quartermaster, who was watching over the regiment's wagons a few miles behind the lines. As the wagons moved forward, they suddenly encountered Union wagons flying in the other direction mingled with the private carriages of spectators who had come out from Washington.[31] The rebels had regrouped, and before the infantrymen of the Second knew it, they found themselves stampeding off the field. Tom Leaver, the Concord corporal, spoke for many in describing his consternation at this turn of events: "I never thought of retreating until I was fairly under way being carried on with the crowd, and when I look back upon it now it is with feelings of pain to think that we should have lost all the ground that we had gained."[32]

The mob withdrawal took a heavy toll on army wagons. Finding the road out so jammed up that it was impassable, Lt. John Godfrey, the Second's quartermaster, detoured through a field and returned to the road farther along. "The scene was now mortifying in the extreme," he wrote, "and at the same time it was laughable. Everything was in full flight and any wagon was apparently driven as fast as it was possible for the wagons to move. Whenever a ditch was found wide and deep enough, a wagon was sure to be overturned bottom upward." Cut loose by the teamsters, the horses were soon marketed to the highest bidders among foot soldiers. Cluttering his way, Godfrey soon encountered "a perfect avalanche of kettles, pots & pans, barrels of provisions, boxes of bread, coils of rope" along with shovels, spades, pickaxes, and other implements. "It seemed like a ride through an agricultural warehouse with a tin shop attached."[33]

Chaplain Parker remained at the Sudley Church, a mile behind the last stand of the Union line. After bringing several gravely wounded men to this field hospital, which was crowded with soldiers from both armies, he had decided he could be more helpful there than on the battlefield. Many of the worst wounds were similar, caused by musket fire at close range. In most cases all the surgeons could do was extract the ball, if possible, and apply a dressing moistened with muddy water from Sudley Creek. As Union fortunes disintegrated, "a medical officer of rank" told the surgeons they were free to leave. Soon only three caregivers remained: a Massachusetts surgeon, a local doctor who had showed up to help, and Henry Parker. Of the wounded men in his regiment, the chaplain believed that all but Private Rice, who "seemed impossible to move," had been brought to the hospital. Parker and the others remained there until six o'clock, by which time "all the wounded capable of moving" had been sent on their way.[34] The departing army left an estimated 180 severely wounded men behind, all of whom fell into the hands of the enemy.[35]

Of the retreat, Parker told his wife: "It sickens me to look back upon what then passed before my eyes."[36] He happened upon two soldiers from his regiment helping a wounded comrade along and stopped so they could lift him on the horse's back. As Parker and his passenger rode on through the woods toward Centreville, the man moaned or cried out each time his leg struck a bush or a tree or a soldier on foot. The chaplain delivered him to the town's Stone Church, which was being used as a field hospital. Colonel Marston was already there, and the surgeon who had treated his shoulder wound advised Parker to see that the wound was dressed again as soon as possible in Washington. Parker readied a baggage wagon and the party soon departed. The chaplain, who had been on the move for seventeen hours, could barely stay awake in the saddle as he hurried ahead to the capital to arrange for Marston to be treated at the home of Salmon Chase, the secretary of the treasury and a New Hampshire native.

For most of the men without horses, the retreat was a long, lonely ordeal full of peril and horror. Charles Putnam, a Second New Hampshire private from Claremont, was one of many who told his story in detail.[37] During the battle, the man who marched next to him had been one of the first in the regiment to die. Putnam had also watched in distress as Confederate troops wiped out a Union battery, killing several men, blowing most of the horses to pieces, and seizing five cannons. When he took flight, he could find no one from his regiment along the way. For half a mile, rebel cannonballs "struck so near that they would throw the dirt all over me." He walked into the Stone Church in Centreville to ask about his regiment. Repelled by the gore and agony he witnessed, he left praying that he "would never witness another such a sight." Moving on, he recognized two wounded men from his company lying beside the road. Cannon fire had blown off the left leg of Andrew Straw below the thigh, but he still had the strength to beg for water. Putnam gave him some and moved on. He saw Union cavalrymen on a hill ahead, figured they were covering the retreat, and started toward them. Before he could reach them, he heard the bullets flying around him and changed course. He finally caught up with the main body of the retreat and reached Washington safely. In thirty-six hours of marching, fighting, walking, and running since the Second had left Centreville early the previous morning, Putnam estimated he had covered sixty miles. Along the way he had removed his boots and soldiered on in his stockings. Now he suffered from "the sorest feet I ever had." Five days later, when he shared his battle story with his brother, he felt "entirely well" and ready for more: "They say we must try them again next week. I am ready to go, and if I fall I know I shall be avenged. I know it is a just cause, and am willing to go where duty calls."

Back at Camp Sullivan shortly before dark on the day of the battle, Harriet Dame asked the cook to prepare tea. She freshened up and struck out for the city determined to hear news directly from the front and find her way there if she was needed. She figured her best hope was Edward Rollins, her congressman and Concord neighbor. He had told her earlier that he intended to go to the battlefield. Congress had adjourned so that its members could ride or be driven there. Gen. James Wilson of Keene, New Hampshire, a guest at the Willard Hotel, was another possibility. His daughter had told Dame he was going. She did not yet know it, but events had dashed any possibility of her reaching the battlefield during the fight. Just when she expressed her plans to do so in her letter to Anna Berry, the Union Army was collapsing thirty miles away and starting back to Washington.[38]

In a chance meeting with her Concord friend Henry McFarland of the *New Hampshire Statesman*, Dame heard that Rollins had indeed left for the battlefield and had, in fact, already returned. McFarland was standing with a friend on the south edge of the White House grounds when he saw Rollins ride back into the city.[39] McFarland had also spoken with Chaplain Parker after his dash to Washington to prepare for the care of the wounded Colonel Marston. Parker had told McFarland he feared the rebel victory at Bull Run would lead to official recognition of the Confederacy by Great Britain and France.[40]

Dame, meanwhile, attended an evening service at the Episcopal Church. Later, at the National Hotel, where seven or eight soldiers had just arrived from the battlefield, she shouldered her way through the crowded doorway in hopes of learning more about her regiment. She witnessed wild excitement but gathered little intelligence. Escaping the throng proved to be a challenge, as more and more anxious people had jammed into the entrance in search of battle news. When she did wriggle through and reach the street, Dame had the good fortune to find a ride back to Camp Sullivan.[41]

By daybreak on Monday, the first soldiers from the Second New Hampshire began limping into camp. As Lt. Joab Patterson put it, the "grand army" that had marched singing into Virginia six days earlier had "returned with broken ranks and saddened hearts."[42] They came, a sergeant remarked, "with one shoe on, some barefoot, some in their stocking feet."[43] As the men waited to see which of their comrades would make it back and which would not, they began to process what had happened to them. Like Parker, a few men earned praise, including Dame's friend Leonard Drown, whom Marston called "the bravest captain on the field." For the most part, however, the men were left to speculate about who and what had caused their defeat. "The fact is the Federal Army was not ready," Patterson lamented. Never shy with his opinions, Lieutenant Godfrey, the regiment's quartermaster, blamed newspapers for "constantly calling out for a fight."[44] As for the inglorious retreat, he faulted "the headlong panic of civilians who came out to see the fight." He was confident the army would recover, but even five days after the battle, eighty men of the regiment remained unaccounted for. During the time of second-guessing and nose-counting that followed, what Dame heard about the captured and wounded only reinforced her resolve never to be left behind again.

Back home in New Hampshire, the cold print of reality chilled the public's zeal for war. Casualty lists made their debut in newspapers all around the state. Surgeon Hubbard, who had invited Dame to join the regiment, had observed much of the carnage the regiment suffered at Bull Run. In a note accompanying the casualty list he sent to the *Mirror* in Manchester, he said he had lost all his medical gear except for his instruments. "Our ambulances were fired on by cannon during the retreat," he lamented, "and we were forced to leave them and run for our lives."[45] But it was the terse phrases of the list he appended to his note that struck home in a small state where people tended to know their neighbors well. Isaac Derby lost left arm. Charles H. Chase wounded in thigh and left prisoner. John F. Lord wounded in head. Hugh Lewis wounded in breast. Henry A. Bowman foot shot off and left a prisoner. Wells C. Haynes severely wounded in thigh—missing. Brothers Elbin and Woodbury Lord wounded and captured. On and on it went. The list of missing men evolved during coming weeks, causing grief and anxiety as names came and went. Elbin Lord, for one, died in Richmond two days after being taken prisoner. For news of who had made it back to Camp Sullivan and who might be in a prison camp or dead somewhere near the battlefield or on the road back, many families waited in distress for letters from their loved ones.

Moments of relief sometimes eased this anxiety on the home front. The Durgin family of Fisherville had two sons in the regiment, Abner, the quartermaster sergeant, and Hiram, a nineteen-year-old infantryman. The first news to reach town was "that you wer all killed," their father Jeremiah informed them eight days after the battle. "Your mother did not sleep at all that night."[46] A dispatch the next morning from the Second's major assured the couple that both sons were alive and had excelled in battle. Then Captain Drown, a blacksmith who had made wagon axles in Fisherville before the war, praised both Durgins, writing that "Hi fought like an old vetron." Mail from the front became a communal affair in Fisherville. Young Scott Durgin, the brother of the two soldiers, rushed to the post office the moment the mail coach came into view, and many townspeople followed close behind. From a raised platform, a prominent businessman and civic leader read dispatches from the front to a crowd of a hundred cheering people.

An accurate count of the regiment's losses would be months in coming. A full postwar roster of those who served in the Second New Hampshire indicates that fifteen men died during the battle, later of their wounds, or in Confederate prison camps. Thirty-nine were captured, including eleven men left wounded on the battlefield or during the retreat. The total wounded, including the captives, was fifty-six.[47] Many more were missing, although some stragglers returned to camp. A few returnees soon deserted, and the fates of many prisoners echoed through the Second's camp for months. Pvt. William Conner died in captivity in Centreville on July 31. Pvt. Charles Chase, the man Hubbard had listed as wounded in the thigh and captured, lasted in Richmond until September 1. Both were nineteen years old. Andrew Straw, whom Charles Putnam had found with his leg blown off during the retreat, was never heard from again. Many captives would be paroled and exchanged after eight or nine months, but some suffered in rebel prisons for well over a year. After three months in Richmond, Pvt. John Wheeler of Claremont was taken to New Orleans.[48] From there, on February 6, 1862, he started on foot for Salisbury Prison in North Carolina. Finally paroled and put on a ship nearly a year after the battle, Wheeler died before reaching New York Harbor.

Not everyone who left the regiment and went home to New Hampshire that summer had behaved honorably at Bull Run. Perhaps some had not even made it to the battle. Or at least Drown suggested as much to his wife. After learning in early August that Cpl. Joseph Sweatt and Pvt. Jacob Baker were in town, he wrote her: "I suppose they are looked upon as heroes. Wonder if Baker has shown his discharge to anyone. Should advise all the young ladies to get a look at the cause that is written on it."[49] As their company commander, he knew why they had been dismissed from the regiment. State records say only that they were discharged for disability.

After the battle, President Lincoln called on Maj. Gen. George B. McClellan to take over the eastern armies. By July 26, McClellan had combined various commands around Washington to form the Army of the Potomac. Considering the defeat at Bull Run and the accolades McClellan had received for two victories over rebel forces in western Virginia, most men in the Second New Hampshire welcomed the change. "We have great confidence in Gen. McClellan as he is known as a smart and active man besides being loyal," declared George Ladd, one of the sharpshooting privates from Concord.[50] Pvt. John Odlin, Dame's neighbor in the city, thought McClellan got off to a good start by "confining the men to camps without a special pass. [This] put a stop to drunkenness and rowdyism in the streets of Washington."[51] The general began preparing the men for battle through a regimen of close-order drill, tactical training, target practice, and physical conditioning. Based on McClellan's successes west of the Alleghenies, Odlin proclaimed that "a succession of brilliant victories may be expected," snuffing out "the treason of Virginia forever."

Many months would pass before Harriet Dame had another chance to go to battle. Seventeen days after Bull Run, she and the rest of the regiment packed up to move. They marched just six miles north, to Bladensburg, Maryland. Dame had been with the Second for a little more than a month and was still figuring out what it meant to be a matron. She knew how to tend to sick soldiers and had liked helping Hubbard treat men wounded after Bull Run. Because of her dressmaking career before the war, she was a wizard with a needle and thread. She had baked and cooked for herself and her boarders for years. In addition to these skills, Dame took on any challenge. In the regiment's new camp, this combination of ability and determination would further define her role.

Maryland

Soon after settling into Camp Union at Bladensburg in August 1861, Harriet Dame decided she liked her new surroundings. The regiment occupied the estate of a wealthy Maryland landowner, and pathways through flowers and trees surrounded Dame's tent near his mansion. "Instead of having (as of old) a beautiful garden adjoining our grounds, we are in a beautiful garden," she wrote Anna Berry.[1] She continued to make friends with the officers and men, who treated her "with kindness & attention. Why shouldn't I like them?" While taking a shortcut to the kitchen one morning, Dame nearly collided with Gen. Joseph Hooker on a shrub-lined path. She knew he boarded in the mansion but had not yet met him. Hooker, a West Pointer from Massachusetts with a rakish reputation, bade her "a very cordial good morning." The flustered Dame replied that the path was narrow. "Yes," Hooker said with a glance at her skirt, "for hoops."

Her first impression of the camp had been less positive. The day she arrived, it was raining so hard that no one could pitch her tent.[2] She and Mary Marden, the other matron, slept on the ground in the surgeon's tent next door. It rained all weekend. Although the campsite looked grassy, the ground consisted of "regular Maryland clay," and the rain turned the clay into a quagmire. Captain Drown, whom Dame had met in Concord when he stayed at her brother's boardinghouse during jury duty, visited her tent and blacked her dirty boots, but it was no use. The boots constantly sank deep in mud when she made her rounds or slogged to the regiment's hospital tent to care for the sick.

Once the place dried out, Dame described her surroundings as "the most beautiful country I ever saw." Her domestic arrangements also improved.

When Ai Thompson, her former boarder, left the regiment for a promotion, he bequeathed her his bed and chair, and the surgeon gave her a longer tent to accommodate the new furniture. She now slept alone on the bed. Mary Marden—"My Chum," Dame called her—"still sticks to the mattress & the floor, but she is fat—her bones don't mar the floor."[3]

Dame quickly became known as a light eater and a good, if frugal, cook. During the Second New Hampshire's early days at Bladenburg, her friend Henry Parker ate with the officers and boasted to his wife Mary that few soldiers "live as well as the officers of our mess do at present."[4] Even General Hooker dined with them. The chaplain saved table scraps for Dame and Marden, and when churchwomen in Concord sent him a box of food, he gave Dame the bread his wife had baked. He could think of no one in the camp who needed the bread more, as Dame's diet consisted of "*nothing to speak of.*" In time, the officers' mess broke up, and Parker and the surgeon began eating with Dame and Marden "in a very humble but wholesome way. No more of those superabundant & luxurious meals, I assure you." He missed dessert but enjoyed the company of "a very genteel set over our tea and toast sitting around a rickety apology for a table."

With good reason, doubts about the loyalty of Marylanders ran rampant in the camp. John C. Breckinridge, a Southern diehard who would later serve the Confederacy as a general and secretary of war, had carried the state in the November presidential election with Abraham Lincoln winning just 2 percent of the vote. Early in the war, Maryland proclaimed "armed neutrality," but secession remained a popular idea. Women wore Confederate pins, and men destroyed roads and railroad bridges to obstruct federal troop movements. On April 19, rioters killed four men from a Massachusetts regiment who were changing trains in Baltimore, including Luther Ladd, a private from New Hampshire, who became the first Union soldier to die for the cause in a clash of arms. In the end, because Maryland's fortunes depended on ties with the North, its governor led a movement to keep his state in the Union, and many dissenters decamped for Dixie.[5]

Bladensburg had been a major seaport for nearly a century from its founding until 1840, when even frequent dredging could no longer control the silt in the harbor. Large ocean ships carried enslaved people and indentured servants to and from the port, along with tobacco, rum, molasses, and other commodities. Those days were gone. The region grew tobacco now, its large farms worked by enslaved people.[6] As Dame would learn during a chance visit to a foundry, Bladensburg's proximity to Washington had bolstered its manufacturing economy. From a strategic perspective, the town was a key point in the string of federal forts and camps guarding the capital. Many of the million three-year volunteers called up by Lincoln shortly after Bull Run passed through its station on the way to Washington. Dame and the soldiers could see the trains on the railbed at the edge of their campground. While knowing that the men of Hooker's brigade would rather be on the march to avenge their defeat at Bull Run, she soon realized that "an enemy more deadly than the bullet was constantly lurking in the atmosphere."[7] She had come to nurse the sick, and here they were.

To win his first command of the war, Hooker had gone directly to Lincoln after the defeat at Manassas. He had been at Bull Run during the battle, he told the president, "and it is neither vanity or boasting in me to declare that I am a damned sight better General than you, Sir, had on that field."[8] Hooker had received his brigadier's star just days before his encounter with Dame at Bladensburg. The Second New Hampshire was the first regiment to arrive at his brigade rendezvous and thus the first to serve under him. "We felt he belonged to us and we followed his career with an interest that was born of that early comradeship," Dame later observed.[9]

Hooker soon joined the hierarchy of the Army of the Potomac. At its pinnacle stood Maj. Gen. George McClellan, a self-important but talented officer who set out to create a large, battle-ready force. Although the New Hampshire men longed for quick redemption after their flight from Bull Run, they were now on McClellan's timetable. His idea was to protect the capital while carefully turning a mob of eager civilians into soldiers. He would prove to be far more adept at creating an army than using it.

Although the men did not know what to expect from McClellan, they had begun to put their July defeat behind them. Parker expected the next battle soon but thought it would be different. Because Confederate cannon fire had inflicted so many casualties at Manassas, he accepted the "universal opinion" that artillery would play a far greater role than infantry in the next fight. "None of us will object to this," he wrote. Wrong as he was about this, Parker clearly understood the war's strategic picture: "Even if our battles were all to be like the last, the enemy would become worn out much the sooner: they are far less able to bear such a loss as they met with at 'Bull Run' than we are ours."[10] Dame's friend Drown adopted a similar perspective, advising his wife Molly to ignore newspaper speculation about Bull Run's significance and reminding her that he had left home expecting a long, hard struggle. "I have not changed my mind," he added. "Rest assured that the *right* will prevail. Whether I live to see the end or not, I shall not have lived in vain."[11] Pvt. Charles Jewett welcomed a shipment of Springfield rifles. "When we go to the bulls run again," he predicted, "we shall have something that we can reach the rebbels with."[12] By mid-August, less than a month after the battle, the sting of defeat had healed enough for Capt. Simon G. Griffin to use it in a pun. To a musical friend back home, he quipped: "For want of a good conductor, we made a good *'Bull'* of it and *'Run'* the wrong way."[13]

Camp life was rigorous, consisting mainly of training and fatigue duty. Hooker soon had his brigade drilling six hours a day with the first session beginning at five thirty in the morning, ninety minutes before breakfast. When not at drill, Drown wrote, the men cleared away trees or did other chores on "a chain of works on the hights commanding the approaches to Washington on the Maryland side."[14] Some men groused about all the drilling, but Cpl. Tom Leaver embraced the new regime, assuring his brother that when the next battle came, "we shall be prepared to give the rebels fits." Strenuous activity dominated the men's time even during leisure hours. Frank Fiske, their lieutenant colonel, had purchased ten balls for them. "The boys keep them going pretty much all the time," Leaver remarked, either "playing base ball or kicking foot ball."[15] Fiske also provided comic relief one August day when his out-of-control horse bolted into the tent of a lieutenant who was reading a newspaper. "Down went tent, horse and rider in one grand mix-up," Pvt. Martin Haynes reported. "Out of the ruins crawled the worst-scared man since Bull Run."[16]

Dame expanded her circle of acquaintances during these early days in Maryland. She had ready access to the Second's staff officers, Marston, Fiske, Hubbard, and Parker, and often interacted with captains and lieutenants. But she also befriended many enlisted men, who over time would make up a far greater portion of the sick and wounded she treated. She knew Leaver from home and came to admire Haynes for his independence of mind.

Among the regiment's keenest chroniclers, the two were both printers who, like many in their trade, longed to write for newspapers.[17] The twenty-one-year-old Leaver's letters home detailed his every action and frustration. He knew Dame from home as a family friend but reintroduced himself during the regiment's early days at Camp Union.[18] Haynes, two years younger than Leaver, seemed less susceptible to the bothers of army life. A foot soldier to the core, he shunned promotion and gladly remained a private. He was a lively writer who would in time become the historian every regiment wished it had.

The Leavers were well known in Concord, where, as Dame understood, tragedy had shaped their lives. Tom was the second-born son and namesake

Left: Cpl. Thomas B. Leaver (from 1896 Second New Hampshire regimental history); *right:* Pvt. Martin A. Haynes (from *The Girl I Left Behind Me,* by Haynes, 1916)

of a Baptist missionary who had left his native England to preach and pros-elytize in the Bahamas. Tom was born there. In 1846, Thomas Sr. brought his family to Concord, where, now an Episcopalian, he was called as the rector at St. Paul's Church.[19] Before the family could settle into its new life, Pastor Leaver fell ill and died, leaving his Welsh-born wife Mary to raise five children between the ages of one and eight.[20] To help with the bills, Tom left home at fourteen to work at a farm and then a machine shop in western New Hamp-shire. He later returned to take up the printing trade at the *New Hampshire Patriot* office, earning twelve dollars a month.[21] By the time the war began, the family lived in a house with a free African-born servant and two boarders, both printers like Tom.[22]

Haynes, who had begun reporting in his teens, submitted accounts of life in the Second New Hampshire to the *Daily American* in Manchester, his home-town. He also wrote regularly to Cornelia Lane, his betrothed. He would later use his reporting skills and material from his letters to compose not one but two superb histories of the regiment. Half a century after the war, he would publish a selection of the letters to Lane. *A Minor War History,* he called it, a tip to readers that unlike the fat memoirs of generals, his book conveyed "an idea of what the men in the ranks were talking and thinking and doing." His one worry in publishing it was that its contents would dispel his grandchildren's illusions "as to their grandfather's relative importance in the war."[23]

One August Sunday morning at Bladensburg, with no inkling of the eventful day in store for her, Dame walked to the field where Henry Parker was to preach. The chaplain loved the Sabbath, whether in his Concord pulpit or outdoors on a sunny morning with his regiment. "We have a prayer almost every night and a meeting on the ground every Sunday so you see that we are kept steady," one private wrote.[24] The soldiers had plenty of company in church. "Mr. Parker is good to draw a house," observed Sgt. Abner Durgin. "All the gals within reasonable distance come to hear him preach."[25] As Parker awaited his congregation that morning, the sun shone through the trees and a breeze tempered the heat. Parker appreciated how neat and clean the arriving soldiers looked. After sitting on the grass for his sermon, they sang along—many of them badly, in Dame's opinion—to the band's renditions of familiar hymns. Afterward, as the field cleared out, Parker introduced Dame to Charles Beck, chaplain of the Twenty-Sixth Pennsylvania Infantry, another regiment in their brigade. Beck's pulpit stood fifty yards from Parker's. Feeling she had no choice, Dame stuck around for his service, too.[26]

While recovering from her gospel overdose back at camp, she learned that the kitchen had no milk for supper. She grabbed a pail and set out with a junior cook to find some. The couple at the nearest mansion had none to spare but directed them to someone who might. After walking two miles farther without finding the place, the searchers spied a peculiar two-story octagonal building with ramparts. From its center rose a two-tiered tower, and beneath that, painted above the structure's large wooden door, a sign identified the building's owner and his purpose: "Clark Mills, Sculptor."[27]

A native of Charleston, Mills was not just any sculptor. He had created the equestrian statue of Andrew Jackson in Lafayette Square across from the White House and a mounted bronze likeness of the nation's first president in Washington Square. The octagonal building was Mills's showroom. Workers at the nearby foundry were engaged in his grandest project yet. He was not the sculptor of this work in progress. Instead, the United States government had rented his foundry and hired him as an artisan to oversee the casting of the statue. The plaster model of what was then known as *Freedom Triumphant in War and Peace* had arrived at the foundry the previous year. The challenge of disassembling the enormous model so that it could be rendered in bronze fell to Philip Reid, an enslaved Black man. The government contract for Reid's work provided a wage of $1.25 each Sunday, the only day that enslaved people

Clark Mills's show-room on Bladensburg Road, 1862 (Library of Congress, LC-USZ62-116438)

could legally work for wages. More than a year after finishing the work, Reid was paid $41.25 for thirty-three Sundays. Any money for work he did on the statue during the rest of the week presumably went to Mills. Anyone looking for a metaphor for America's willful blindness to the cruelty of slavery needed look no further than to the irony of an enslaved man casting a monument that became known as *The Statue of Freedom*. The foundry would produce a stellar work that stood nineteen and a half feet tall and weighed seven and a half tons. Two years later, it would be raised atop the United States Capitol.[28]

When Dame and the cook happened upon the foundry, they were disappointed to learn that Clark Mills's workers kept only one cow at the complex and had no milk to give them. One of the workers did direct them to Mills's house in the distance.[29] The Northern couple living there served them cake and milk and filled the bucket for the trip back to camp. They also warned Dame against scrounging provisions in Bladensburg. Many local people, including Mills himself, favored secession, they said. They told Dame that she, the cook, or anyone else from Camp Union looking for food in this vicinity might "accidentally get a little poison."

James Pottinger McGill, twenty-seven years old and single, owned the estate on which the brigade camped and trained. His dwelling was about the size of Dame's boardinghouse in Concord. She referred to him as "the bachelor" and considered him a secessionist, too.[30] In the previous year's census, he had valued his property at $45,000 and his personal worth at $250,000, a handsome sum for the time.[31] McGill had learned only on the day before Hooker's brigade arrived that he would be host to more than three thousand soldiers. His first thought was to vacate the premises, but he decided to stay, possibly after assurances from Hooker that he would be safe. Dame found the estate splendid but was alarmed by the damage the soldiers were inflicting on the terrain. She hoped they would at least spare McGill's trees.

Because she made lemon pies and brown bread for the Black women who worked in McGill's kitchen, they allowed her to brew tea any time she wished.[32] One day she departed from her spartan diet and ate a meal from the kitchen. "Well Anna," she declared afterward, "we have had dinner & I have taken a nap in the big chair."[33] The menu confirmed her notions of the South. "Indeed this is a lazy country," she wrote. "The most important thing is to eat and sleep. Let me tell you what we had for dinner: fried chicken boiled ham shelled beans corn cabbage sweet potatoes." Peaches and cream topped off the meal. "Do you wonder at peoples being lazy & sleepy after dinner?"

The enslaved people who made the meals and worked the property called McGill "Boss."[34] They must have sensed that the war might improve their lives, but perhaps change came sooner than some of them expected. Just months after the first federal soldiers occupied Camp Union, President Lincoln signed an act freeing the enslaved people of Washington, DC, and compensating their owners for their loss. As a Marylander, McGill could not be paid under the act, but Sarah Allen, whom he owned, lived with her husband and four children in the district. After the act was broadened to include enslaved Washingtonians whose owners lived in Maryland, Allen petitioned for her freedom and that of her four children. Her husband George was owned by a woman from Washington who described him as "a very fine Restaurant cook, market gardener & handy with all tools—sound body & mind, and good morals." A note in her petition for compensation said he had been purchased only to keep his family together when he was on the verge of being sold into Georgia. Thus was the Allen family reunited in freedom.[35]

At Camp Union many men in the Second New Hampshire interacted for the first time with Black people, enslaved and free. Haynes wished his fiancée could visit the camp on a Sunday. This was "the negro's holiday, and they swarm into camp with their apples, peaches, chickens, or whatever they happen to have that can be turned into money or old clothes. Each one has a basket, with a crooked stick on which to swing it over the shoulder. The plantation negroes—mostly slaves—are a quaint lot, not a bit like the bright colored people you see north. We used to think the stage negro at the minstrel show was a burlesque. He wasn't."[36] The slavery issue and local hostility to the presence of Union troops shaped Leaver's thoughts. "There is a curse on these Southern homes which shows itself in everything—Slavery," he wrote. "Within sight of our camp poor slave women toil at men's work hoeing corn, pitching hay &c."[37]

One Sunday, Parker draped a banner over the table he used for a pulpit and began his sermon, an old standard about the Prodigal Son.[38] The banner had been given to the Second by the Sons of New Hampshire of New York City when the regiment stopped there on the way south. At Bull Run, the rebels had shot the eagle off its staff and perforated the banner with bullets.[39] Parker was about two-thirds of the way through his sermon when a handsome black barouche arrived behind his pulpit. He ignored the commotion it caused and kept on preaching. The Rives family, whose house Dame had visited during her recent search for milk, had come to the service with other civilians from the neighborhood. Having spotted them from the pulpit, Parker set out to greet them just after the service ended. Only when he reached them did he recognize "the President's towering form" hovering over them. Lincoln and his son Robert had arrived in the barouche with a party that included Secretary of State William Seward, Naval Secretary Gideon Welles, and Gen. Joseph Mansfield. As pleased as Parker was, he wished he had known "such illustrious visitors" were coming so that he could have prepared something grander for their ears. "Didn't my vanity and pride fall clear down into the grass with awful suddenness?" he confessed to his wife Mary. When others praised his sermon, he "fired up quickly" and his "vanity lifted its head a little above the grass." Parker spoke at length with the president and his son, a Harvard student on summer break, and liked them both.[40]

For some soldiers, Lincoln's unexpected visit proved to be a thrill with a catch. As Parker chatted with the Lincoln party, Hooker bustled about readying his brigade for a presidential review. Officers of the Second New Hampshire ordered their men to leave the church and prepare for inspection. Leaver's captain, Simon G. Griffin, marched his company quick time to its quarters. The men threw on their equipment, grabbed their rifles, and joined the regiment on the left of the brigade. To his mother, Leaver described what happened next: "We passed in review before 'Old Abe.' It took two or three hours and was very hot work. I don't care about another visit from him if they mean to put us through that way every time."[41]

By contrast, Pvt. George Ladd of Leaver's company was "highly honored" to be in such distinguished company.[42] Ladd was nurturing a romance with a girl he had never met. While heading south with the regiment in June, he had scribbled his name, unit, and marital status—"eligible bachelor"—on a card-board scrap and tossed it out the train window at a station in Pennsylvania. Sixteen-year-old Carrie Deppen, a judge's daughter who had come to cheer the passing troops, picked it up and wrote to Ladd. By the Sunday when he marched before the president, he was smitten. In his long letter to "Dearest Carrie," composed in three sittings, the last to the flickering light of a candle stuck on a bayonet, he poured out his feelings: "Do not believe that I am play-ing you false. [I] sincerely hope that the ties of love that bind us together will last as long as life itself."

Dame nursed daily in the camp hospital, but her work hardly ended there. Anna Berry asked on behalf of her mother if Dame ever "had time to take a stitch." Dame responded: "If she had seen the quantity of linen thread & silks I brought with me she would know I had taken *many many* stitches." Her workload caused her to miss the president's second visit in October, but she decided to attend Hooker's review of his brigade a few days later. She didn't make that either. After pulling his best trousers on for the review, John God-frey, the quartermaster, dropped his everyday pants off for her to mend by day's end. Dame often sewed into the night, usually for soldiers in the hospi-tal, until her eyesight failed her. "I darned stockings when every other body was asleep," she wrote. "I like to do for the poor sick fellows that are far from their mothers." Nor did she lack for creature comforts. She had acquired two of "the prettiest cats this side of N.H," although they were so wild that she needed a stick to control them. Flowers long gone in New Hampshire by early October remained in bloom in Bladensburg. "The roses are still beautiful as even I made a bouquet of eighteen, the most splendid roses I ever saw," she wrote. After placing a yellow rose at the peak, she gave the bouquet away.[43]

Despite Dame's confidence that October that none of the thirty-two hospi-talized men from the Second were dangerously ill, events proved her wrong. An eighteen-year-old patient just back from a morning visit to his company complained of stomach pains, then collapsed and died of typhus. The regimen-tal band played at his funeral and that of a Pennsylvania soldier who had been shot by a comrade playing with his weapon. One day there were four burials. "It is a sad sight to see a soldier's funeral," Dame wrote. The coffins were placed on a gun carriage, draped with the flag, and drawn away. All the members of the Third Michigan Volunteers wore white gloves as they followed their dead to the burying ground. When a private from Dame's regiment was unearthed and shipped home, she knew another man would soon occupy the grave. She disliked seeing "these young men die & be buried in a strange land." In one

Maj. George Hubbard, surgeon of the Second New Hampshire ("Maj. George Hubbard," MOLLUS-Mass Civil War Photograph Collection Volume 128, U.S. Army Heritage and Education Center, Carlisle, PA)

case, Dame consoled herself with a verse: "It matters not what spot on earth, Receives my frail & lifeless clod, If born to an immortal birth, I wake in heaven a child of God."[44]

That fall, the army summoned George Hubbard, the Second's surgeon, to run the medical department of northern Missouri. Hubbard was a fine doctor and a charming man. After the departure of Ai Thompson, he had become Dame's best comrade. "I loved him dearly," she later remarked. "He was so kind to me, always full of funny stories." She liked James Merrow, Hubbard's assistant and successor, well enough, but things were not the same. Hubbard took three excellent hospital stewards to Missouri with him, another reminder of how rapidly people came and went in the army. During Dame's first three months in the regiment, ten of the sixteen men in the hospital corps departed. "This reg't is worse than a boarding house," she complained.[45]

When word spread in October that the regiment would soon move, most men welcomed the idea even though, typically, they did not know where they were going. Because the news might augur another battle, Dame's friend Captain Drown carried out a task he must have been thinking about for some time. In his best hand, he shared with Israel, his ten-year-old son, his ideas about an honorable life. Bull Run had sharpened his sense of mortality, and the passage of the months since the battle had heightened his guilt as an absentee father. Yet his mind soared above the personal nature of his letter to express the power of the Union cause and the sacrifices Northern men and women were willing to make for it:

> Not knowing whether I may ever have the privilege of seeing you again, I write this for your future reading that you may know something [of] what I wish you may be, and my reason for wishing you to defer opening this is that you will then be old enough to give the words due thought.
>
> Never forget that there is an overruling power that orders all things for the best. Let the first of your earthly cares be for your Mother; she has no son but you to provide for her, and remember that as you deal with her so will your children deal with you.
>
> Do unto others as you would have that they should do unto you is a safe rule. Ask yourself when you are about to do a thing, How would I like to have it done to me? Remember that your sisters have no brother but yourself. Never degrade yourself enough to tell a lie, and remember that a man's word of honor is the strongest pledge that he can give.
>
> Chose some ocupation [sic] and strive to be one of the first in it. Remember that nothing is worth doing that is not worth doing well. Live within your means and avoid debt as it is a curse. Strive by all reasonable means to acquire knowledge; you will feel the need for it as you grow older.
>
> Do not let military affairs have too many charms for you, but if ever the foot of the invader presses your native soil, or Treason raises its head, be ready to pour out your blood as freely as water at your country's call.
>
> Never do anything but what you would be willing your mother should know and you will save yourself from sorrow. That you would be a good man is the ernest [sic] prayer of your
>
> Father[46]

During the brigade's final weeks at Camp Union, no hospital bed stayed empty for long. Some men died, some improved enough to be transferred to military hospitals in Washington. Funerals were so frequent that the burial ground was "fast filling up," Dame noted, and sick soldiers "who would have faced a battle without flinching were not ashamed to give vent to tears." When orders came for the regiment to pack up, Dame prepared to stay behind to care for men too ill to march. The surgeon of the Twenty-Sixth Pennsylvania took charge of the sick with Mary Marden and Dame as his nurses. "One cannot realize except by an experience of the same kind, what were the feelings of these men as the regiments marched away with the martial airs of bugle and drum quickening their steps toward the scene of conflict," Dame observed.[47] Among the men still in the hospital was Pvt. George Ladd, who lay weak and lonesome on his cot. It irked him that all mail, especially his, was being forwarded to the regiment. If it were his choice, he wrote Carrie Deppen, "I should like to come see you and go home."[48] Dame toiled at the tent hospital for six weeks. As patients suffered and died, she reflected on the causes of so much sickness. She concluded that instead of keeping the men on the move, "some mismanagement at our head departments" had consigned them to idleness in a camp where disease spread quickly.[49]

For tactical rather than humanitarian reasons, McClellan's reluctance to move had raised concerns at the White House that would fester as the months passed and the Army of the Potomac sat idle. Dame understood this frustration as well, articulating a chilling but perceptive view of the army's delay. "If they intend to get through without sacrificing lives," she asserted to Anna Berry, "I don't believe it can be done. Only when they are willing to go into battle with fifty thousand brave souls & come out with one third of them & a glorious victory, then & not till then shall we see anything like coming home."[50]

As well as anyone, Dame later summarized how nearly eighty days of marching in place at Bladensburg had sapped the morale of her regiment. "With nothing to do but the usual routine of the soldier's life; with no realization of the belief with which we had started that the rebellion would be crushed in ninety days; with none of the glamour surrounding active duty in the field; above all, with young men recruited from the plow, the counting house, the trades, and from every avocation of New England life, the stagnation created homesickness, regret, and lassitude." These words reflected her own keen disappointment. She had come with the regiment to help the men put down the rebellion and instead found herself nursing the sick and serving as a cook and seamstress to an idle army. Yet even these feelings failed to dull her sense of purpose. "I found," she reflected, "that a friendly woman's face, suggesting memories of home and mother and sweetheart, was no mean panacea for lonely young soldiers."[51]

"My Hands Were Never Idle"

For all the excitement of pulling up stakes, the four-day slog down the Maryland side of the Potomac turned out to be a miserable journey. Hooker's division headed south from Camp Union on the morning of October 24, 1861, with thirteen regiments, nine of infantry and three of artillery, and a cavalry battalion.[1] Because the Second New Hampshire had traveled light to Bull Run, this was the men's first long march with all their gear. To Cpl. Tom Leaver, the narrow, muddy path was the most difficult the men had traveled so far. They slept in the open the first night, then nearly froze and went to bed hungry the next. When some were reprimanded for stealing cows and shooting sheep, Leaver wondered why the officers "could not allow us to help ourselves to what we wanted from the miserable secessionists, who are as thick as bees in this part of the state." Most commanders allowed foraging in enemy territory, but because Maryland had stayed in the Union, it was forbidden there. As the division neared its destination, Leaver trailed behind. "Feet too sore to catch up, fell to the rear," he lamented.[2]

One unexpected pleasure relieved the drudgery of the march: timely mail service. Since Chaplain Parker was on horseback while the men were on foot, he took a cue from the Pony Express. He rode to Washington to post the soldiers' letters and returned with mail from home, completing this wearying mission twice during the move. "You have no idea how grateful the men felt for my enterprise in obtaining their letters for them," he wrote his wife Mary.[3]

The regiment's new home, Hill Top, impressed no one. "What we are down here for, I can hardly tell," Leaver observed.[4] John Godfrey, Hooker's division quartermaster, wondered what the horses would eat. "This is the poorest country I ever saw," he complained, "& how we are to subsist the Horses of which we have some 1500 God only knows. We shall sweep this country clean as a floor."[5] Meager rations prompted the men to name the place "Camp Starvation." To make the hard bread palatable, Pvt. Martin Haynes gave it a good soak in hot coffee and a slathering of butter. Still, he craved soft bread.[6] Leaver noted that each tent held nine men "eating & sleeping just like pigs." They alternated positions, four laying their heads to one side of the tent, five to the other. At six feet tall, Leaver felt cramped, but at least the tentmates stayed warm. "We would surely freeze if we did not lay pretty thick," he wrote. Haynes, meanwhile, puffed up the mission with his typical wry humor: "For some weeks the Second was stationed in the important village of Hill Top, consisting of one dwelling-house, one store, and two negro cabins."[7] The regiment soon moved from a soggy hollow to higher ground. And the cuisine improved, as local Black people "brought in coons, possums, gray squirrels, rabbits and chickens, all cooked, and well cooked."

Leaver learned from the enslaved men who came into the camp in the evenings that they all considered the abolitionist martyr John Brown a saint. Whether true or not, they also told him they knew the war was being fought not to free them but to preserve the Union. Fearing that once the soldiers left, they would be beaten for visiting the camp, they hoped the army would take them along when it left. Leaver thought that "the mere stationing of a regiment of Northern men in a slaveholding district will strengthen the love of liberty in the hearts of these poor men." Despite claims of loyalty from local white men, he considered them all secessionists: "If the Negroes are to be believed, and I think they are, not a Union man, at heart, can be found."[8]

By the time Harriet Dame helped to transfer the last of the sick men at Bladensburg to hospitals in Washington, the regiment had moved several miles to Camp Beaufort at Budd's Ferry on the Potomac shore. She boarded the *City of Richmond* at the wharf in the capital and steamed downriver to rejoin the Second there. In eastern Maryland, the blaze and blush of autumn came far later than in New Hampshire. Dame caught it at its peak as "the Virginia shore hung out its audacious red from every hilltop in its vivid shrubbery."[9] She quickly moved into what she generously called "our *Village*," although Haynes considered it "about as near to being no place at all as it could and still be on the map."[10]

Lieutenant Colonel Fiske, who commanded the regiment in the absence of the wounded Marston, welcomed Dame, as did several Concord men. When

Captain Drown dropped by, she asked if he was officer of the day. No, he said, he had special orders to look after her. Abiel Colby, the grocer who now commanded the Concord company, was becoming one of her model captains. She admired the sturdy log cabin he had built for his lieutenants. Fiske lived in a similar cabin and offered to have one made for Dame, but she told him log houses were too dark inside and said she was satisfied with her tent. When winter came in earnest, she would change her mind. Dame shared the tent with Marden, the other matron, but slept on a mattress on the ground with a doubled-up blanket and a few clothes thrown over her. Because she lay near the stove, she could reach the woodpile without getting up. A fire of green wood usually lasted until five in the morning, when she would add logs and sleep till daybreak.[11]

Dame was a cat lover who, given the circumstances of army life in the field, would later adjust to dogs. Friends had taken in her cats before she left Concord and she had left two frisky felines behind at Bladensburg, but at Budd's Ferry she decided it was time for a new one. An enslaved man who lived with her egg supplier thought he could catch her one, but the cat he had in mind escaped his clutches. "In all this county," she lamented, "there is no cat worth feeding." Still longing for something to pet, she vowed to "get a cat, dog or tame our big rat that scampers around my head nights."[12]

Beyond digging in for winter and training, the regiment's mission was to harass an inept Confederate blockade and keep the Potomac safe for Union ships. The infantry served mainly to protect the artillery, which fired on any rebel vessel within range.[13] Nothing came of frequent camp rumors that the men would soon cross the river's two-mile expanse and attack the enemy, and as the weeks passed, Godfrey worried about the idleness of the Army of the Potomac. "There is nothing that looks like a movement here more than at any time for a month," he wrote, "but if they don't do something soon, it will ruin somebody, either the Administration or McClellan or both."[14]

Dame had become annoyed with Marden and was glad when she decided to leave. Though just two years older than Dame at forty-eight, Marden had borne six children and inherited four from her late husband, a farmer.[15] Her girth, clumsiness, and constant chatter led to talk behind her back. Sitting together as the drums beat tattoo one evening to announce lights out, Dame, Surgeon Merrow, and a private from Concord made Marden the butt of their jokes. "We are all having such a riot & dreading her coming back," Dame wrote. "Her everlasting tongue is never still, only when she is asleep. Then her nasal engine catches the strain."[16] Referring to the capture of the mail boat from Washington that day, the three of them speculated about which Confederate prisoner would be exchanged for Marden if the rebels seized the boat that was bringing her back to camp. Although she did, in fact, leave the regiment for good, Marden would later report to Dorothea Dix and nurse at Gettysburg, in Beaufort, South Carolina, and at Point of Rocks Hospital in Virginia, where she and Dame would again cross paths.[17]

Surprisingly, the weather turned pleasant enough for a day or two in mid-December that a gingham dress without lining in the waist kept Dame warm till the cool of the evening. As she curled up by the fire to write Anna Berry one night, her dough for the next morning sat rising beside her. She had a three-legged spider pan for baking bread over a fire. It took her half a day to make all the food she needed. "I have such a large family in the hospital, fourteen to cook for," she explained. "I send bread & tea three times a week. Yesterday eight of them had steak for dinner, the rest soup. Today they all had oysters."[18] She also made goodies for Colonel Fiske and prepared meals for her own table, which included two hospital stewards. One of them, William Stark, liked tomatoes for breakfast, and a friend in Concord supplied Dame with canned tomatoes for him. They ate at nine in the morning, after sick call.

Dame was closer now to the sounds of war than she had been during the Bull Run battle, but still it was not quite war. When big guns shook her awake one night, she threw on her clothes and ran out to see the flashes that usually followed the pop of a cannon, but there was no further firing.[19] A few days earlier, the *Harriet Lane,* flagship of the Union's Potomac Flotilla, and other gunboats had attacked across the river after sailors spotted a rebel caravan approaching buildings near the beach. Steamers destroyed the structures, and marines went ashore to burn the stores.[20] Dame heard cannon fire for an hour that day but was too busy to go look. When she did witness artillery fire, it surprised her that, despite the thunder that sent the shells flying, they seemed to strike little or nothing of importance. One day, Pvt. George Ladd counted twenty-eight rebel shots on a Union frigate on the Potomac, all of which missed the mark.[21] When a sixty-two-pound Confederate shell flew close enough to the Second New Hampshire's camp to cause an involuntary duck before it landed without exploding on the parade ground, Captain Colby paid a soldier ten dollars to dig it out for him. Early in the regiment's stay at Budd's Ferry, the men had watched rebel artillery wreck a Union schooner, but this proved to be a rarity. "Thousands of shots were fired by the rebels during the winter," Haynes observed, but except for the schooner, "not a vessel was hit from the beginning to the end of the blockade."[22]

Disease and the close winter quarters in which it spread emerged as the true dangers at Camp Beaufort. "Typhoid fever goes pretty hard here," Dame wrote.[23] Three bodies were carried to the cemetery one December day. Soldiers disinterred one of them the next day when a relative arrived to take him home. One gravely ill man was a private from Keene whose fifty-one-year-old father, a musician with the regiment, had carried the wounded son back to Washington from Bull Run in July. The ordeal had so disabled the father that he had gone home and was unavailable to watch over his son. The day the son died of disease, two other men in his company also succumbed, including one who had slept in the same tent. As Hiram Durgin, a private in Drown's company, languished for weeks in the hospital, his mother asked the captain to remind him to write. To her relief, Hiram soon informed her that he was walking again and thought he was receiving the best care an army field hospital could provide. "I feel satisfied," he reassured her, "but it is not like home."[24]

Hiram Durgin's lukewarm review would not have surprised Dame, who found hospital tents "inadequate to shelter the miserable patients." She toiled in these tents daily. "My hands were never idle," she later recalled, as "malignant diseases, smallpox and diphtheria filled the days with menace."[25] She wiped her patients' fevered brows, cleaned them as best she could, fed them broth, and tried to nourish their hope. Although the death toll discouraged her, the sick soldiers taught her "the profoundest lessons of sublime endurance to suffering." At the same time, her efforts left her deeply depressed. Untold horrors lay before her, but she would remember these days as the "severest test of my love of my work."

Even amid such trials, Dame continued to provide hearty meals for some of her comrades. Cooking kept her warm. "The fire looks bright & keeps popping," she wrote Berry during one cold night. "My mother used to say it was a sign of rain."[26] For her messmates that day, she had prepared beefsteak, boiled potatoes, and biscuits for breakfast, stewed oysters with soda crackers and bread at midday, and fried oysters and cornbread for supper. The new regimental quartermaster, who was accustomed to eating often at General Hooker's table, joked that Dame's cooking made him think he was boarding at "the National Hotel on the lower Potomac."

Recovered from his wound at Bull Run, Gilman Marston returned to the regiment but was almost immediately shot again. This time the assailant was one of his own officers, who accidentally pulled the trigger while cleaning his pistol in another tent. Marston was lying on his divan when the bullet struck his left hip and exited through his abdomen. Somehow, the wound proved to

Maj. James Merrow, surgeon of the Second New Hampshire (USAHEC) ("Maj. James Merrow," MOLLUS-Mass Civil War Photograph Collection Volume 107, U.S. Army Heritage and Education Center, Carlisle, PA)

be painful but not disabling. Six days after being shot, Marston sat up for three hours.[27] When he could not get comfortable in his own bed, Dame traded tents with him, and he slept on her new mattress and pillow. In January, she remarked that camp life must have agreed with him as he had grown "fleshy" since his return.[28] For the new session of Congress, he took his cooks to Washington with him. In Marston's absence, Chaplain Parker anointed Dame the chief cook for the regimental staff. It took nearly all her time outside of her hospital duties, but she was glad, as always, to be doing something useful. She moved into the tent Marston had left behind and gave her own tent a good cleaning.

Captain Drown visited her on New Year's Eve, and they chuckled over a joke he had recently played on her. Drown had helped Merrow, the new surgeon, into a fancifully trimmed woman's dressing gown and then rushed to Dame's tent to tell her Merrow needed her. She arrived to find Merrow prancing about in the dressing gown.[29] Back in his tent shortly after midnight, when the clock tolled in 1862, Drown found himself still wide awake with a soldier's holiday blues. "As I do not feel disposed to sleep as yet let me talk with you a little tonight," he began a letter to Molly, as he called his wife. "When I look back it seems like a dream my being from home. I think Molly we shall love one another better for this separation. Let us bear it as patiently as may be, hoping that it is for the best. But let me tell you when I do get hold of you again, I will make up for lost time. Am longing to come back for the sake of one of those baths which used to be administered at times."[30] To this message of love, he added a warning that "Miss Dame" had threatened to expose the trick he had played on her.

Dame did her best to stay in touch with people and events back home. When she heard that a friend was having a hard time, she sent her a dollar. Parker forwarded the money, asking his wife Mary to add "a trifle" from church funds to Dame's gift.[31] Life in the field was hard on clothing, and Dame needed more dresses. With no material to make her own, she asked a Concord neighbor to buy the dresses, then arranged for a furloughed soldier to bring them back. In asking Berry to oversee this relay, she also sought information on a girl back home on behalf of a private in the regiment. She offered Berry a photograph of the private. "I see his *moustache* and all whenever I want," she teased.[32]

Early in the new year, Dame made time to visit the sights, such as they were, and to meet local people, few as they were. One cold day she hiked out to watch Union artillery fire on a rebel battery. Shells landed in the enemy camp, but Dame could not tell whether they had inflicted any damage. On a walk with Drown she got her first glimpse of a rebel flag flying across the river and returned to camp to see it again through a glass. Thinking the regiment might spend the rest of the winter at Camp Beaufort, she wondered if there was not at least "one decent family in this county we could occasionally call on." She found one, a poor woman half a mile away who seemed civil and had three lovely children. They were ragged and dirty, and Dame promised to bring them clothes.[33] Before she could follow through, the woman fell ill. On one of Surgeon Merrow's daily tours, he "found her all broken out with Small pox," Dame wrote. "Of course we must stay away from them for a while."[34]

During these monotonous days, Dame pondered quitting the regiment for a better offer. George Hubbard, the regiment's original surgeon, whom she liked and admired, now served in the West as medical director of the Army of the Frontier. Dame had toiled at his side for less than three months, but that had been long enough for him to recognize her skills, work ethic, and dedication. He invited her to serve as chief of nurses at the hospital in Paducah, Kentucky.[35] Even though nearly all Union surgeons still resisted the idea of women as nurses, Hubbard had been on Dame's side since she first proposed accompanying the regiment to war. He valued competence and resisted the gender prejudice of his peers. His offer tempted her, as "Anything was preferable to the stagnation." Chaplain Parker urged Dame to consider the possible move carefully, but he also informed Marston in Washington that the regiment might lose her.[36] Then Dame began to have doubts. A colleague who had gone west with Hubbard reported that "he never saw such rough people as those in the hospital" where he now worked. Hubbard himself told her he might soon be transferred to Texas. She also felt guilty about leaving behind "the familiar faces of the boys I had known in their beardless days." In the end, Marston settled the matter by giving Dame a direct order to stay put. He was her commander and she obeyed him. "Down deep in my heart," she reflected in a letter to Anna Berry, "rose a quiet thanksgiving that duty had been made so plainly to lead inclination."[37]

Because of Hooker's promotion to command the division, the Second New Hampshire needed a new brigadier, but the man chosen for the job was no Hooker. Henry Naglee, a West Pointer and a veteran of the Mexican War, arrived in February. The men were soon cursing him for his "three-cent airs" and his habit of punishing any man who committed the slightest infraction of military rules. Though "thoroughly hated by everybody from highest to lowest," in Leaver's opinion, Naglee considered himself the epitome of leadership.[38] "I am very agreeably surprised to find that my duties come very naturally to me, and so far have had no difficulty," he wrote his girlfriend, a San Francisco actress. "On the contrary, although but two weeks here, I have succeeded in capturing the confidence and respect of all of my officers, and am received in the most flattering manner by all."[39] In fact, without the moral support of Dame and Marston, the regiment might have revolted.

One night, Leaver had the misfortune of serving as sergeant of the guard at Naglee's headquarters. In keeping with army custom, parts of his squad alternated shifts, half of them sleeping or resting while the others manned the posts. A bench collapsed late at night, spilling its sleeping occupant onto the floor. As Leaver tried to quell the curses and guffaws that followed, Naglee's aide-de-camp, "a little snob of the first order," burst into the room to admonish him. The next morning, Naglee ordered Leaver arrested and court-martialed for neglect of duty. He was acquitted, but "Old Grizzly," as Leaver called Naglee, lost whatever respect he had with the men of the Second.[40]

Private Haynes picked his own fight with Naglee by mentioning in a dispatch for the Daily Mirror in Manchester how much the men loathed him. In response, the War Department sent Editor Simeon Farnsworth a message that "scared him stiff." Farnsworth shared it with Haynes's parents. "I guess they went wild—expected me to be taken out at sunrise and shot for high treason," Haynes wrote his fiancée. In camp he looked over his shoulder for days. Then a comrade told him "Harriet Dame wanted to shake hands with the private soldier that the War Department had to sit up and take notice of."[41] Because Dame was close to Marston, her comment convinced Haynes that Naglee's sour reputation in the regiment started at the top. The ruckus over his *Mirror* letter suddenly became "the best joke of the season."

A better joke soon came along, and it was Marston who played it. During a visit to the Second New Hampshire's guardhouse, Naglee raged over how airy and comfortable the building seemed. He ordered Marston to have a new log cabin built "without a crack or an opening, so that it is completely dark." When Naglee returned to see if his order had been carried out, "his eyes beamed with satisfaction as they rested on the gloomy structure." Then, walking around it, he realized something was amiss. "Where's the door?" he asked Marston. "Oh," the colonel replied, "that's not my lookout. I have obeyed orders." "Naglee's Dungeon" instantly became a landmark and remained one for the rest of the regiment's days at Budd's Ferry.[42]

When Naglee ordered the colonel of the First Massachusetts to find an enslaved man in his camp and return him to his owner, Northern newspapers reported "Negro Hunting" in his brigade. This report correctly described Naglee's racial attitudes but not those of a great many of his troops. Dame and most of the New Hampshire soldiers sympathized with the Black people who labored at the piers and did laundry, delivered messages, and performed other duties in camp. One formerly enslaved man told Dame that he and others had escaped as soon as the Union soldiers arrived. Former owners who came to retrieve them had little luck in the Second's camp, where Marston set the tone. Dame knew that the colonel sometimes allowed enslaved men working near the road to join his passing column. As she described one incident, a Black man "left mules and plough standing where they were & came back with our folks."[43]

When the troops crossed the Potomac to the Virginia side in early April, many formerly enslaved people went along.[44] Most were among the sixty porters who helped move goods from boats to wagons at the Budd's Ferry landing. As Leaver's company marched into Dumfries across the river, most of the Black people with the regiment scurried to the nearby huts of enslaved people.[45] Using the cover of the Union troops, they ushered family members and friends back to Maryland. Maintaining his campaign to resist this rising tide of liberation, Naglee later ordered his regiments to leave Black people behind when they moved out.[46] To the extent possible, some would ignore his wishes.

The local white population dismayed Dame. The practice of slavery was one reason, but she also found white Marylanders unfriendly and heard many tales of violence, including one about a man being gunned down near the camp. "What we hear of the Southern people, they are more like Savages than civilized people," she wrote Berry. "The women are about as bad as the men. I think if the women living near here dared, they would possess every one of us. Things I know they have said make me believe so. Their shooting that man today was cold-blooded murder."[47]

Until an incident in early April, Dame had had no such qualms about the crowd of men with whom she camped and spent her days. Engrossed one afternoon in a search for dandelion greens near another regiment's camp, she failed to notice two soldiers lurking nearby until one of them accosted her. She shooed him away, but he pursued her and blocked her path again and again. Realizing he was drunk, she hastened along, but the man menaced her until she "trembled like an aspen leaf." At last, several men from her regiment came into view, and her pursuer retreated at the sight of them coming her way. It amused her to see how angry her comrades were, but she was upset, too: "It was the first time any one had ever treated me uncivilly." While wishing "rum could be kept away from soldiers," she knew this was a forlorn hope, having just seen so many men in camp who could hardly walk.[48]

General McClellan had signaled to the men in mid-March that the Army of the Potomac was about to move out. "For a long time I have kept you inactive," he began, "but not without a purpose." They were "a real Army" now, and the moment for action had arrived. When battle came, he assured his soldiers, "I am to watch over you as a parent over his children; and you know your General loves you from the depths of his heart."[49] Whatever the men might have thought of McClellan's grandiloquence, they cheered the notion of moving. The usually upbeat Private Ladd spoke for many when he called the Maryland camp "the most lonesome place I have ever been in."[50]

The general did not name their destination, but southbound traffic began to increase on the Potomac, and one clue followed another. Thirty ships steamed past one day carrying the regiment's Third Corps comrades downriver toward Chesapeake Bay. The mail stopped coming because boats could not be spared to deliver it, according to Haynes, who worried about all the equipment they would have to carry.[51] Leaver hoped they would not be packing their tents, which had so many holes that the rain dripped into them. Recalling Bull Run, he wondered if the men would sleep under the sky.[52] Haynes knew better, having heard that new French tents would soon arrive. Each man would pack a section of one of them. By buttoning together four bedsheet-size pieces, the soldiers could make a shelter for four, open on both ends but providing some protection from the elements.

Quartermaster Godfrey wondered what would become of the formerly enslaved people now living amid Hooker's division. "About all the slaves in Virginia opposite here have been sent back in the country or have escaped," he
informed his brother Horace. "We don't know what to do with them, & the
Administration is too cowardly to say boldly what to do with them."[53] Some of
the Black men built piers for the soldiers to board a steamer when one finally
came. Orders to leave were issued one day only to be withdrawn the next.

Even with connections in Washington and at Hooker's headquarters,
Chaplain Parker couldn't pin down the timing of the move, but he prepared
for it. He made a farewell visit to the family of the free Black woman who had
done his washing that winter. At the request of her and her husband, Parker
baptized their four youngest children. He also suggested to his wife Mary that
they hire the eldest of the four to care for their younger son in Concord and
teach him to read. "Her parents, too, I think would like very well to have us
take her," he wrote. The parents wanted a good education for her, something
unavailable in Maryland. "Slavery curses the free-colored people about as
much as it does the slave," Parker observed. The chaplain's subsequent letters
did not disclose whether the girl went north to New Hampshire.[54]

While also eager to leave Budd's Ferry, Dame had other concerns. The rent-
ers of her boardinghouse in Concord were moving out and she needed a new
tenant. If her brother George, who ran an inn further up Main Street, could
not find one, she wanted him to sell her furniture. When she mentioned this
to Marston, he joked that he and she would not need furniture after the war,
as they had learned to "sit on boxes and sleep anywhere, bake in an old Dutch
oven, &c, &c."[55]

Dame's chief worry was Henry Parker's state of mind. She asked Anna
Berry not to mention the chaplain's gloom to his wife, but it would not have
surprised Mary Parker. Since returning from a furlough, Parker had constantly
complained in his letters about how miserable he was. It did not help that on
the eve of the second birthday of the Parkers' son Henry, the chaplain had
attended Willie Lincoln's funeral at the White House. "Poor Mr. & Mrs. Lincoln!" he wrote. "They are in the deepest affliction." His wife knew how much
Parker wanted to come home because he had told her so: "It has been very
hard for me to come back, and I know our renewed separation has cost you
many a bitter hour already." He found camp life dreary and expected the regiment's move to be a "cheerless experience." Wherever it took him, he prayed
to God to open a useful place for him and grant him the grace to fill it.[56]

Dame had an impeccable source on the timing of the move. General
Hooker himself had told her that it would come soon. Then, in early April,

after a meeting with McClellan, Hooker sent a coat for her to mend. She told the young man who brought it she could not fix it till morning. "The general must have it this evening," he replied, "for he expects to leave tomorrow." Busy as she was, she went right to work.

In recent days she had found it "splendid to go out & see the hundreds of big boats pass down the river loaded with troops, Stars & Stripes flying & bands playing." Yet, unlike most of the men, she felt ambivalent about joining the parade, seeming to sense the dangers that lay ahead. "I long to go & yet I dread it," she told Berry. As Dame took a last look around, she hated what she saw. "It is unpleasant to stay in this filthy camp," she observed. "If we don't move from here soon, we shall all die." She loved and respected nature, and it troubled her deeply that the men had cut trees willy-nilly to build log structures and burn for heat. "When we came here it was mostly woods and now where are they?" she asked. "Our camp was in a thick forest and now I don't believe there are fifty trees left."[57]

The Second New Hampshire broke camp on April 5, 1862. As the soldiers struck their perforated tents, the fine spring weather also broke, and a hard rain began to fall. "We did not heed it much, as all were eager to be on the march for new scenes and places," wrote Leaver.[58] With four companies of the Twenty-Sixth Pennsylvania, the Second marched to the pier and boarded the *South America*, quickly overloading the "crazy old riverboat."[59] When Dame's regiment set out for Bull Run in July 1861, she had stayed behind. This time, she moved with the men toward the battle they had all been longing for.

And yet, after casting wistful eyes on the ships streaming past Budd's Ferry day after day, the Second found itself on a different sort of journey. The *South America* chugged out and anchored in the stream, where it sat for nearly two days. The first morning was a Sunday, but with twelve hundred soldiers packed onto the ship, Parker decided to forgo a church service. The ship weighed anchor before dawn on Monday but soon docked at Point Lookout, a summer resort that jutted out into Chesapeake Bay at the mouth of the Potomac. A big storm was coming, and the men were ordered off. On short rations and without most of their belongings, which were on another boat, they spent two days and nights at the resort.[60] After filling every berth and all the floor space aboard the *South America*, they had mixed reactions to resort living. As the storm howled outside, Haynes sat in a cottage with a fire to warm him.[61] Leaver shivered away the night in the inn, which had no stove.[62]

Six days into a trip that should have taken less than a day, a surprise awaited Dame and the soldiers aboard the *South America* when they reached the tip of the Virginia Peninsula. The Union ironclad *Monitor* pulled alongside to inform the officers and crew that the CSS *Virginia,* its Confederate rival, was heading out of Newport News and the two might soon fight. The passengers could see the *Virginia* in the distance with its battleship escort, and their hearts leapt at the chance to witness a battle. "We got to Fortress Monroe just as the order was given to clear the harbor, but as our boat had no coal and the regt no provisions, we stayed there over three hours," Dame wrote. "Everything looked like a battle & I assure you we were not very anxious to leave."[63] "The Yankee Cheese Box, the *Monitor,* and the rebel champion, the *Merrimac,*" as Leaver called the two ironclads, using the *Virginia's* original name for the latter ship, had fought to a draw a month earlier at Hampton Roads.[64] This time, the *Virginia* turned back to port without engaging the *Monitor* or the Union gunboats lurking nearby.

The *South America* took on coal and provisions at Fortress Monroe and delivered the Second New Hampshire to nearby Shipping Point on the York River. The men pitched their new French tents at Camp Winfield Scott. "There is a tremendous army before Yorktown and in it, and there will be a great battle," Private Haynes predicted to his girlfriend, giving voice to the expectations of the Union legions then gathering.[65]

Fourteen Miles to Richmond

After witnessing the ironclads' little dance off the tip of the Peninsula, Harriet Dame boarded with local women while the men of the Second New Hampshire set up their camp. With an air of defiance, her hosts on the night of April 12, 1862, told her the Yankees would never capture Yorktown. For months, they said, the town's defenders had been destroying houses and constructing fortifications in their place. When Dame moved to Camp Winfield Scott the next day, the new French tents reminded her of chicken coops. "They are better than no tents & that is all that can be said of them," she informed Anna Berry. Her tent was larger than the men's, but the camp was so crowded that it could not be opened to its full size. It bothered her to be in such close quarters. Even so, after hearing news of a battle on the Tennessee River at a place called Shiloh, where casualties had totaled twenty-four thousand men, she preferred crowded conditions to the possibility that a battle might reduce the number of men around her. "Soon I fear we shall not have so many," she confided to Berry.[1]

So much water ran under her tent that hospital stewards had to dig a deeper drainage trench around its edges. A brown ooze covered its inside. After a teamster brought her a feedbox from his wagon to use for a bed, she spread her mattress in the box, and all was well. "At least it kept me from sinking, in life, into the bosom of mother earth," she joked. As she watched the stewards slay ticks and other insects in the muck at their feet, she wondered if she could have slept at all with her mattress on the ground. She saw a big lizard scamper past outside, but it was "moving so fast from me that I didn't even scream."[2]

For weeks, General McClellan had been resisting President Lincoln's doubts about his plans. While Lincoln cared more about destroying the enemy's armies

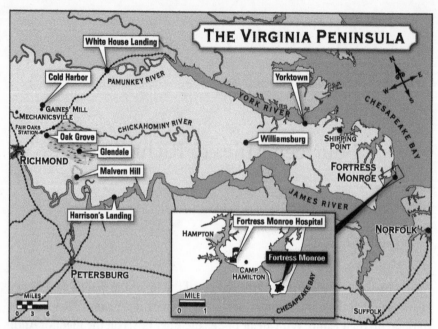

The Virginia Peninsula

than capturing points on a map, McClellan, like much of the Northern public, remained fixated on Richmond. His plan was to land his army of more than one hundred thousand men on the tip of the Virginia Peninsula between the James and York rivers and lead them seventy-five miles to take the Confederate capital. As Lincoln suspected, once the rebel commander Joseph E. Johnston caught wind of the move, McClellan's army would face the same enemy and the same problems as it would have had he attacked Johnston near Manassas. But Mc-Clellan had gotten his way, and now his army had now arrived and encamped.[3]

The soldiers worked at all hours, giving Dame a sense of urgency that had been absent in the Maryland camps. The rules were stricter, too. During the night the men were ordered not to speak while digging rifle pits near enemy lines. Buoyant and confident, they used bootblack to scrawl names on signs identifying their patches of the camp as "Granite State Row" and "Yankee Park." They admired their new commander and envisioned a bright future.[4] Sgt. Tom Leaver was sure that when McClellan attacked, he would astonish the rebels "with the number of his guns and the magnitude of his preparations."[5]

After lunch one day, Dame ventured out to explore her new surroundings. Although it was just mid-April, the heat and humidity made it feel like July in New Hampshire. She intended to stroll into the woods but changed her mind when she reached the Union picket lines. She and the army were in a potential battle zone before a Confederate force defending its capital. "As I was alone, I wasn't safe," she decided. "They might take me for a spy or shoot me accidentally." On her way back, she drank in the glories of spring, the violets and the peach, pear, and cherry trees in full bloom. Even with battle looming, she saw the world around her in a way that most of the men, in their letters at least, seemed not to. "It is said there are two hundred thousand troops in the vicinity," she observed. "I can go out by my tent & look over the large fields near me & see nearly all of the camps of 50,000. I tell you it is a grand sight in the evening when they are all lighted. Notwithstanding all this bustle & confusion the birds sing just the same & all night long in the woods quite near us the whippoorwill keeps up her plaintive cry."[6]

Dame often caught glimpses of McClellan, whose efforts she, too, appreciated.[7] In her view, all his brigades stood prepared to march into battle anytime day or night, and he seemed eager to move them. The forest of tents made it seem that "the entire army of the United States was under the shelter of that white canvas."[8] She cast aside her hurt feelings over being left behind during the Bull Run campaign and expressed pride in seeing herself as "an integral part of its immensity." McClellan had commandeered the only house of decent size that Dame had seen since arriving in Virginia. It reminded her of the houses in the farthest reaches of Chichester, a farming town east of Concord. Sometimes she saw the general riding around behind it "just like any other man."

Neither she nor the men perceived the rift between McClellan and the president. Like Joseph Hooker, McClellan had benefited from the Union debacle at Bull Run. The day after the battle, he had received a telegram from Washington that began: "Circumstances make your presence here necessary." In informing his wife Mary Ellen that he had been given command of the armies of Gen. Irvin McDowell and Gen. Joseph Mansfield, he described having suddenly become "*the* power of the land. I almost think that were I to win some small success now I could become Dictator or anything else that might please me." On his thirteenth day in command, he opened a relentless crusade to inflate the strength of the enemy forces opposing him as reason to delay an attack. "I am induced to believe that the enemy has 100,000 men in our front," he wrote Gen. Winfield Scott, adding that rebel reinforcements were headed for Richmond. Lincoln would soon add Scott's job as the nation's general-in-chief to McClellan's duties. Even so, the president complained about the general's exaggerated assessment of rebel might and reluctance to advance. At one critical moment, McClellan told Lincoln he had just 80,000 men available to face as many as 160,000 Confederate troops standing between his army and Richmond. The enemy's actual strength at the time was 62,500. Before York-town, McClellan had set his army to work chopping trees, digging trenches, and creating obstacles in preparations for a siege, not a movement.[9]

Being in the presence of the enemy day after day changed the routines of camp life. Dame noticed a few days after arriving that there had been "not a note of music, not even the beat of a drum, since we landed in Dixie." The offi-cers kept the troops on constant alert. Before four o'clock one morning, Dame awoke to find her regiment and the nearby Pennsylvanians ready to move out. The muster was so quiet she did not know it had happened until a steward told her. "I went out just before sunrise & just as far as I could see were one mass of soldiers all ready for battle." Another night, a commotion outside her tent con-vinced her an attack was imminent. She stepped out to find every regiment in sight in formation. "Hardly a word was spoken, but there was a rushing sound that made me think of Niagara when we [were] about a mile from it," she wrote Anna Berry. The soldiers stood down, returned to quarters, and were called out again before dawn. Hearing musket and cannon fire, Dame thought there had been a skirmish but could learn nothing more, "as every such thing is kept quiet in camp these days."[10]

Maj. Gen. John B. Magruder, the local Confederate commander, had pre-pared for the Union invasion. He was at Yorktown when McClellan's army arrived, although his main defenses stood near Williamsburg, twenty miles closer to Richmond. When he took command, he considered Williamsburg a crucial point in protecting Richmond from invasion but also believed the city was unprepared to defend even itself. The main threat at the time came from the small Union garrison at Fortress Monroe. Williamsburg sat in the middle of the Peninsula, four miles from the York River to the north and the James to the south. Shortly after arriving the previous spring, Magruder and Col. Lafayette McLaws had begun using enslaved and hired Black men alongside soldiers to entrench and fortify a line that stretched from river to river. To in-crease his Black labor force, Magruder sent out patrols to seize enslaved men who had run away. The workers built the earthen Fort Magruder just outside Williamsburg on the road to Yorktown and a string of redoubts on both sides of the fort for more artillery. McLaws added a touch to the design of the de-fenses that would pay dividends. He ordered Georgia infantrymen to clear out the oak grove that blocked the batteries' view and to see that the trees fell "across each other and in the direction the enemy is supposed to come." That way, any attacking force would have to pick its way through this obstruction before even reaching the open area in front of the artillery redoubts. This would expose the enemy to fire throughout its advance, keeping "a large number from rushing suddenly upon us."[11]

Considering McClellan's reluctance to attack and fondness for engineering, Magruder proved to be his perfect foil. When the Union troops landed, he had just over a tenth of McClellan's manpower. Rebel artillery kept up a harassing fire on Camp Winfield Scott. It was only natural for an opposing general prone to exaggerating enemy strength to conclude that the constant shelling was the work of an entrenched and formidable army. As time passed and the Army of the Potomac sat motionless, Confederate reinforcements arrived to strengthen Magruder's force, although it never equaled McClellan's. By April 18, Magruder had fifty-four thousand men to McClellan's one hundred and ten thousand.[12]

Like their compatriots, the men of the Second New Hampshire continued to march out morning and night, rain or shine, to build roads and defensive works to hold off Magruder's phantom horde. "One has little idea of the immense amount of labor such operations as we are now engaging in necessitate," Chaplain Henry Parker observed. "For long, long years to come how many portions of our country will be marked by the works of attack and defense constructed during the present campaign?"[13] One day after a rainy night of guard duty, Leaver and his comrades hung their blankets and overcoats in a tree "and marched off with rifles slung over our backs and their places on our shoulders occupied by shovels, axes & picks."[14] Two days later, they toiled all night digging an infantry trench behind an artillery emplacement.

Most days, the men saw Prof. Thaddeus Lowe's hydrogen balloon rise from its mooring across from Gen. Samuel Heintzelman's headquarters and float over the trees to spy on the rebels.[15] Lowe, who had overcome poor beginnings in far northern New Hampshire, was the Union Army's chief aeronaut. Private Haynes described his flights as "by no means safe operations . . . as the appearance above the tree tops of his aerial monster was almost invariably the signal for a well-directed fire from the rebel guns." Although the balloon returned unscathed each day, chunks of shell rained on the camp. No one in the Second New Hampshire was ever hit, but there was one close call. A shell fragment struck the haversack that a sleeping soldier was using as a pillow, scattering his hardtack supply. He jumped up angry, looking for the culprit who had played what he took for a practical joke on him.[16]

Sgt. Enoch G. Adams accompanied a detail one day to dig a trench for ten mortars. While his men worked, he ventured forward to the Union sharpshooters' rifle pits, which, like Magruder's line, stretched across the Peninsula from the York to the James. As these men lay on their bellies protecting the laboring soldiers, Adams watched them "peek over the ridge in front of the pit to catch sight of a rebel. [One man] lifted up his cap for the Enemy to fire at. It suggested to my mind the words of one of our statesmen, 'that eternal vigilance is the price of liberty.'"[17] A great admirer of McClellan's tactics, Adams found the entrenchments "a wonder to behold" and thought the war's final reckoning might be at hand. Union forces had just seized New Orleans, and if the sieges succeeded at Yorktown and Corinth, Mississippi, he wrote, "Secession may be considered at an end."

The one hitch in Adams's case was the ripping sound of shells passing overhead as he wrote, but at least the regiment had learned at Budd's Ferry that artillery fired randomly from a distance rarely struck anything important. Some men described the shells as "teakettles without snouts." Adams glanced up from his letter to watch a shell fly over his tent and land without detonating in the camp of the Twenty-Sixth Pennsylvania. Another exploded harmlessly near Heintzelman's headquarters. When Harriet Dame stopped by to chat with Adams, she told him a shell had passed within a few yards of her during her stroll through a nearby ravine.[18]

The men knew they occupied historic ground. As Adams reminded his brother in his letter, Lord Cornwallis had surrendered to George Washington at Yorktown. "The old rifle pits of the Revolutionary war of 1781 cross our present works in every direction," he wrote.[19] Haynes noted that these parallels "could be traced as easily as if created only the day previous."[20] The Union men unearthed many relics of those days, including the bones of soldiers who had died there. They solemnly reinterred these skeletons far from their works. Capt. Abiel Colby, whom Dame knew from his days working at a downtown Concord grocery, was one of many Union soldiers who had a Revolutionary War ancestor. He thought the coming battle would "almost bring up those who so nobly fell defending their country in 1781." During their labors, his men found flints and small cannonballs "such as Old Uncle Tom Colby used to have up in his old home chamber." Were his uncle still around, the captain mused, he could have "edified the boys of the next generation." As he contemplated the past, Colby's thoughts about the future darkened. "I sometimes feel that every letter is my last," he told his parents.[21]

If Dame harbored such fears, they did not show. During a stroll amid Confederate salvos, she encountered a frantic lieutenant running toward the camp shouting, "They are shelling the woods!" She reminded him that they were also shelling the camp. Perturbed, he asked why she was even there when she could go home whenever she wished. A few days later, a mule kicked the lieutenant in the face, injuring him badly enough that he was sent home. In Concord he spread the word that Dame was foolish to stay in the field amid such peril. Friends begged her to come home. Later, when she recounted this story, she speculated that the lieutenant, who was discharged from the army, now had "a new set of teeth [and] a pension for the mule kick."[22]

With trees concealing their work, many men surmised that the rebels, who had no aeronaut, did not know what McClellan's army was up to. "If they should find out what we was about, they would stop us, for we are rite under their guns," wrote Charles Jewett, a twenty-four-year-old private. But if all went well, as it had seemed to until now, "the Rebeles will wake up some morning and find the wodes all cut down and some Big guns pointing write at them." Jewett envisioned the army taking Yorktown and moving on to Richmond and Norfolk. After that, he wrote, "I think we will come home."[23] McClellan had informed a Union flag officer that he intended to open fire on May 5 with the expectation of taking Yorktown after two or three days of artillery fire.

Before he could act on this intention, reality spoiled both his plans and the men's vision of rebels peering in shock down Union cannon barrels. During the evening of May 3, General Heintzelman learned that the rebels might be abandoning Yorktown and ordered Thaddeus Lowe to investigate. Lowe ascended twice before daybreak but could not confirm the report. Heintzelman joined him for his third flight at daybreak. "We could not distinguish any guns or men in or around the fortifications of Yorktown and the smoke of their camps was very much diminished," the general reported.[24] On their return, Heintzelman and Lowe shouted to a signal officer below that no one remained in the enemy works. Magruder's force was gone. Like many men, Leaver put the best face on the Confederate evacuation. "We had driven out the rebels with shovels and picks just as effectually as though they had waited until we commenced with the more deadly instruments," he wrote. "It was full as hard a way, too, if it was not quite so glorious."[25]

In fact, General Johnston, who commanded the Confederate Army, knew he lacked the manpower to defend Yorktown. Magruder's trenches there were so wet, muddy, and pestiferous that his men could scarcely sleep in them. The rebel death toll from disease had mounted throughout April. It was only a matter of time before the rebels withdrew toward Fort Magruder and its artillery redoubts before Williamsburg. The exodus began on May 2. Late the next night, the Confederates mounted an artillery barrage meant to suggest an imminent attack. In fact, the intense shelling covered the departure of the infantry force.[26] All the Union men's work in preparing McClellan's siege had been for naught.

With the rest of Heintzelman's Third Corps, the Second New Hampshire headed out on the Williamsburg Road in pursuit of the rebels at about one o'clock on the afternoon of May 4. As night fell, the regiment encountered wounded Union cavalrymen who told them the rebel line of battle lay just ahead. The news "sent an electric shock through the ranks," Haynes reported.[27] In the darkness, the army trudged through a dense pine wood before finally lying down to sleep in a clearing. Rather than pitch tents, the men drew their tent quarters over themselves and slept as well as they could.[28]

The rebel evacuation also set Harriet Dame in motion. Now that Yorktown had been abandoned to Union forces, she accompanied the sick soldiers of her regiment and several others to new quarters there. Among them was her friend Captain Colby, who had shared his fear of dying with his family less than two weeks earlier and was now gravely ill. Her destination was the Nelson House, the town's most prominent building. Cornwallis had made it his headquarters in 1781, and the rebels had used it as a hospital before moving out toward Richmond. When Dame arrived, she found the house dirty and cluttered.[29]

Here, for the first time, Dame met Dorothea Dix, the army's superintendent of women nurses. Women nurses in the field were rare in part because Dix opposed their accompanying regiments on campaign. At the Nelson House, she implored Dame to leave army life to the men, telling her that "it was folly my thinking of such a thing as living on the field." Dame responded that being with the regiment and sharing its hardships were the very reasons she had gone to war and that she would stay with the men for as long as she could. The two would remain cordial throughout the war and beyond, even as Dix's rigid rules made her a host of enemies. Perhaps their similar backgrounds helped them become friends, as both were mature women, and Dix, like Dame, had been born in a small town in northern New England and later moved to Boston. They also shared a passion for helping people in need. Dix made Dame a standing offer: anytime she wished, she could have a job in a Washington hospital at twelve dollars a month, a dollar less than a private's pay.[30] Dame declined, even though the offer would have doubled her wages and provided a roof over her head. Dix's purpose on the Peninsula was to inspect Union medical care. Finding it woeful, she took a boat back to Washington to arrange for supplies to be shipped down, then returned to the Nelson House hospital to lend Dame a hand.[31]

Dorothea Dix, who would remain Harriet Dame's friend for life (Library of Congress, LC-DIG-ppmsca-59721)

Left in charge while Dix was away, Dame had little rest from daybreak till late at night. She had fifty patients to care for in a house she described to Berry as "more than filthy (it was alive)," underlining all six words. When every surgeon but one left for Williamsburg with his regiment, Dame and another nurse organized a team of formerly enslaved people to help. Before Dix's return, they had scoured the house from attic to cellar and washed all the linen. The two women managed this work and helped out whenever they could while nursing the sick and feeding them citrus fruit and whatever else they could scrounge. With her sidekick supervising the Black workers and looking after other sick men in nearby tents and houses, Dame was often on her own at the hospital. "One of the most laborious weeks of my life," she called it, telling Berry that every moment was "devoted to poor suffering soldiers." She doubted her ability to convey to the girl the suffering she witnessed. "After all, you can never know anything of what we see every day," she wrote, adding that she preferred to omit the details. "Why tell you this tale of horror? It was enough to bear myself."[32]

On May 5, as the men of the Second lay with their weapons at their sides in the clearing before Williamsburg at two o'clock in the morning, rain woke many who had fallen asleep. Dame's friend Godfrey, the former regimental quartermaster who now did the same job for Hooker's entire division, managed to light a small fire in the clearing, but the fire lit him back. "Somehow it got loose," he told his brother, "and the first I knew I was in a blaze. I had a couple of horse blankets wrapped round me and it nearly used them up." Hooker himself put the fire out, saving Godfrey from serious injury.[33] At four o'clock, the Second marched on with the division toward Fort Magruder. "The mud was awful, and we had to wade right through it," Pvt. John Dean groused to his mother. "Our clothes and blankets being wet, and our legs covered with mud, it was with difficulty we could get along."[34]

Once they arrived, Colonel Marston chose two companies as skirmishers, including Leaver's, and sent them into the jumble of trees the rebels had felled and then arranged to impede a Union advance. The sharpshooters lay down, using the stumps for cover.[35] Pvt. Frank Morgan found their rifles "just the thing for this type of business for we can load them in almost any position."[36] Hooker ordered Marston to move his other companies forward and have them take cover as best they could in the treefall. Rebel artillery opened on them from six hundred yards as they emerged from the woods. "We distributed ourselves behind stumps and logs, and quite a number had genuine earthworks, made by punching holes through a thick mass of dirt that clung to the roots of an overturned tree," Haynes wrote.[37] The first cannonball killed a man and wounded two others in Private Dean's company. The soldiers advanced one fallen tree at a time until they came to the field that faced the rebel works. Hooker sent a battery forward, but several Union artillerymen were hit during the advance, and one gun stuck in the mud. When the battery finally opened, rebel sharpshooters began picking off the gunners. Shells killed every horse and disabled all but one gun. With his men practically immobile in a torrent of shells and musket balls, Marston ordered them to withdraw. They had remained in position for more than six hours, "constantly under fire of the enemy's batteries, and the rain all the while falling in torrents," he reported.[38]

When the order to withdraw reached his company, Dean lay behind a log with his friend Charles Putnam. As they retreated over the timber-strewn terrain, they lost touch with their company. When they finally reached the woods, they threw off their knapsacks and overcoats, determined to continue fighting. They moved from tree to tree, loading and firing from behind each one. While driving a ball into his musket, Dean glanced up and saw Putnam "pitch forward, his face down." He rushed to his friend's aid. "Oh! My God!" he wrote afterward, "what were my feelings at that moment! I was immediately at his side, turned him over, and found that he was shot through the brain. The ball passed through the front piece of his cap, entering the head just above the left eye, and coming out exactly opposite on the back side of the head." Dean gathered $10.45 and a few items from Putman's pockets to send to his family.[39]

Other companies of the Second also failed to remain in formation during the move. As Marston acknowledged, "The regiment had become very much broken in making its way through the almost impenetrable thickets in which we had lain for so many hours." Captain Drown had led his company in as skirmishers at the outset of the battle. When the company fragmented, he welcomed strays from other regiments to join his men and cheered them all on until his courage cost him his life. His fate became a matter of dispute. In his official report, Marston wrote that Drown and his men had come upon a "rebel barbarian" leading a group of soldiers in the woods. The leader shouted from under a white flag for his men to trail arms, a nonthreatening stance, and begged Drown's men not to shoot. When Drown complied, "the whole body of the enemy suddenly fired on him, killing him instantly."[40] This may be true, but rebel prisoners contended that "the flag which deceived the brave captain and cost him his life was only a battle-flag, faded until the figure upon it was hardly visible."[41] As the New Hampshire men reached safety, it was "raining as hard as it could," in Pvt. Frank Morgan's words. He paused briefly to watch another Union regiment bring its wounded from the field, then reconsidered, deciding he "had rather be in a fight a thousand times than to be a spectator to another such sight."[42]

The dispute over who won the battle began immediately after the smoke cleared and continued long after the war. It was a fight neither McClellan nor General Johnston, his Confederate counterpart, wanted. McClellan ignored the sounds of battle and stayed fourteen miles to the rear till near the end of the day. Johnston understood that his mission was to defend Richmond, not Williamsburg. His army turned back to fight only after realizing that the Yankees were in such close pursuit. When the shooting ended with both sides in the positions they had occupied at the outset, Johnston continued pulling his troops back toward his capital. The battle had bought him time and space to withdraw his army.[43] McClellan blamed "the utter stupidity and worthlessness" of his corps commanders for a near-defeat and credited himself with having saved the day and forced the rebel army to retreat.[44] Hooker thought otherwise, citing McClellan's "great indisposition to go forward" despite urgent requests beginning at ten o'clock in the morning on May 5.[45]

Despite this testiness at the top, the Confederate withdrawal at least gave the Union men reason to think they had carried the day. As Quartermaster Godfrey put it, "Every man in the Division is as large as life, & swears by the General." The battle had taught Godfrey something. "I never knew till that day what men & horses could do & live, nor what I could do either," he marveled to his brother.[46] For nine months, regiments like the Second New Hampshire had sought redemption for their wild retreat from Bull Run. Now, as the normally circumspect Haynes saw it, "The battle had been fought and the victory won. . . . [Hooker's] division had carved a page upon American history which no true lover of his country can read without feeling a glow of pride."[47] Leaver boldly predicted "our entry into the City of Richmond and when three more months have passed, into the city of Concord."[48]

The numbers suggested a draw. The Union force had outnumbered the Confederate, and the casualty ratio, 2,283 Union, 1,682 Confederate, reflected the rebels' advantage of better cover.[49] The Second New Hampshire lost twenty-three men killed or mortally wounded among more than a hundred casualties.[50]

While other Union troops moved out to pursue the enemy, the Second stayed behind as part of the force occupying Williamsburg and vicinity. With a touch of disdain, Leaver assured his brother that "Williamsburg is nearly as large as Concord but cannot be compared with it as much as a mud hole to the Garden of Eden. . . . Any quantity of hogs, dogs and negroes can be seen wallowing in the 'sacred soil.'"[51] The Union men camped near the College of William & Mary, also a temporary hospital. Some slept in officers' tents abandoned by the enemy. Pvt. George Ladd's bore the name of Lt. G. B. Olmstead of the Tenth Georgia. "We live high and sleep on a mattress," he wrote to his sweetheart Carrie Deppen.[52]

The morning after the battle, many men returned to the field to bury the dead or just to see them. "Men went around and covered the faces of the dead from the gaze of curiosity, but it was four days before the dead were all buried and the smell had got to be fetid from the heat," wrote George Gordon, a lieutenant in Haynes's company. It horrified him "to contemplate so many so young and fair lay cold and senseless upon the cold earth."[53] Haynes discovered that "in some spots I could have walked comfortably on dead bodies."

He saw a dead rebel "prone on his breast, his gun thrust through between two rails, a finger on the trigger, and a little round hole in the top of his head." He collected spent bullets and enemy coat buttons from the field as souvenirs.[54] Private Dean and four other men from his hometown found their buddy Charles Putnam and buried him beside a stream. "A pine tree marks the head of his grave, and a small beech tree stands at his feet, upon both of which we cut his name and the letter of his company," Dean wrote home.[55]

Eight days after the fight, with the regiment still on provost duty at Williamsburg, Chaplain Parker rode to Yorktown to visit the men in Dame's hospital. The detritus of battle depressed him all along the road. "Every disagreeable & unsightly mark you can conceive of, almost, met the eye every rod of the way," he told his wife. There was "not one pleasant object to relieve the whole." Dead horses lay unburied everywhere. "War at a distance and in history is one thing," he observed, "and war before your eyes and of which you may be part & parcel is quite another thing. The former may thrillingly interest, the latter is unutterably revolting."[56]

Sad news awaited Parker at Yorktown, where Dame was caring for many men, including her friend Captain Colby. Parker made it just in time to see Colby in the final throes of typhoid fever. He died that day. He had commanded Goodwin's Rifles, the Concord company of the Second.[57] Sergeant Leaver sent a private to take his body for embalming at Fortress Monroe and shipment home to Concord, paying for these services out of his own pocket. "No member of the Goodwin Rifles will be buried in this soil if money can get his remains to New Hampshire," Leaver vowed. "There is nothing our company would not do to testify to our love and respect for him." The same did not apply to George Boyden, the lieutenant who had led the company in Colby's stead. After Boyden fled during the battle, Leaver circulated a petition demanding that he resign or face a court-martial. The entire company signed it.[58] Boyden, a silver-plater of kitchenware in civilian life, resigned and returned to Concord.

Dame also worried about Frank Fiske, the Second's lieutenant colonel, who could not seem to shake typhoid. After the battle he was sent north with a shipload of two hundred wounded men. Eliza Woolsey, a nurse on the ship, noticed Fiske lying on the slats of a bed with just a knapsack for a pillow. She made him comfortable and left him happier than she had found him.[59] Fiske recovered but never returned to the regiment.

Nearly two weeks after the battle, Dame and Dorothea Dix visited the battlefield and a military hospital in town. Because guerrillas had killed army teamsters on the road the night before, the military governor at Yorktown told them they needed a guard. "Neither of us was afraid & concluded we would go unguarded," Dame wrote. She quailed at the sight of so many ruined houses in Williamsburg. As she and Dix spoke with the sick and wounded, Dame decided that she had never seen anyone more disheartened than the Confederate prisoners. One man told the two women his story, claiming he had been deceived into enlisting and begging to take the oath of allegiance to the Union and go home. Dame cut a lock of his hair, and Dix promised to send it to the soldier's mother.[60]

The New Hampshire regiment soon marched toward Richmond again. During a rest at Kent Court House, "a village of half-a-dozen old tumbled-down shanties," someone recognized Samuel Langley, the Second's former adjutant, passing by.[61] The men lined both sides of the road to watch the Fifth New Hampshire, Langley's new regiment, march past. Many of the men of the two regiments knew each other, and they all shouted greetings. Back on the road again, while crossing the Chickahominy River after a swampy stretch, the men spotted a signpost informing them that Richmond lay just fourteen miles ahead. Their confidence soared. Leaver fretted more about the hilly terrain he expected on the way to the Confederate capital than about the army defending it.

On that very day, May 25, 1862, Dame finally left Yorktown to rejoin the regiment. After missing the westbound mailboat, she persuaded McClellan to issue her a pass to travel on any of the many hospital and supply ships plying the York River. She boarded the *Rockland*, a steamer stacked with hay bales on its way east to Hooker's division. There were just a few other passengers, including six soldiers, two of them from the Second. A doctor and his family boarded at one stop with a fifteen-year-old girl they had rescued from the shameful treatment of her married sister. When the family left the boat at the next stop, the girl declined to go live with them. Dame stayed with her but knew she could not bring the girl along once she landed and headed back to her regiment. The idea of leaving her alone was another burden on Dame's already heavy heart. Two of her favorite captains were dead. "It's so useless for me to say one word about the death of our dear Capt. Colby or Capt. Drown & many other dear friends of mine who fell in the battle, only that I am situated where every moment of my time is devoted to poor suffering Soldiers," she lamented to Anna Berry. "I could hardly bear the loss of these more than friends. They were like brothers to me."[62]

Back home, Colby's body lay in state at the capitol in Concord, two blocks from Dame's boardinghouse, until a funeral party delivered it for burial in neighboring Bow, his birthplace. In the flag-draped Baptist church in Fisherville, townspeople accorded similar honors to Drown, a forty-two-year-old father of three who had been a community leader. The volunteer firemen of the Pioneer Engine Company, of which Drown had once been foreman, came to his funeral en masse. For all the pomp at his service, what most impressed a local reporter was "the host of sympathising people, now brought face to face with a palpable memorial of the disaster which has overtaken our once happy land."[63] Drown was the first New Hampshire officer killed in battle.

The *Rockland* delivered Dame to White House Landing on the south bank of the Pamunkey River. She headed straight to the hospital tents on the plantation grounds to find the sick New Hampshire boys. Afterward, she visited a colonel's wife in the mansion, where she learned the history of White House. George Washington had courted and wed Martha Custis there in 1759. Robert E. Lee later married a Custis descendant, and one of their sons had lived at White House with his wife when the war began. The wife had left a note before abandoning her home asking that Union soldiers not "disturb the house of Washington's descendants." Dame found the estate beautiful and wished the sick and wounded of the battle at Williamsburg had been sent to tents on the mansion's lawn rather than a miserable Yorktown hospital with foul water.[64]

After she returned to the *Rockland,* the steamer moved offshore amid a mass of vessels until workers were ready to remove its cargo. She used the time to finish a letter to Berry, sharing the history of the place and a bitter complaint. "Up in the tents are 1,500 sick and wounded [and] not one female nurse," she wrote. "If some of our good women would come and take care of them, how many lives would be saved?" On ships that transported the sick and wounded she had seen "many of the first ladies of New York & they have their servants to wait on them. What account are such people?"[65]

Dame rejoined her regiment just before it arrived at Fair Oaks, where the Fifth New Hampshire had fought a bloody battle on June 1. This settlement consisted of two houses surrounded by what Leaver called "a cluster of the most magnificent oak trees imaginable."[66] The Confederate capital was visible in the distance from the upper branches of one of the oaks, and many men climbed the tree to catch a glimpse of their objective. The regiment camped on the battlefield, where scores of dead horses lay near a Union artillery emplacement, their carcasses "perforated by thousands of bullets." The men gagged on the fetid air when the horses were burned. Ominously, rain washed the dirt from the shallow graves of soldiers. "Here and there a leg or hand or head could be seen protruding," Leaver wrote, and corpses were scattered about the swamps and woods.[67]

Dame's first stroll across the campground near sundown unsettled her. She accidentally kicked an arm, lifting it from the face of a dead soldier. To overcome her revulsion at the gore and the stench, she resorted to a philosophical thought that often eased her wartime trials. She forced herself to see the suffering around her as the price of "the final goal of my country's triumph."[68] In coming days, under constant artillery fire, she despaired that there was no safe place for her sick and wounded. The constant threat of death, she believed, weakened some men to the point of giving up.

Dark thoughts preyed even on the healthy. "It almost deprives a man of humanity to follow the fortunes of war," Lieutenant Gordon wrote. Nearly eighteen hundred men had been killed outright during the fighting at Seven Pines on May 31 and Fair Oaks on June 1, and total casualties had exceeded eleven thousand.[69] Two weeks after the battle, there were still so many dead that it was "impossible to bury them decent." In many cases, "animals have dug bodies quite out of the ground."[70]

With just two hundred yards separating the pickets of the two armies in some places, the men put in long, watchful days and nights on guard duty or under arms. If they looked up the Williamsburg Road, they could see the enemy pickets. It seemed to Leaver that McClellan was planning another siege. Although this possibility appealed to Leaver, he also believed that another battle could not be avoided for much longer. He was confident that Union troops could withstand any rebel attack. On June 24, 1862, he closed his letter home with these words: "Keep up good courage, Mother. 'The end is at hand.'"[71]

The Killing Summer

The summer of 1862 brought one trial after another for the Second New Hampshire Volunteers. Harriet Dame was there for all of them, marching and camping with the men on campaign. "Sometimes I would go several weeks without any clothes but those I had on," she later recalled. "When we were marching, I could carry nothing but a haversack. When I could get a chance, I would go down to the creek, wash the clothes I was wearing and put them right on again without drying. There was no other way."[1] While she did not accompany the men into battle, she worked so near the fighting that she was briefly captured not just once but twice.[2]

In June, Dame rejoined her regiment on the Fair Oaks battlefield before all the dead were buried. Much later, the mere thought of the stink and the green flies on that campground made her ill. She lived with the soldiers under more intense artillery fire than the daily barrages at Yorktown. Although direct hits remained rare, one shell whizzed through Dame's tent. She and the medical steward Joseph Janvrin were outside making gruel at the time, and the shell failed to explode. "We heard another shell scream over us," she said. "[We] dodged at the same time, and we hit our heads together so hard that each of us thought the shell had struck us."[3]

Peril always seemed near even though the rifle pits on the camp's perimeter lay some distance from the hospital tent where she treated the sick. As everyone awaited battle at any moment, outbreaks of typhoid, diarrhea, and dysentery sent many men to the hospital and some to their death. Doctors believed that foul air carried the germs that caused these diseases, but the real culprits were the green flies that Dame loathed and bacteria from the foul water supply. The flies picked up and spread germs from fecal matter and decaying bodies. An assistant surgeon who had been at the Fair Oaks battle estimated that the bodies of three thousand soldiers and scores of dead horses had been haphazardly buried on the field. This "filled the air with noxious effluvium, and the only water was infiltrated with the decaying animal matter of the battlefield."[4]

After three weeks at Fair Oaks, Pvt. Charles E. Jewett sat behind an oak tree to avoid incoming shells while writing to his family. He was on guard duty twenty-four hours every third day and assigned to fatigue details during the days between. The men could not move about without treading on shallow graves and exposed body parts. A man had awakened in his tent one morning to see a hand sticking out of the earth inches from his face. "It is very warm here now and you can judge for your self that it aint a very sweet smelling place," Jewett complained. He doubted the armies could "lay so snug together much longer with out fighting."[5]

Indeed, Robert E. Lee, the new Confederate commander, was plotting to exploit McClellan's decision to park his army in place. Lee had taken over on June 1 after Gen. Joseph Johnston was wounded. McClellan, who knew Lee, expected him "to be timid and irresolute in action."[6] With the gift of time, Lee instead built up the army protecting Richmond to one hundred and one thousand men and planned his offensive. McClellan's army dug in while its general harassed Washington for more troops and claimed that Lee's army was even larger than it was.[7]

Lee was not the only new commander in the vicinity. Cuvier Grover, a thirty-three-year-old brigadier general from Maine, had replaced the despised Henry Naglee as the Second's brigade commander. The men liked Grover. On June 23, he personally led a "sneak-up" into the woods beyond the rifle pits. As Private Haynes's company crawled through the brush to the rebel picket line, the only exposed member of the brigade was Grover, who sat on his horse with his torso visible above the bushes.[8] The general directed the action as the men drove the pickets back and pushed on toward the main body of Confederate troops. Satisfied that he knew the enemy's position and had tested its strength, Grover pulled his men back.

The divisions of Hooker and Philip Kearny attacked over the same ground two days later, also with a limited objective. They were to clear the way through a field of trees known as Oak Grove to a staging point for an assault on Richmond. This proved easier said than done. As they had at Williamsburg, the men of the Second entered a thick wood with orders to pick their way through, scatter the rebel pickets, and gain control of the open ground beyond.[9] On the day after Tom Leaver had written his mother that the end was near, his company of sharpshooters, now just forty-two strong, took the lead as skirmishers. "The spiteful crack of their Sharp's rifles soon rose above the din of conflict," Haynes wrote. He would later say that in all its "proud history, that company never showed to better advantage than on this occasion. . . . [T]he rapid and accurate fire of its breechloaders soon cleared the front."[10] The men struggled through brush and trees, meeting fierce resistance, and then fired away as the enemy crossed the open field to the woods beyond. The advance and the fighting lasted for hours. Nine men of the Second were killed or mortally wounded.[11] The three Union brigades in action suffered 626 casualties, the Confederates 441.[12]

Dame spent much of June 25 as near a battle as she had ever been, fulfilling a wish she had often expressed. The hospital tents began to fill soon after the sound of battle at Oak Grove reached its crescendo. With "no available space for the freshly wounded" in the hospital tents, she cared for men in the open air.[13] Some were conscious and could see their wounds and sense their severity; others were insensate or semiconscious or had been hit in a place they could not see. All were sweaty and dirty. Dame approached them with empathy and confidence. She cleaned and bandaged open wounds to stop the bleeding if she could. This task required lint, much of which soldier-aid groups formed by women back home had produced by fraying and scraping old linen.[14] Once she had cleaned the wound, Dame folded the lint to the proper size and spread a thin coat of astringent, probably alum, a potassium compound, on one side to help with clotting. She pressed the lint gently into the wound and secured it with an adhesive. Dame gave her patients water if they could drink and food if she thought it would help them. No matter how severely men were wounded, she reassured them. After she had done what she could, she passed many of her patients on to the surgeons. Because balls shattered men's bones, amputation was common. Once the field hospital had done everything possible for the wounded, ambulances and other wagons carried them to White House Landing on the Pamunkey River. From there, transport ships evacuated them to Hampton Hospital near Fortress Monroe and, in many cases, on to hospitals in Washington and farther north.

These established hospitals equipped their nurses for long-term care. Hannah Ropes, a sixty-four-year-old Maine native who answered Dorothea Dix's call, started work at Union Hospital in Washington shortly after the battle of Oak Grove and treated wounded men for the first time in early July. On her first emergency call, she beheld a sad sight: "Fifty soldiers, grim, dirty, muddy, and wounded," bent with pain and clinging to railings, crowded together inside the entrance to the hospital. Each nurse collected her share of the men and began washing them one by one. This took four hours. "Everything they had on was stripped off," Ropes wrote. She found her patients "helpless as babies" and eager for care, but she struggled not to hurt men with broken bones. Once all were washed, the nurses dressed them in clean shirts, drawers, and stockings before turning them over to the surgeons.[15] Because field nurses seldom had time for thorough washing or a change of clothes, Dame's labor amounted to triage. Although she cut away parts of uniforms to access and clean wounds, the men were not bathed, and there were no fresh clothes to give them.

Dame knew many men who were brought in from the fighting at Oak Grove. At one point during the crush of work, she stepped away to examine two bodies that had just arrived at the field hospital. She lifted the single blanket that covered them both and gazed upon the familiar faces of a sergeant and a corporal from the Concord company. "My God! It is Tom Leaver," someone heard her say.[16] The other man was Leaver's twenty-four-year-old corporal, George Damon, who had left a job at a woolen mill to join the regiment.[17] Possibly they had been shot by sharpshooters firing from treetops behind the Confederate battle line. Leaver had recently sworn that the body of any member of the Goodwin Rifles would be sent home for a proper funeral, but Dame's only option was to prepare the two corpses for burial on the field. Late in the day, she watched their pine caskets being lowered into a grave at the foot of an oak tree. "Thomas was killed instantly," Chaplain Parker wrote his wife. "He had been doing his duty nobly, and fell just as he had laid down the body of Corporal Damon of his own Company who fell into Thomas' arms mortally wounded." Parker added: "Poor, poor Mrs. Leaver!"[18] Mary Leaver, long a widow, had lost not only a beloved son but also a faithful provider. She would receive a monthly widow's pension of just eight dollars, about half her son's military pay. Although the graves of the Union dead were marked, there is no evidence Thomas's body ever made it home. His space in the Leaver family plot at Blossom Hill Cemetery in Concord would remain forever vacant.[19]

The battle at Oak Grove opened what would later be known as the Seven Days battles. Lee attacked the next day at Mechanicsville and the day after that at Gaines' Mill.[20] To strengthen his army, he left only Gen. John B. Magruder's thin line to defend Richmond, but demonstrations by these troops convinced McClellan that he was outmanned. Had his force counterattacked on June 27, it might have captured the rebel capital. In his battle report, Magruder wrote that McClellan's "failure to do so is the best evidence that our wise commander fully understood the character of his opponent."[21] The two battles, especially Gaines' Mill, where ninety-one thousand soldiers fought, were far deadlier than Oak Grove. Union casualties exceeded seven thousand, Confederate nine thousand.[22] McClellan informed Secretary of War Edwin Stanton that he had lost these battles because his force was too small, adding: "You must send me very large reinforcements, and send them at once."[23]

The Union retreat, which McClellan tried to sell as a "change of base," began the day after he made this demand. When General Grover's brigade took up arms that morning, the men of the Second New Hampshire thought they were preparing for picket duty or a turn in the trenches on the camp's perimeter. To their surprise, they were ordered to take their tents with them. As they headed away from Richmond rather than toward it, they saw that the Union artillery crews and their cannons had left their redoubts. The pickets were ordered in, and the men marched to the Williamsburg Road, abandoning their camp to the enemy.[24]

Dame was surprised, too. She saw the movement for what it was, describing McClellan's army as "On Skedadle."[25] Hooker's order to leave behind all sick men who could not walk alarmed her. "The outlook was disastrous," she later said. "Before us lay unknown dangers, behind us an insatiable encroaching enemy, and in our presence death and suffering in the saddest phase."[26] Such a crisis, she decided, required her to act. When many of the sick vowed to walk with the retreating army, Dame decided to lead them.

Their prospects were dim. Colonel Marston warned Dame that anything loaded on the wagons "would never be seen again." She and the stewards could not carry all the medicines or her personal belongings, but she took along everything she could. Because it was summer in Virginia with temperatures reaching ninety, Dame normally wore only her hoop, a long cotton dress, and her "chemistry," as she called cosmetics. For the skedaddle, she put on layer upon layer of clothing: drawers, her "old, pathetic corset," a cotton dress with a Victorian support skirt known as a Balmoral over it, a flannel garment, a dress that the regiment's major had given her, and her shawl. She carried a haversack with bread, butter, and condensed milk and a bundle in which she had tied her best dress, a change of shoes, a coffee pot, and coffee. "It was no small load," she assured Anna Berry in a letter. She was glad that a box of dresses sent by Concord friends had yet to arrive because she could not have carried it.[27]

Before the regiment departed, a soldier destroyed the rest of Dame's wardrobe to keep it out of the hands of rebel women. One exception was her bonnet, which another soldier wrapped in a horse blanket, a gesture she would later describe as tender but "questionable as to the result." Crushed by the time she got it back, the bonnet "would never go on anybody's head again."[28] In its absence, she tied a scrap of green mosquito netting in her hair to shield her from the torrid sun. She pulled on the only footwear she had left, a pair of rubber boots.

Destruction ruled the day, as her little party would discover when it reached Savage Station, the second rail depot east of Fair Oaks. The soldiers with her must have blanched at the sight of so many sick and wounded comrades left lying at the depot by the fleeing army. To keep the vast store of supplies and ammunition at Savage Station from the enemy, Union troops torched them. At White House Landing, the supply depot on the Pamunkey, fires consumed not only stores but the big house owned by the Lee family that Dame had visited a few weeks earlier.[29] After the hospital stewards caught up with her and her sick squad, they all walked on in the din of rattling wagons until another horse-drawn train blocked the path of Hooker's division. By then, a sick Georgia soldier had risen from the roadside to join Dame's party. He feared the enemy might mistreat him, a dread shared by the Union sick who had left their beds for the perilous journey.[30]

When Dame had such thoughts, she reacted with stoicism and even a touch of humor. Her party's glacial pace and the obstacles ahead caused her to worry at times that the pursuing Confederate Army would capture them all. "Well, let them come," she wrote Berry. "We have a long time been talking about going to Richmond. If they overtake us, of course, we'll know the shortest route."[31]

What she witnessed that first day on the road—the great fires, the dreary slog of man and beast, the vastness of the retreating army—appalled and astounded her. "Oh Anna," she lamented, "you can never dream of the horrors I have seen & it is well you don't know what we do." She could not bear the suffering of the horses and mules that pulled the supply wagons, ambulances, and cannons in the steamy heat. They had "little to eat & muddy water to drink [and] hardly a breath of air." She pitied the soldiers with her, too, especially after she and the men covered only three and a half miles the first day. "Poor fellows," she wrote. "It makes my heart ache to see them parading so sick." While she had marveled at the flickering evening lights of fifty thousand men at Camp Winfield Scott in April, the actual size of McClellan's army astonished her. "In all my life I never saw anything like the teams and troops," she observed. "Really did not know we had a tenth part as many in the whole army. It is one of the grandest sights I have ever seen." A wagon driver told her the roads had been just as thronged the previous day.[32]

On June 30, the party of sick men that Dame called her "little forlorn hope" remained on its own as her regiment joined the fight against the pursuing rebels at Glendale.[33] The New Hampshire men served mainly in support, suffering just a few wounded, including Martin Haynes. "I was hit in the groin by a spent ball and crippled about as I would have been if a mule had kicked me," he wrote. Stunned, he thought he "was shot through and through. I saw some of the boys look back sort of pityingly as the line went on." In fact, he had been fortunate: the ball had struck his belt buckle, and he soon caught up with the regiment.[34] The Second stood in reserve during the battle of Malvern Hill on July 1 and reached the James River the next day.

The two battles, Glendale and Malvern Hill,[35] were as deadly as Mechanicsville and Gaines' Mill had been. McClellan's forces suffered nearly sixty-five hundred casualties, although a high proportion of these were missing men, many of whom later returned to their units. The rebels lost eighty-five hundred, including fifteen hundred killed, compared with six hundred Union dead.[36] An alert, aggressive commander might have recognized this victory as reason to turn around and resume the Army of the Potomac's advance toward Richmond. Marston, for one, believed his men were ready for more. Reporting on the Malvern Hill battle, he said he had "never seen the men of my regiment so eager for a fight. . . . Every individual man seemed anxious to come to close quarters with the foe and to strike telling blows for the great cause in which they had voluntarily engaged at the peril of their lives."[37] But McClellan had fixed his mind on retreat.

When Dame and the men with her reached Glendale, night had fallen and only the wounded, dead, and dying occupied the battlefield. Ambulances and wagons stood near the field. In the quarters of the Black people who had been left behind by their enslavers, Dame found cornmeal, milk, cooked gruel, and meal cake for the exhausted men in her care. It had been a long day, and by midnight she was exhausted and "generally in need of reconstruction." Soldiers tried to find her a room in the main farmhouse, but the white women there claimed it was full. Dame spread her blanket in the hallway and left to tell her charges where she was sleeping. When she returned, a young Black man showed her to a room with a bed. The same man woke her in the morning. "You'd better get up," he said. "They're going to fight." She rushed to her sick soldiers and saw that the teams that had blocked their way were gone. Before the army departed for Malvern Hill, someone had ordered a sick rebel officer who was under guard to guide Dame's party to the best road toward the James River.[38]

Their wagon soon joined an ambulance train, and she and the men rode all day before stopping for the night in a dense wood. Her friend John Godfrey, quartermaster of Hooker's division, came to check on her. Ordered to send her ahead if he thought she was in danger, he found her resting with a dog that a soldier had given her. She had named it Skedaddle. Godfrey decided to stay and watch over Dame's party. Years later, whenever his wartime nightmares preyed on him, Godfrey recalled that scary night in the woods on the way to the James. He and Dame found milk the next morning for the sick men. "I wonder if it killed any of them," he joked in a letter to her.[39]

Shortly after Dame's party headed out, bursting shells panicked the animals that were pulling the wagons. After the corps quartermaster ordered the caravan to move on, she and her comrades somehow became separated from the others and found themselves stalled in a cornfield with no obvious way out. Dame borrowed the teamster's knife and began cutting corn and filling empty space in the ambulances with it. "If Nero could fiddle in sight of burning Rome," she decided, she could surely harvest a little corn under cannon fire. When it seemed that a battle might be fought on that very field, she and her charges hurried blindly away. She had just enjoyed a "short interval of peace and beauty" as the wagons passed a field of blooming flowers when the driver suddenly halted. Dame found herself staring into the eyes of a rebel picket. He tried to interrogate her, but when she evaded his questions, he marched her and her party off to his commander.[40]

It is fair to ask whether her conversation with her captor was as spirited as she later recalled it, but her account is typical of the courage, spunk, and independent spirit she exhibited throughout the war. "Got too far into Dixie, hey?" the Confederate officer asked. "No," she answered, "not as far as I'm going." "How far might that be?" "As far as Richmond." He thought he had her now: "And going as a prisoner?" "No," she said, "I am going under the old flag." With both armies in constant motion, she correctly guessed that the Confederates had no secure place to keep prisoners, especially sick ones. In the end, she and the others simply slipped away during the chaos of two armies on the move.[41]

Dame soon arrived at the crowded camp where the Army of the Potomac was gathering at Harrison's Landing on the James River. Of the sick men she had led across the Peninsula, only Pvt. Josiah Taft of Fitzwilliam, New Hampshire, had died along the way. With the help of others in her party, she had made sure he had a proper burial beside the road. As for the rest, Martin Haynes believed that "it was to her devotion and inspiring courage that most of them owed their liberty and some their lives."[42]

Sickness ran rampant at this new encampment, a circumstance that once again tested Dame's skills and stamina. General McClellan had brought his army here to recuperate under the protection of Union gunboats on the river. The men were now thirty miles by water from the Confederate capital, which some of them had seen from a treetop just a month earlier. The Second New Hampshire pitched its tents two miles from the landing, where a lookout posted in a pine tree and Professor Lowe's balloon kept an eye on the rebel line with instructions to signal the Union ships if necessary.[43] These precautions were not altogether reassuring to the regiment. At Malvern Hill, the Second had been in the line of fire of these gunboats and come to regret it. Haynes described how their shells passed right over the enemy and "came howling about our ears, so that at times we were really in greater danger from our friends than from the enemy."[44]

Dame's breathless June 29 letter, written during her march to Harrison's Landing and datelined "On Skedadle," was the last one pasted in Anna Berry's notebook.[45] It seems an unlikely conclusion to their lively correspondence; both were prompt with their responses, and Dame had depended on Berry's help to stay in touch with friends and neighbors in Concord. Berry turned seventeen in 1862 and may have begun her courtship with Huntington Porter Smith, a prosperous merchant of woolens in Boston. A Congregationalist like Berry, Smith distributed goods to soldiers in Virginia for the US Christian Commission, a national aid organization that passed out religious tracts at the front along with supplies and medical assistance.[46] In 1864, Dame's friend Henry Parker would officiate at Smith and Berry's wedding from his Concord pulpit before the couple settled in Cambridge, Massachusetts.[47]

As the Second New Hampshire dug in again along the James, Lt. George Gordon summed up the situation: Despite horrible recent losses on both sides, "we whipped the rebels in every engagement and the army now lies on the banks of the James all quiet and resting from three days and nights fighting without rest or sleep."[48] Gordon believed a few more such fights would "exterminate the whole rebel army and our own." After a week of fatigue duty and sickness in the ranks, he wished the army would fight more and dig less. "More men have died by diseases contracted from exposure than have been killed in battle by long odds and we are sick of shoveling and chopping and such works," he told his wife Angeline.

The men's French tents, now tattered and holey, could not protect them from the storms, humidity, and germs of a southern July. When rain dripped in, their occupants slept in the mud. To remedy this situation, Haynes and his tentmate gathered clapboards from a nearby house that was being torn down and built a platform for their sleeping bags. They made an arbor of boughs to shade one end of the tent.[49] Like Gordon, Haynes was eager to get on with the fighting. "I hope the North will send reinforcements on quickly," he wrote, "for I want to see our army advance again on Richmond and end the war."[50] His company had lost ten men on the retreat and could muster only "a pitifully short line now."

As much as the regiment needed replacements, recent times had done little to entice friends back home to join. Pvt. Charles Jewett complained to his brother and sister that during the Second's months on the Peninsula "we have been marching, shoveling or fighting about every day . . . and I can tell you we have got pretty much used up."[51] For a friend considering volunteering, he passed along this advice: "If he wants to try it, tell him to go out dores and sleep on the ground through two or three rain storms without any thing to put over or under him. If that don't disharten him, put half bushels of corn on his back and march all day then take a shovel and shovel all night without any thing to eat or drink."

While Dame shared the men's urge to get on with the war, she endured the same weariness they did. "I was ragged," she admitted. She had arrived at Harrison's Landing with neither a tent nor a wardrobe other than the layers she had worn during the retreat. After friends at home sent her fabric, she sat up all night making a calico dress. She slept with Skedaddle on a stretcher under a tent of blankets fastened to a tree. When it rained, she pulled an India rubber blanket over the two of them. An actual tent filled with smallpox patients stood nearby. Thus Dame "lived without a single convenience, a woman in an army of men." After two weeks, Ann Harlan, wife of an Iowa senator, visited the landing with a companion. They were the first women Dame had seen since her arrival. They shared with her reports from Washington about army surgeons mistreating the men, a subject about which she was becoming an expert. The women promised to send supplies to the hospital at the landing. "Don't remember that they ever did so," Dame later remarked.[52]

Lieutenant Gordon's worries about sickness in the ranks proved prophetic. Because Hooker's division had not been alone in leaving medicine and hospital tents behind, the army desperately needed supplies and shelter for ill and wounded men. Sick rolls soared as scurvy, malaria, typhoid fever, and chronic diarrhea prostrated many soldiers. Dr. Jonathan Letterman, the new medical director in the Army of the Potomac, reached the James encampment on July 2. He ordered that the birthplace of President William Henry Harrison, the only substantial structure at the landing, be converted into a military hospital. He also sent for hospital tents to accommodate the expected overflow. A relay of steamers carried 6,000 of the most gravely ill and wounded men to a hospital near Fortress Monroe, but 12,795 remained. By Letterman's count, one in five soldiers was sick or wounded. Harriet Dame's labors never ceased.[53]

Chaplain Parker, one of her closest companions in the regiment, finally decided at Harrison's Landing to resign his commission and leave the army. He and Dame had joined the Second as unarmed comrades to offer the men spiritual and bodily care along with sterling examples of duty and courage. Both lamented the state of the war, but unlike Dame, Parker had young children at home, including two-year-old Henry Horatio Parker, whom he hardly knew. Being an absentee father had been hard from the beginning, when the mail became his chief means of following young Henry's progress. Even letters from home sometimes caused him pangs of guilt. Months earlier, former president Franklin Pierce had written him after stopping in to visit Mary Parker in Concord. "She was looking well," Pierce wrote, "but the little boy has been suffering a good deal from teething—but I should not give you domestic items as Mrs P. intended to write last evening or today."[54] Despite Pierce's kindly intentions, the details surely reminded the chaplain that he had left his wife to bring up the boy on her own. The recent campaign, meanwhile, reinforced Parker's belief that the end of the war remained distant. "This Virginia campaign both above & below Richmond has been managed most bunglingly," he complained to his wife in early July. "It is too bad, too bad, to kill off such an army as this by disease & battle and have it all amount to so little." He had considered quitting earlier, but recent events sealed the decision. "It is unspeakably painful to have nothing occur from day to day to inspire one with hope & confidence," he wrote. "It is now the darkest day that has ever hung over the army of the Potomac." Marston opposed his leaving, and the chaplain's conscience troubled him. "I am afraid it will have the appearance of turning my back upon the cause just when . . . the greatest sacrifices were demanded, if I leave it now," he confided to his wife. Parker preached to the men for the last time on August 10, 1862. Although he was still officiating at a funeral almost daily, he saw better days ahead, writing: "All our sickest men were sent off to a boat on the River last evening to be taken to some good hospital on the sea-side."[55]

Dame had boarded this boat with Joseph Janvrin, one of the Second's stewards, to accompany many of their patients to the hospital at Fortress Monroe. She tied her green mosquito netting over her head for the journey.[56] To her surprise, after reaching the fort hospital, the captain stopped only briefly and steamed on to New York City without unloading the sick. Several women from the US Sanitary Commission had boarded at Fortress Monroe. A private agency approved by Congress, the commission supported the medical care of Union soldiers in the field. Working out of the Treasury building near the White House, the commission sent inspectors to crowded Union camps and field hospitals and recommended and carried out reforms to make them healthier. The women with Dame aboard the ship "looked at me rather suspiciously at first," Dame recalled, "for I was both ragged and dirty, having been on the field for several weeks without change of clothes."[57] By the time the ship arrived to deliver the sick men to New York hospitals, a woman who had befriended Dame lent her a proper hat so that she could shop for a new bonnet of her own.

When the ship returned Dame and Janvrin to Fortress Monroe, they found that their regiment had left with the rest of Hooker's division to reinforce Gen. John Pope's Army of Virginia west of Washington.[58] The Second had begun its march back across the Peninsula on August 15, stopping for a night near Williamsburg, where the men had fought in May. The owner of a cornfield nearby asked Hooker for a guard to protect his crop. The general replied, "Yes, you shall have seven hundred and twenty in just fifteen minutes." This was no exaggeration, Lieutenant Gordon wrote, "for in the morning he did not have an ear large enough to cook in all his place."[59] The Second boarded a transport at Yorktown and headed up the Potomac toward Alexandria.[60]

The men's summer of fighting was not over yet. In fact, the worst was yet to come.

Dame and Janvrin caught up with the regiment at Alexandria, and soon they all packed into cattle cars for Warrenton, twenty miles beyond the Bull Run battlefield. At a stop along the way, cavalrymen guarding Manassas Station seemed terrified that Confederate general Stonewall Jackson was in the vicinity. Hooker's men dismissed their fears, but the next night Jackson's army "came down with a swoop like a hawk" and captured the cavalry. By then, Haynes wrote, the Second had been "dumped, late at night, in the fields on the side of the road."[61] Almost immediately the regiment turned back the way it had come to pursue Jackson's troops.[62]

On the Peninsula, fighting and sickness had shrunk the Second as McClellan's caution gave Lee time to reinforce his army and outmaneuver the Yankee invaders. Now, back in the vicinity of the regiment's first defeat, the men came under an even less capable commander in Gen. John Pope.[63] The Confederate Army, by contrast, had no shortage of aggressive generals who knew their business. After arriving near Bull Run with his four divisions, three of infantry and one of cavalry, Jackson learned that Pope's army had amassed supplies at the Manassas depot and "deemed it important that no time should be lost in securing them." He dispatched Gen. J. E. B. Stuart with a cavalry contingent and five hundred infantrymen on a thirty-mile night march. Early on August 27, Stuart's men overwhelmed the depot's defenders and captured eight cannons, three hundred prisoners, nearly two hundred and fifty horses, and immense quantities of food and supplies, including two hundred new tents. They also "recovered" two hundred formerly enslaved people. Other forays ordered by Jackson cut Pope's telegraph connection to Washington and interposed rebel troops between Pope's army and the capital.[64]

That night, when Pope realized that a rebel force occupied ground in the rear of the Union position, he sent Hooker's division back to challenge the enemy. Behind two companies of skirmishers, the Second New Hampshire marched along the railroad at the head of the column. At Kettle Run, five miles from Manassas depot,[65] they fought troops from Gen. Richard Ewell's division. Ewell, who had already accomplished his mission, withdrew to rejoin the main body of Jackson's army. In the abandoned rebel camp, the Yankees found ample evidence that Ewell's men had received their share of the Union stores captured by Stuart's cavalry and infantry. Haynes saw many bayonets "decorated with fresh meat speared from the ground or from kettles simmering over camp fires."[66] In the dark sky toward Manassas, the men beheld the immense fires set by Jackson's army to burn anything it could not carry, a sign that it was readying for battle. By morning, Jackson was deploying his army along one side of an unfinished railroad bed on the old Bull Run battlefield.

Dame had endured a miserable tramp to reach Kettle Run. In the steamy pitch-black night, she, a barefoot cook, and a few others fell in behind the Second on the march. When her companions heard that the rebels had destroyed the bridge across the run, "they were discouraged and insisted on waiting for daylight," Dame wrote. "They spread their blankets and slept."[67] She sat on the ground, leaned against a telegraph pole, and noticed, for the first time, "that beautiful music, the singing of the wires."[68] Come morning, an ambulance train pulled up, and Dame decided the casualties in the ambulances needed to eat. She and a cavalryman heated canned meat and other food for them. When supplies ran low, she sent a runner for more. Edward P. Vollum, an army medical inspector, found the little group eating and realized he had not even thought of feeding the wounded. He apologized for not pitching in earlier.

After a short nap Dame headed to Centreville, four miles beyond Bull Run. Expecting a bigger battle, she prepared to nurse the wounded in a house converted into a field hospital. She would later shuttle between the house and the hospital at the Stone Church, where Marston, Parker, and other men of her regiment had stopped during the wild retreat from the first Bull Run battle. It was one of many reminders that after more than a year, the New Hampshire soldiers were back where their war had begun.[69]

Hooker's division camped at Blackburn's Ford on August 28 and marched east along Centreville Heights early the next morning. In the distance the soldiers could see ribbons of dust rising from the paths of the comrades who had gone before them. Further on, the smoke of battle hovered over the rolling hills at Bull Run. The men braced themselves to face Jackson's formidable army with no inkling that Maj. Gen. James Longstreet's five divisions of Confederates would soon arrive to support it.[70] Pope was similarly clueless about these reinforcements while also waiting in vain for General McClellan to come to the aid of his army. McClellan had already ignored a direct order to send a division Pope's way; he now decided "to leave Pope to get out of his scrape" alone, claiming that his army was needed to protect Washington.[71]

With the rest of Gen. Cuvier Grover's brigade, the Second reached the battlefield and paused opposite the center of Jackson's line at about eleven o'clock on the morning of August 29.[72] The situation favored Jackson, as did Pope's erratic management of his army. The bridge-builder Washington Roebling, a member of Pope's staff, complained to his father that very day: "A dozen orders were given and countermanded . . . and the troops subjected to a lot of useless marching." Pope deluded himself that he had the rebels just where he wanted them.[73] Jackson, meanwhile, had deployed his men in what Haynes described as "the alternate cuts and fills of an unfinished railroad," shielding most of them behind the raised railbed or in rifle pits beyond. A wide strip of woods blocked Grover's men's view of this line, although they heard the fighting beyond the woods as they awaited Pope's orders.[74]

Hooker later recalled his revulsion when Pope ordered a frontal assault on Jackson's center. He showed Pope the formidable rebel defenses and told the general that even if a charge succeeded, enemy artillery would force his men to abandon any ground they gained.[75] Hooker suggested a coordinated attack with Gen. Philip Kearny's division on Jackson's left flank. Pope agreed, but the maverick Kearny ignored orders to attack for the second time that day.[76]

Grover, whose brigade numbered fifteen hundred men, designated the Second New Hampshire to spearhead the assault with a regiment on each of its flanks and two more behind those three. Expecting Kearny to advance on his right, Grover moved his brigade in that direction as it passed through the thick woods.[77] When the Second reached open ground and halted, Marston and the other regimental commanders told the men to fix bayonets. Grover rode along the line shouting that they should halt and fire a single volley before attacking with bayonets.[78]

At three o'clock, Grover's brigade moved out. Haynes left a riveting personal account of what happened next. With the Second leading the way, the brigade "showed its mettle as it never had before." Just after the men moved onto the field, "there was a crash of rebel musketry [and] an answering roar of Yankee cheers, and almost instantly the 2d was pouring over the railroad embankment." The rebels had braced for a return volley, not a charge, but the regiment did not pause to fire. When his company reached the enemy position, a rebel lying on the ground aimed his musket at a soldier beside Haynes. "He never fired, for I gave it to him from the hip and doubtless saved the life of some Second Regiment man—I'll never knew who." Under savage Union attack with bayonet thrusts and point-blank firing, the rebel line collapsed "in less time than it has taken to write it." The Second rushed eighty yards through the trees to the next line, where the sides scrapped with bayonets and rifle butts. The result was the same, but the rapid advance had carried the New Hampshire men beyond its comrades, and the reinforcements who might have exploited the success of Grover's brigade never arrived. Enemy infantry fired into the Union flanks, causing the line to crumble and turn back. During this flight, "Something tickled my upper lip and the roots of my nose," Haynes wrote. "One inch further, in the wrong direction, would have spoiled my beauty, and three inches would have spoiled me."[79] The men paused at the railroad embankment to re-form, but enemy fire felled many of them. The rest straggled back to the woods where they had begun their advance.[80]

The exhilaration of the moment and brushes with death like Haynes's glazed over the truth about one of the few bayonet charges of the war. The Second was devastated: a third of its 332 men were casualties, including 36 men killed or mortally wounded. Haynes would later call the assault "a wild turmoil of murder." While in the thick of it, he had helped a comrade carry the wounded Lt. Sylvester Rogers toward safety. Rogers had been shot in the knee, and blood gushed from a second ball in the small of his back. Despite encouragement from his comrades, he gasped and died a few rods down the path.[81] Charles Jewett, the private who had complained bitterly in July about the regiment's labors on the Peninsula, survived the charge and made it back to the railroad bank, where he was shot in the head. "He fell upon his face, turned partly over, rolled back and died," his sergeant informed his family.[82] As Pvt. William Morgrage lay shot through the body, a comrade asked how he was. "A man can't live long, suffering as I am," he responded. Moments later he was gone. Cpl. Charles Smiley simply disappeared. After being appointed lieutenant colonel of the Eleventh New Hampshire infantry, Capt. Joshua Littlefield had decided to stay with the Second until his new regiment was fully formed. He was hit three times at the railroad embankment. Union medics found him alive five days later and sent him to a Washington hospital, where he died on September 17.

Even survivors told gruesome tales. A ball struck thirty-eight-year-old Cpl. Bill Dunton in the lower right cheek and destroyed his upper jawbone before exiting below his left eye. As he lay bleeding, rebels stole everything but his pants and shirt. When his throat swelled nearly shut, he cut out mangled flesh with a knife to keep from choking to death. After nearly a week, a Union burial party found him still breathing on the battlefield, and army surgeons somehow restored him to life.[83] Dunton returned to Fitzwilliam, his hometown, where he would marry in 1889 and live without a palate until he shot himself to death at the age of seventy-seven.[84]

From a hospital where George Gordon was being treated for his head wound, he captured the melancholy mood of a regiment that had sacrificed many lives that summer with little to show for it. "What is to be the result of this war is more than I am able to conjure but it seems a land of mourning," he wrote. "When I stop to look at the inmates of these various hospitals and think of the thousands that have already been killed in this unholy rebellion, it most turns my head." Yet he could not abandon his belief that "the war must be prosecuted with all vigor although every home in the nation shall be made desolate." Failure to conquer the Confederacy would lead to "slavery and nothing more."[85]

The night after the charge, the Second's survivors slept on Matthews Hill, almost exactly where they had formed their first battle line at Bull Run in 1861. The fight raged on, but after Longstreet's divisions joined in, Pope's army retreated in defeat. The Second had encamped at Alexandria by September 3.[86] The next day, with the rest of the army moving out, a brand-new Pennsylvania regiment marched onto the Bull Run battlefield to bury the dead during a truce. This was no trial by fire, but few regiments endured such a cruel indoc-

The Stone Church, one of two Centreville field hospitals where Dame worked during and after the Second Battle of Bull Run. (Library of Congress, LC-DIG-ppmsca-19930)

trination in the wages of war. "The bodies had been lying in the summer sun for several days and were in terrible condition," a historian wrote. The Pennsylvanians buried 1,799 dead comrades.[87]

Despite the defeat, the battle assumed a storied place in the Second's annals. In his official report, General Grover summed up his brigade's role in these words: "Though forced to retire from the field by the immensely superior numbers of the enemy, supported by artillery and by the natural strength of his position, men never fought more gallantly or efficiently."[88] Lt. John D. Cooper reported that the regiment had made "what is often talked about, but seldom witnessed, a bayonet charge," leading to "a deadly encounter with cold steel in which many a rebel soldier yielded his life to that king of weapons."[89] To Cooper, the 143 officers and soldiers of the Second who fell that day were "heroic fellows as ever faced a foe." He did not mention that he happened to be one of them, having survived a serious wound.

Dame had spent the battle and its aftermath at the field hospitals in Centreville. On the way to Alexandria, the regiment stopped nearby to retrieve her and any Second New Hampshire soldiers who could travel. "Our folks sent for me to go with them," she wrote, but the hospital's head doctor asked to keep her until all the wounded were gone, and she complied with his request. Ambulances from the battlefield had kept both hospitals filled since Dame's night propped up by a telegraph pole. She bandaged, medicated, and fed scores of men, including Pvt. Michael Dillon of her regiment. Shot through a lung during the bayonet charge, he had reached the Stone Church feeling "as though the heavens were about to fall." Dame thought he was sure to die but set right to work caring for him.[90] In recalling his personal crisis, he later said that hundreds of men, including many rebels, would bless her for doing "for us as our mothers would have done." Long after the war, Dillon would become the Second's only recipient of the Congressional Medal of Honor.[91]

George Ladd, the private who was courting a girl he had never met, had been struck by a shell fragment during the battle. He was found alive during the truce and sent to Dame's hospital in Centreville. From there, the surgeon transferred him to a Georgetown hospital, where Ladd died after an amputation.[92] Carrie Deppen's insistence in her last letter that she was too young to marry had failed to dampen Ladd's ardor. After his death, her letters to him were packed into a bundle of personal effects and forwarded to his mother in Concord. The mother, Susan Abbott, informed Carrie of his death, and the two women began corresponding. By early 1863, Abbott was addressing Deppen as "My Beloved Daughter."[93]

During the Union retreat, the task of evacuating the wounded fell to Thomas McParlin, medical director of Pope's army, and Edward Vollum, the medical inspector. Vollum, whom Dame had met before the battle, directed the first phase, sending the wounded from scattered field hospitals to Washington. In all, he helped move twelve hundred men out of harm's way. The truce, meanwhile, brought so many more wounded to Centreville that the hospitals remained busy until September 9.[94] Dame faced the usual obstacles, filth, dirty water, and shortages, but at Bull Run another was added to the list: renegade ambulance drivers. The medical examiner accused the drivers of stealing blankets, food, and medicine during the evacuation of the wounded. "Very few would assist in placing the wounded in their ambulances," Dr. Richard Coolidge wrote. "Still fewer could be induced to assist in feeding them or giving them water. Some were drunk; many were insubordinate." In many cases only physical force induced drivers to return stolen goods.[95]

After all the wounded had been treated, the doctor who had begged for Dame to stay reneged on his promise to send her on to the Second.[96] She asked Vollum for advice on what to do next. He was a naturalist and a photographer as well as a doctor, and she had come to admire him. Before the war, at Fort Umpqua in the Oregon Territory, he had compiled Pacific Coast weather conditions and sent them to the Smithsonian Institution along with his animal finds, including birds, eggs, shells, skins, and the preserved carcass of a fog shrew.[97] Vollum gave Dame the choice of moving to the Stone Church or remaining at the house hospital.

With the wounded gone, Dame decided to stay at the house. She was "just played out—had not slept much for two or three nights." Black helpers, the only other people who remained there with her, warned that certain white people in Centreville planned "to kill that Yankee woman." Dame laughed this off and told the women "that as we had plenty of coffee and meat, to get some bread and give me a good breakfast to die on." Union stragglers in town "had got at the whiskey among the medicines and were decidedly too jolly for comfort." Worried about them, Dame asked a soldier she trusted to travel with her, and they left together.[98]

Two miles along the road, they walked right into a rebel guard post. Captured for the second time in three months, Dame asked the guard what right he had to arrest her when Union soldiers left Southern women alone. He sent her to a guardhouse filled with drunken men, which she refused to enter. Her captor fed her soup while they waited for his commanding officer to arrive. As she later recalled, when her guard bragged that the soup was made of Yankee beans, she replied that "a Yankee did not make that soup, sure, or it would have been better." The commander, Thomas Flourney of the Sixth Virginia, sent her back toward Centreville with the wounded prisoners. Packed into ambulances, they traveled over "a road so rough that in fact it wasn't a road at all." Some men died along the way.[99] When the party reached Stonewall Jackson's headquarters, Dame noticed the rebel soldiers "sleeping out of doors as close as sardines." She detected a cunning design in this, later telling an interviewer: "You would never suspect how large a number they had until you came upon them. They avoided campfires or anything else that would attract attention." She did not see General Lee but believed he was in the camp. She did see Stonewall Jackson when he read an order paroling the prisoners, including her. "They did not say much to me, and I went right on caring for the wounded men as soon as I got back to our lines," she said.[100] Afterward, she found Vollum, who helped her find a ride on an ambulance train carrying wounded men to Fairfax Station.

Bull Run was the last act of a summer of agony and defeat for the men with whom Dame had gone to war. Two sentences near the end of the battle report written by the Second's corps commander put the season's human cost in stark terms. "General Hooker's division had above 10,000 men when it landed near Yorktown last April and after the battle of Fair Oaks was re-enforced by about 3,000 more," reported Maj. Gen. Samuel Heintzelman. "At Fairfax Station it drew rations for 2,400 men." Of the five regiments involved in the bayonet charge, he noted, the Second New Hampshire had suffered the most.[101] In June 1861, the regiment had reached downtown Washington a thousand men strong. Now, fifteen months later, when it bedded down just eight miles from its original camp in Washington, 80 percent of the original soldiers were gone.[102]

"The Great Army of the Sick"

In the late fall of 1862, after two months in Alexandria, the remnant of the Second New Hampshire again marched toward Manassas. On stretchers and in ambulances, the sick and wounded moved with the regiment under the care of Surgeon James Merrow and Harriet Dame. The journey ended at Centreville, seven miles north of the old battlefield. An agent appointed by the governor to look after New Hampshire soldiers in the field traveled from Washington to check on the Second. He found the men in good spirits but unable to hide the fatigue of the recent campaign.[1] They had been ordered to the heights above Centreville to guard the nearby railroad tracks against enemy attack. In camp, they set to work restoring the barracks they had inherited from the departed rebels near Wolf's Run Ford on the Occoquan River. When the season's first snow came on November 7, they "basked in the genial warmth of the fires which blazed in their rude fireplaces."[2]

On nicer days, soldiers ventured out to the battlefield at Bull Run, some to satisfy their curiosity, some to reflect, and others to look for comrades they had left behind. "It is visited very much for relics although I have not seen it yet," wrote Capt. George Gordon, who had recovered from his head wound.[3] Near the railroad bank where the regiment had tried to regroup after its bayonet charge, the teeth of a decaying body reminded one man of the face of Frank Robinson, his first sergeant. The soldier brushed dirt from the corpse's chest and found Robinson's name on the shirt. When Robinson was shot through the bowels on August 29, his company commander had seen at once that the wound was mortal. "I might have brought him out," Capt. James Carr said at the time, "but he was dying—is dead now—so I helped out one of my men who has a chance to recover."[4] The return to the battlefield brought a sense of closure to Sgt. Abner Durgin, whose brother Hiram had been killed there. "Experience teaches a very dear school sometimes, and I think we are receiving a very dear one indeed, although we shall come out right side up yet," he assured their mother.[5]

After just two and a half weeks of easy duty on Centreville Heights, the Second departed to rejoin the main body of the Army of the Potomac near Fredericksburg. President Lincoln had recently dismissed General McClellan and appointed Maj. Gen. Ambrose Burnside to command in his place. The veterans of the Second knew Burnside, who had been their brigadier at the First Battle of Bull Run.[6] The night before the men moved, Merrow and Dame rode ahead on baggage wagons carrying the sick and wounded to Fairfax Station. When the regiment caught up with them, Merrow returned to it, leaving Dame alone to care for the patients.[7]

Larkin Mason, the governor's state agent, came to her aid, bringing food and supplies from Washington. The two hit it off and would soon work as a team in other crises. A farmer, merchant, and public servant from just south of the White Mountain forests, Mason had been assigned to act as Gov. Nathaniel Berry's eyes and ears at the front.[8] While apprising Berry of the status of New Hampshire soldiers, he was to help solve their problems and meet their needs. After finding Dame and her squad of sick and wounded men, he described their plight to the governor. From this report, it is easy to see why Mason and Dame bonded in ministering to soldiers in need. He was a man of empathy and energy. The soldiers with Dame at Fairfax Station had lain in the baggage train all night in a pouring rain and eaten nothing for thirty-six hours. "Our men actually suffer more than ten times as much as any of us thought they did," Mason informed Berry. "I am able to give some little relief but come awfully short of their necessities. . . . Day and night I cannot lay down and sleep and let a man die with neglect when I can relieve him."[9]

Dame soon moved on to rejoin the Second on the Rappahannock River opposite Fredericksburg, where the men awaited orders to cross into the city. Confederate general Robert E. Lee had deployed his infantry and artillery along Marye's Heights above the downtown, which his troops also held. Burnside, who felt pressure to take the offensive after Lincoln's sacking of the sluggish McClellan, gathered his army across the river and made his plans to capture the city and attack Lee's army.[10] From their camp on the bluffs, the men of the Second could peer through a glass and read the names on the city's street signs. Federal guns firing on Fredericksburg echoed down the bluffs as the regiment prepared to move out on December 11, but rebel riflemen on the opposite bank delayed the laying of pontoon bridges.[11]

The Second crossed two days later but stopped on the downtown riverfront to guard the pontoon bridges as the rest of Burnside's army prepared to march up the hill and assail the enemy. The battle was a Union disaster, as the well-protected rebels on Marye's Heights gunned down wave after wave of advancing Union soldiers. "In no position did we ever witness such a mixture of sad and ludicrous incidents as at the bridges," Pvt. Martin Haynes wrote.

With explosions pounding in their ears, the soldiers of the Second were to permit only the wounded and men with passes to recross the river. During the battle, predictably, many "lay-backs" headed for the pontoon bridges, grimacing as they pointed to bullet holes and bloodstains on their uniforms. "A close inspection generally discovered these holes to extend no farther than the skin and the blood to be that of some braver comrade who had been wounded," Haynes observed. At one point during the battle, he ascended a nearby hill to watch the right flank of the attacking Union force beyond the trees and houses of the city. "The rebels had an enormous advantage in position, upon the hills and behind breastworks, and our men charged across the open plain only to be slaughtered by the thousands," he wrote. The Army of the Potomac suffered more than twelve thousand casualties, twice as many as the rebels.[12] Union tactics, in Haynes's opinion, had been "worse than useless."[13]

After the fighting ended, the Second settled back in across the river near Falmouth, where rumors soon circulated of a possible reassignment. The men hoped Colonel Marston would pull strings and have them sent for a rest out of harm's way.[14] This wish soon became a reality, and the regiment went home to recruit. It was no coincidence that the men would arrive in time for New Hampshire's gubernatorial election in early March. By law, they could vote only if they were home, and in the wake of the Union military disaster at Fredericksburg, Marston agreed with other Republicans that the party needed every vote it could get to hang onto the New Hampshire governorship.[15]

Even though Dame loathed the camp at Falmouth, she did not go to Concord. With another winter setting in, she was miserable in the wet, cold weather. "I like to died," she would later say.[16] But her duty, as she saw it, was to care for the men too sick to move and the Second's few casualties from the Fredericksburg campaign until the last of them could travel.

As Dame wrapped up this work, a group of prominent men from the state decided they needed her for a new purpose. In mid-1862, they had joined together to create the New Hampshire Soldiers' Aid Association in Washington.

Among its leaders were Mason, the governor's agent, and Edward Rollins, Dame's congressman and onetime Concord neighbor. The association's main purpose was to assist the state's sick and wounded soldiers at hospitals in and around the capital, but the mission had expanded to include connecting people at home with their loved ones in the field. With demand for the association's services surging, its leaders invited Dame to open storage rooms for donated goods pouring in from New Hampshire. "They had several times written to me asking me to come and get the rooms fitted up, then put some one in charge and go back if I wished to do so," she wrote. As she had told Dorothea Dix on the Peninsula, Dame wanted to work in the field, not in Washington. She turned down the offer. When Colonel Marston asked her to take the job, she said no again. Then, after sending his regiment home, the colonel ordered her to report to the capital to supervise the work of the association. For the second time in her nineteen months at war, she decided she could not disobey his order.[17]

Dame joined a multitude of caretakers in Washington. All the surgeons there were men, as were the stewards and orderlies. Despite the opposition of many doctors and federal officials to hiring women as nurses, scores of them had arrived to work in the hospitals that sprang up in the capital's churches, hotels, and vacant buildings.[18] With these makeshift buildings still in use, the New Hampshire Soldiers' Aid Association initially served sixty hospitals. Although many of these closed as the government opened large new hospitals, the number of sick and wounded soldiers in the city continued to climb.[19]

Like Dame, the poet Walt Whitman had just come to Washington, where he produced a vivid account of the hospitals. Whitman had gone to Fredericksburg to help his wounded brother, but when the wound proved minor, he devoted himself to visiting other men in hospitals near the battlefield. He liked this work and resumed it when he moved to the capital. After seven weeks on the job, he described his experience for the *New York Times*. His story, which ran under the headline "The Great Army of the Sick," opened with this description: "The military hospitals, convalescent camps, &c. in Washington and its neighborhood sometimes contain over fifty thousand sick and wounded men. Every form of wound, (the mere sight of some of them having been known to make a tolerably hardy visitor faint away,) every kind of malady, like a long procession, with typhoid fever and diarrhea at the head as leaders, are here in steady motion."[20] John Swinton, a onetime drinking buddy of Whitman's who edited the piece for the *Times*, especially liked a section of the story with the subheadline "The Field Is Large, the Reapers Few":

A benevolent person with the right qualities and tact, cannot perhaps make a better investment of himself, at present, anywhere upon the varied surface of the whole of this big world, than in these same military hospitals, among such thousands of most interesting young men. The army is very young—and so much more American than I supposed. Reader, how can I describe to you the mute appealing look that rolls and moves from many a manly eye, from many a sick cot, following you as you walk slowly down one of these wards? To see these, and to be incapable of responding to them, except in a few cases, (so very few compared to the whole of the suffering men,) is enough to make one's heart crack. I go through in some cases cheering up the men; distributing now and then little sums of money—and regularly, letter-paper and envelopes, oranges, tobacco, jellies, &c., &c.

Whitman's words captured the challenge Dame embraced in her new job. She had many more duties and worries than a volunteer like him, but her principal charge was similar: to find the New Hampshire men in the capital's maze of hospitals and to see that they were treated as family. While she had a large team to help her and a dedicated organization to supply her, she also took on many other responsibilities. The association helped New Hampshire families contact their sick and wounded loved ones in the field hospitals near the fighting in Virginia. Whenever possible, it delivered food, clothing, and supplies directly to these men. Dame's initial priority was organizing the rooms rented by the New Hampshire Soldier's Aid Association on the third floor of a Seventh Street building. These offices became the agency's meeting place, distribution center, and information-gathering hub. John Gass, who had owned the American House in Concord, now ran a hotel in Washington. He joined the association's executive committee and donated even more storage space for goods sent from home.[21] "We had heaps of things that we distributed among the soldiers at the different hospitals, and found plenty of work all winter," Dame wrote.[22]

She and other association members regularly visited about thirty hospitals in Washington and perhaps a dozen more nearby. Each member was assigned to a hospital, and they all met with Dame at the rooms once a week to report on their activities. The association spelled out its expectation that its members would go to their assigned hospitals "constantly and regularly, ascertain the name of every New Hampshire soldier, whether enlisted within or without the borders of the State, find out his wants, and relieve his necessities." Families back home asked constantly about men who had suddenly stopped writing, and Dame and her crew tracked them down. By this point in the war, the families feared the worst. Many had already lost a loved one.[23]

As one visitor's experience demonstrated, the association had a long reach. Sarah Twombly found her way to Dame's offices after traveling twenty-seven hours to the capital from Alton, New Hampshire. She knew her husband Moses, a corporal, had typhoid, and she had come "to alleviate the anguish of a sick bed, if not restore him to health and duty again."[24] At the association, she "found a lady of intelligence who gives her whole time to the cause." Although Twombly did not name her, the "lady" was either Dame or Miranda Swain, Dame's capable chief assistant. It turned out that Twombly's husband was still at the division field hospital of his regiment, the Twelfth New Hampshire Volunteers. This was near Falmouth, where Dame had camped before and after the battle of Fredericksburg. To procure a pass and passage to the hospital for Sarah Twombly, either Dame or Swain sent a clerk to the War Department with her husband's letters home. On a government steamer to Aquia Creek, a Union-held landing forty miles into Virginia on a tributary of the Potomac, Twombly found "six other ladies on board, all on errands of mercy." Most were bringing goods to the field hospitals. From Aquia Creek, Twombly took the train to Falmouth. Dame's office had telegraphed ahead, and a soldier met her at the station. The men at the camp were kind to her.

It pleased Twombly to find the hospital well equipped with iron bedsteads, mattresses, and blankets. Caring male nurses tended to the sick, she observed, "but of course their labors are hard and they cannot give that attention to each patient which we desire to do when we have a sick friend, or that which a very sick man requires."[25] Despite his wife's attentions, Moses Twombly died on February 25. A man of thirty-nine, he left four young children in addition to his wife. In Sarah Twombly's public letter describing these events, she praised the men she had met, cheered on the Twelfth, and had this to say about Dame's enterprise: "I believe our people at home are little aware of what this Association is doing or how much it might do if it had more means. A knowledge of these facts would no doubt procure them the cooperation of many citizens at home who are now inquiring how they can aid the soldiers."[26]

For a young woman, Miranda Swain, Dame's caring and efficient right-hand woman, had seen more than her share of sorrow before coming to the capital. A Welsh ancestor of hers had purchased the entire township of Grafton, New Hampshire, where Swain was born four generations later, in 1835. A good student, she became a teacher at fifteen, married at twenty-one, and had a daughter,

Lena Belle, in 1860. The family lived in Pittsfield, a town adjacent to Barnstead, Dame's birthplace. Swain's little girl and her husband died in quick succession, leaving her a childless widow at twenty-seven. A year later, she joined Dame in Washington. Both women did far more than manage hospital visits and the flow of goods. Swain often traveled to the far reaches of the area served by the association, including Annapolis, where paroled Union prisoners-of-war usually arrived from the Confederacy. She found these soldiers "wretchedly debilitated and pitiable." Whenever one begged her to stand at his side during surgery, she granted his wish. She conveyed the last words of many a dying soldier to his family. At the Soldiers' Aid Association, Swain proved to be a superb administrator, often handling office details so Dame could solve problems elsewhere. She would later succeed Dame as director of the operation and remain at the association's Washington rooms even after the war ended.[27]

In late February, a visitor from New Hampshire stopped in to seek Dame's counsel. Oliver Pillsbury, a brother of the radical abolitionist Parker Pillsbury, served on the state's Executive Council, an elected body that advised the governor. He had come to investigate a problem. As he put it, "There is nothing for which we are receiving so much censure as for appointing incompetent Surgeons."[28] After Sylvanus Bunton and William Stone, both in their fifties, were sent to the Second as assistant surgeons in 1862, Colonel Marston complained to Pillsbury that these "old *grannies*" had "never slept at home without a bottle of hot water at their feet." Pillsbury also asked Dame about John Moore, a Concord private who had just left the Second to accept promotion as assistant surgeon of the Eleventh New Hampshire. "Miss Dame says he is not nearly so competent as the hospital stewards the 2d now have," Pillsbury informed Governor Berry. Dame's steward friend Joseph Janvrin had recently become assistant surgeon of the Fifteenth New Hampshire, and William Stark, the Second's other steward, would later fill the same role with that regiment. Pillsbury visited fifty sick and wounded men in Washington and came away with a higher opinion of the hospitals than Dame held. He thought two-thirds of the men were "better attended than they would be at home" and praised the hospitals as "the only redeeming feature I have discovered here."

Unlike Pillsbury, Walt Whitman would have seconded Dame's view of the hospitals. He found many workers in them "entirely lacking in the right qualities." He had ended his February piece in the *New York Times* with these words: "There are tyrants and shysters in all positions, and especially those dressed in subordinate authority. Some of the ward doctors are careless, rude, capricious, needlessly strict. One I found who prohibited the men from all enlivening amusements; I found him sending men to the guard-house for the most trifling offence."[29]

Dame spent many days visiting the sick and wounded from the association's offices. An urgent message one night added another name to her list. A nineteen-year-old farmer in the Fourteenth New Hampshire had died of typhoid fever in January, and now the family had been notified that the dead man's older brother was ill. On May 24, 1863, Dame set out from the association's rooms to find Albert Leach, who had been a drugstore clerk before the war. After walking to Campbell Hospital, she learned that doctors there had sent him back to his regiment's camp in northeast Washington. Dame knew this news alone would not satisfy Leach's family. She decided not to write to Cornelia Leach, the sick man's sister, until she had seen for herself how Albert was doing.[30] She walked on into the night to Camp Adirondack, which lay "delightfully though rather unhealthily" in an undulating oak grove near the recently built Finley Hospital.[31] Dame discovered that most of the men in the Fourteenth's hospital tent were "very sick indeed." Albert was there, but she did not know what he looked like. Although the doctor on duty thought it was too late for her to speak with him, he at least told her that Albert had typhoid. The doctor hoped he would rally but doubted he would. It did not help, the doctor said, that Albert "felt very anxious about himself on account of his brother dying of the same disease." Dame asked if she could return the next day to meet Albert face-to-face. The doctor refused her, arguing that her presence might make Leach even more anxious.

To the men, as Dame well knew, disease was a more constant and fearful enemy than armed rebels.[32] As the historian of Leach's regiment would later put it: "To be shot down in battle was to die like a man; but to waste away, far from home, losing day by day the vitality and ambition of life, was a transformation to be dreaded by the victim and deplored by his comrades."[33] Dame was candid in relaying the news about Albert to Cornelia Leach. The only vaguely hopeful note in her letter suggested that in her experience, it was better for a sick man to be cared for in a regimental camp than in a military hospital. "I would gladly do any thing in my power for your brother and if he was in any hos'l in Wash'n could see him every day, but it may be better for him to be where he is," she wrote. "I have seen a great deal of hospitals & surgeons & must say the more I see of them the less I think of them." While acknowledging exceptions, she predicted that the day would soon come "when it will be a disgrace for a man to say he has been an army surgeon."[34] Dame promised

Albert Leach's big sister that she would check on him again, but, alas, he died a week after she wrote. He was twenty-two years old.

At around the time Dame was seeing to this matter, the blacksmith Thomas J. Gale joined the stream of parents, siblings, and wives who came south to look for sons who had been wounded at the battle of Chancellorsville.[35] Fighting in its first full engagement, his son's regiment, the Twelfth, had suffered more casualties than any other in the Union defeat. "Of the five hundred and forty-nine musket bearers who went into the fight . . . only two escaped untouched," the regimental historian reported. "Those who were not killed or wounded had their clothes, blankets, or equipments torn with pieces of shells or pierced with bullets."[36] Half the men in the company of Sgt. Sylvester Gale, Thomas's son, were from Gilmanton. Of the fifty-one members of the company who had fought at Chancellorsville, thirteen reported for duty the next day.[37] When Thomas Gale set out, his son lay in the Third Corps hospital near Falmouth, where Sarah Twombly had nursed her husband three months earlier.

On the way down, Gale stopped for help at the New Hampshire Soldiers' Aid Association. He had been robbed in New York, but a kind stranger lent him a few dollars to continue his journey, and Dame's office helped him get to the Third Corps hospital. Three weeks later, James D. Stevens, the association's corresponding secretary, found Gale "cheerily doing early and late the duties of nurse to the men of the 12th." Gale continued to comfort the men at the field hospital even after his son Sylvester recovered. As Stevens described it, he did all he could to mitigate the poor care of "drunken surgeons." Later, back home in Gilmanton, Gale sent the association a twenty-dollar donation.[38]

During the organization's first year, its members visited 1,765 soldiers, most of them more than once. "I assure you we were not idle or making calls except at the hospitals and the War Department that winter," Dame reported. Forty-two of the patients visited were from her regiment, including eighteen men wounded at the Second Battle of Bull Run. Two of these died. Another, George Carter of the Concord company, had been severely wounded and captured. He would survive the war but only after being wounded twice more, at Gettysburg and Cold Harbor.[39] Dame handled the paperwork when a man died. After disease killed Pvt. Solomon Foss, she ordered a casket from a local undertaker who advertised "improved air-tight coffins, particularly adapted to army use," and sent Foss's body home to Manchester by train.[40]

Dame, whose stubborn streak often served her patients well, learned the ropes at the War Department. "Most or all of the soldiers that were able to travel wanted to go home," she recalled, "and we would get them furloughed or their back pay or discharge." A letter from the governor granted her authority to act on behalf of the state in Washington. She used it as a crowbar to pry loose the documents that ambulatory sick and wounded soldiers needed to get home. She would "*shoulder*" the letter like a rifle and march to the War Department, sometimes showing up there after men from the association had returned empty-handed. "I generally got what I asked," Dame wrote, adding that her gender and appearance were no help in succeeding where men had failed. "We all know youth and beauty can do a heap with some people," she acknowledged, but she was nearing fifty and had never been "a howling beauty." Because the governor's letter was so emphatic, she discovered, "youth and beauty were not necessary."[41]

Dame and her crew of visitors did not enter the hospitals empty-handed. At its founding, the association had informed people in cities and towns all around New Hampshire of its mission and asked for help. "It is purely a charitable institution," the circular read. "There is no diversion of its funds from its special object. Its officers and members serve without charge, and what is sent to the society finds its way at once to the sick and wounded, unchecked and undiminished."[42] The association had to borrow a wagon from the War Department's medical office to haul all the material gifts sent from New Hampshire and even Boston for the state's sick and wounded men. During the war's first year, residents of Greenland, New Hampshire, sent four canes, two hundred pounds of dried apples, and many jars of fruits and vegetables. From Contoocook came a hundred pairs of socks and half a barrel of cider. Portsmouth contributed clothing and foodstuffs of all kinds, including thirty pounds of cod. The women of Amherst made and donated thirty-four flannel shirts and other clothing. Two Boston concerns shipped seven dozen bottles of alcoholic beverages and three half-casks, including one that held the equivalent of one hundred and twenty bottles of brandy. The women of Epping collected thirty-three dollars to be spent solely on soldiers from their town. With the donation of flannel shirts, socks, and applesauce from Boscawen came an eighteen-dollar cash contribution for Dame to disburse at her discretion.[43]

Donations of this nature from women all around New Hampshire had begun at the very start of the war, a year before the association was formed.[44] In Claremont, a mill town in the western part of the state, townswomen met immediately after President Lincoln's first call for troops and began to make bandages and other medical supplies. Then they formed the Ladies' Union Sewing Society, which met daily in the town's Fraternity Hall to prepare kits for the town's volunteers. Each man received woolen drawers, an undershirt, a towel, a handkerchief, wool socks, and needles and thread. The society also raised money for rubber blankets and havelocks, the strips of cloth attached to the backs of soldiers' caps to keep the sun off their necks.[45] Lucy Lambert Hale, wife of Sen. John P. Hale, presided over the aid society in Dover, their home city. It played a role beyond its core mission of aiding the soldiers.[46] Because the senator was a prominent abolitionist, the society also collected money to help the Ladies' Anti-Slavery Society assist Black people. It gave generously to the New Hampshire Soldiers' Aid Association as well.

Unlike many other municipalities, Pittsfield, Miranda Swain's hometown, had no local women's aid society per se, but when state military authorities sent up a call requesting clothing for recruits, townswomen rose to it. As the town war history would report, making three hundred shirts in three weeks was a challenge, but the women met it.[47] One member described how the women came together to work: "When it was time to go home, we took the unfinished garments with us and finished them. We ransacked our houses for old sheets and pillow-slips to make bandages, and every bit of linen we could get we scraped into lint." One woman she knew was too infirm to leave home but did as much for the cause as the rest. After the war, another Pittsfield woman who sewed for the Soldiers' Aid Association recalled the "terrible waiting, the anxiety and expense" of women's lives at home. "We would run to the post-office for a letter, and if none were there we would almost cry. But if there were one from our friends in the army we dreaded to open it, for fear it would bring bad news. Every paper we took up we scarcely dared read, fearing we should see the name of some loved one either killed or injured." Even homecomings tended to be deflating. "We sent forth strong young men," the woman said, "we received back wrecks."

Dame's purpose throughout the war was to do all that was humanly possible to bring about a better outcome for these women and their men at war. As Swain put it simply after more than a year of working for the association at Dame's side, "She is a faithful laborer for the soldiers."[48] In a letter describing the association's work to Joseph Gilmore, the new governor, its secretary pointed out that the state government had contributed nothing to the enterprise. With the battle of Chancellorsville in the recent past and the strong prospect for more fighting in the vicinity of Washington, the secretary, James Stevens, expected expenses to rise. He described Dame as an indispensable leader and asked that the state kick in so that she could be adequately paid. He asked for one hundred dollars a month for rent, fuel, travel, and Dame's wages. Stevens believed the public would support such an expenditure, closing his appeal with these words: "In asking this, we feel little hesitancy, being convinced that making suitable provisions for the wants of her disabled sons ought to be, and will be, New Hampshire's first care."[49]

As the association's treasurer, Matthew Emery, a stonecutter and building contractor, kept the books for Dame and other leaders of the enterprise. A New Hampshire native who lived in Washington, he had been a Union activist since the moment the war began. In April 1861, he had raised and led a local militia that guarded federal buildings until troops arrived from the North. He later visited battlefields near the capital to assist the wounded. His handiwork as a builder was all around him in Washington. He had sold stone to the government for the post office and the Capitol and cut, squared, and donated the cornerstone of the Washington Monument.[50]

During the association's first year, Emery logged dozens of monetary gifts from churches, municipal aid societies, town fund drives, and individuals. A donation of $26.55 came from James E. Murdock, a Philadelphia actor renowned for playing *Hamlet*. He had suspended his stage career to raise money for the care of soldiers by giving patriotic readings. Cash gifts totaling more than $2,100, including $699 from association members, more than covered the first year's expenses of nearly $1,750. Among the expenditures were $755.65 for fruit, wine, sugar, eggs, and clothing; $243 for "embalming, enclosing and shipping home bodies of deceased soldiers whose friends were unable to bear the expense"; and $49 for train tickets home for wounded soldiers who had been robbed or had lost their money. While meticulous in their record keeping, Dame and the association's other leaders wanted patrons to know that for all "the fidelity and self-sacrificing zeal" represented by these donations, the association's good deeds could not be measured by a balance sheet alone. Many volunteers spent their entire Sundays and any time they could spare during workdays ministering to the sick.[51]

All fifteen officers of the association were prominent men. US Senator Daniel Clark of New Hampshire was its president, Senator Hale headed the executive committee. But Dame's role in its day-to-day operations was widely known and appreciated. The association's first annual report singled her out for "energetic, manifold, and untiring labors."[52]

The report also predicted that, if anything, the trials of war would worsen. Wounded men arriving from Chancellorsville that spring had nearly overwhelmed the staff at Armory Square Hospital, which had been designated to receive them.[53] The movement of more long ambulance trains and "the continuous booming of distant cannon" signaled "that other terrible conflicts are already beginning," the report warned.[54] Hospitals south of the capital at Aquia Creek and Falmouth had just closed, sending thousands of patients from the Army of the Potomac to Washington hospitals.

Back in Concord, Dame's regiment was winding up a furlough of nearly three months. The Second New Hampshire had arrived in the city the morning of March 4 to a boisterous welcome from local fire companies and a crowd of waving friends and families, followed by a communal feast. Many of the soldiers voted six days later, helping the Republican railroad magnate Joseph Gilmore to become governor. The election was so close that the Legislature had to decide it after neither leading candidate won a popular majority.[55] During the regiment's stay, the men staged a "sham fight" near the Free Bridge and paraded in the State House yard, where outgoing Gov. Nathaniel Berry addressed them. Some were present on the ensuing Sunday, a bright, sunny day, when a telegram reached Concord announcing that Union troops had captured Richmond. The news was rushed to the city's many churches, where pastors announced it from their pulpits. After services, churchgoers wearing their Sunday best celebrated in the streets until news arrived that the Stars and Stripes did not, in fact, wave over the Confederate capitol.[56] For the most part, the Second used its freedom to recruit replacements and visit with family and friends. For Pvt. Martin Haynes in Manchester, it was a special time. On March 9, he married his sweetheart, Cornelia Lane.[57]

One other notable event affected the fate of the regiment during its long furlough. The Seventeenth New Hampshire Volunteers had begun to assemble as a nine-month regiment late the previous fall. The men had drilled and prepared for months when the regiment, still not fully recruited, was disbanded. A lieutenant spoke for many in calling the Seventeenth's breakup a "bitter experience for true and loyal men to endure." After most of the men transferred to the ranks of two nine-month regiments bound for the pestilence of Louisiana, the secretary of war ordered the rest to merge with the depleted Second New Hampshire. Although they had just five months left to serve, these 103 enlisted men proved to be the best-prepared recruits the Second ever took in. Because of their training in Concord during the early winter, they entered their new regiment as well-drilled soldiers and fine marksmen. "We marched together, and fought together, and drank from the same canteen," Haynes would later write.[58]

On May 27, the Second arrived at Soldier's Rest in Washington on its way to its new camp on Capitol Hill. Three weeks later, Dame's old regiment was well into its longest and most grueling movement of the war.[59] "I think many times I would give anything for a drink of our spring water from home," one of the new men observed after a tramp of twenty-five miles one day. Their direction was north, their destination unknown, but the entire Army of the Potomac was on the move, and the Confederate Army was marching on a parallel track. "We have to be very still because we are on one side of the Rappahannock and the rebels on the other, almost within speaking distance," Pvt. Albert Whipple jotted in his diary shortly after the regiment set out.[60] On the fifth day out, while passing through Frederick, Maryland, the original members of the Second burst into cheers when they caught sight of Gilman Marston, their first regimental commander and now a freshly bestarred brigadier general.[61] They knew the Pennsylvania border was up ahead but had little idea of what awaited the long columns of the Third Corps in which they marched. Few if any of them had even heard of a town called Gettysburg.

Ghastly Harvest

Twenty-nine miles east of Gettysburg, the New Hampshire preacher Joseph H. Foster caught his first glimpse of the carnage of the great battle that had been fought on July 1–3, 1863. When his train stopped at Hanover Junction, Pennsylvania, to allow two outbound trains to pass, he stared into the cattle and baggage cars behind the locomotives. On beds of straw lay scores of wounded soldiers bound for hospitals in Baltimore, Philadelphia, and New York. Volunteers boarded the cars to distribute food and drink as doctors examined wounds and adjusted bandages. Foster reached Gettysburg that evening. It was two weeks after the battle, but thousands of outsiders still roamed the streets.[1] One observer contended that this second invasion of the town had begun when hundreds of people flooded in from all directions "to see the sights, stroll over the ground, and gape at the dead and wounded."[2] How, a resident asked, could a place "overrun and eaten out by two large armies" feed and house ten thousand visitors?[3] The exhausted Foster and eight other boarders stretched out that hot summer night on old carpets in a garret of a private home.

He was no sightseer. His mission was a common one during those desperate days: he had come to retrieve the body of a friend. The armies had departed after the battle, leaving seven thousand corpses lying in open fields or buried in shallow graves. Foster knew time was of the essence, as heat and rain were making quick work of the dead. He had as much company roaming the battlefield the next day as he had had in town. It was true that gawkers, relic hunters, and thieves had swarmed to Gettysburg, but so had doctors, nurses, volunteers, and friends and relatives of the dead and dying.[4]

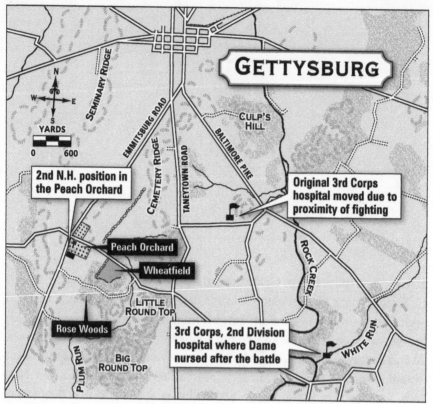

Gettysburg

While exploring the detritus of war on this vast, hilly Pennsylvania farmland, Foster happened upon Harriet Dame in a field hospital. Of the "many noble women" he encountered on his tour, he singled her out for her tireless care of wounded and dying men. "She hastened to this place as soon as news was received of the battle," he wrote.[5] Indeed, after leaving Washington, Dame had reached the Third Corps field hospital by July 6 or 7. Most of the wounded from her regiment, the Second New Hampshire, had struggled or been carried to the hospital tents thrown up on farmland far behind their regiment's battle line. The scale of human suffering in the mud and filth surpassed even the worst hospitals on Dame's rounds in Washington. She dressed wounds, dispensed medicine, and kept the men as clean as she could under the circumstances. She gave hope even to the dying.

Reverend Foster had stopped at her hospital in search of Henry Richards, a sergeant in the Second US Sharpshooters. In civilian life Richards had been a teacher and a volunteer arborist in Portsmouth, planting trees along the road to the cemetery to which Foster now hoped to deliver his remains. The sharp-shooters, who served in the same Third Corps division as Dame's regiment, had been deployed on July 2 at the base of Big Round Top, the extreme left of the Union line. They initially held off the furious attempt by a far larger rebel infantry force to flank and envelop their position. During their inevitable re-treat, Richards was shot below the right knee. The Confederates helped him to a field hospital and gave him water. Back in Union hands, he died on July 5, a day after a surgeon amputated his right leg.[6]

As Foster looked for his friend, he surveyed the horrors of the landscape. It was as though the surviving actors of a garish Shakespearean tragedy had left the stage littered with decaying victims and shattered props. He saw dirt-packed walls that had served as breastworks to protect infantrymen from en-emy fire, hastily dug rifle pits, crashed-in doors and windows, gardens flattened by footsteps and wagon wheels, and fences, trees, houses, and barns pocked and broken by minié balls and shells. In town, Foster had visited three rooms filled with equipment, ordnance, and firearms brought in from the field. More wagonloads were on the way. Yet everywhere on the battlefield, he saw the ac-coutrements and victims of war. Dead livestock lay "wherever the fight was hot," fifty horse carcasses in one field, dozens of bloated oxen in another. Some of these had been burned, others half buried. Even sadder were the human graves visible "in all directions, sometimes singly, sometime in little groups of from 3 to 12." Many were marked, all were shallow, none contained coffins. Fos-ter knew another Portsmouth man who had come to find his son and returned empty-handed. A man he met during his own search dug up eight bodies be-fore finding the one he was seeking.[7]

Foster had better luck. Sergeant Richards "had been carefully buried by comrades who knew his worth, and who had time to do it well." Exactly a week after Foster unearthed him, friends in Portsmouth bore Richards's cof-fin "beneath the trees which his own hand had planted, to rest with kindred dust in our own beautiful cemetery." The next day, at the city's Unitarian Sab-bath School, Foster told a rapt audience what he had witnessed at Gettysburg.[8] Dame was still there, living in the nightmare that Foster had put behind him.

The Second New Hampshire Volunteers who marched north into Penn-sylvania on July 1 were not the same regiment she had joined two years be-fore. Although Gilman Marston, their beloved leader, still looked after the men, another colonel led them now. With Marston's promotion to brigadier general, his command fell to Edward Bailey. A nineteen-year-old Manchester postal clerk when the war began, he had captained that city's Abbott Guards, now the regiment's Company I. Even with the addition of the Seventeenth New Hampshire men, he led a regiment about a third the size of the one that had gone to war in 1861. A thousand men and officers had mustered then, just 354 by the time the Second reached Gettysburg.[9]

There had been other changes. The original enlistees, who still far outnumbered the recent recruits, were hardened veterans, not fresh fish. They had suffered much with little to show for it, but two years of training and hard fighting had made them soldiers. Though green, the men of the Seventeenth had marched and drilled for months. When well led, as they were by Bailey, the men snapped into action before a shouted command could echo. In the fury of battle, most of them knew how to change positions as one and charge screaming into enemy fire without pausing to consider the consequences.

To reach Gettysburg from their camp in Virginia, the men had zigzagged for 150 miles on hot, dusty roads, in railroad beds, along a narrow canal towpath, and through the mud. They camped just south of the Pennsylvania line on July 1 and marched the next morning toward the sound of the guns. As they gathered in the woods on John Rose's farm outside Gettysburg, Lee's army lay before them. Maj. Gen. Dan Sickles, their corps commander, pushed his troops forward on his own initiative. The movement isolated his men, causing a breach in the Union line and giving the enemy an inviting target. If Confederate units could flank the Union left, they could circle behind and attack the Union line from the rear. Sickles's move determined the place and the stakes of the day's fighting. At three o'clock in the afternoon on July 2, Bailey and the Second were sent to support a battery in a peach orchard on the Emmitsburg Road that would soon be known as *the* Peach Orchard.[10] They marched "double quick" to the front, where Bailey aligned them facing south behind the six cannons of Nelson Ames's light battery. They lay for nearly two hours protecting the battery as its guns boomed away.[11]

This was no easy duty. Artillery fire might have been less accurate than an infantry barrage, but the perils of the Peach Orchard were of a different magnitude. For what seemed an eternity, Ames's battery was the main target of seasoned rebel artillerymen. The regiment had hardly settled in when a single shell struck the man beside Private Haynes and two on his other side. A piece of it hit the cartridge box of Sgt. James M. House, who managed to rip the box from his belt as the cartridges began to explode. "Never, in all its history, was the regiment exposed to such a terrific artillery fire as it received while lying upon the ground to the rear of this battery," Haynes later wrote. "The air was fairly alive with bursting shell and whistling canister; the leaves fell in showers from the peach trees, and the dirt was thrown up in little jets where the missiles were continually striking."[12] Wounded men streamed to the rear, leaving holes in the line, but Haynes escaped unscathed. "Talk about luck!" he told his wife.[13]

At about five o'clock, a rebel infantry force threatened to overwhelm the regiment's position. The danger was so grave that Union gunners drove spikes into their cannons' powder combustion vents, rendering them useless should they fall into enemy hands. Then Colonel Bailey ordered a charge. His outnumbered men raced 150 yards toward the foe with "a yell and impetuosity" that chased the flankers into a ravine a hundred yards back. Bailey ordered a second charge on two other regiments. The Third Maine Infantry helped his men force these attackers to seek shelter as well, but the rebels kept pressing. With his regiment now under even heavier infantry and artillery assault, Bailey called for a slow retreat with the men firing as they went.[14] "It was a wild time," Haynes wrote. He found Edwin Kenaston, a thirty-five-year-old private from his company, lying shot through both legs in a field. Haynes left him a full canteen and a small supply of "really tasty pieces of grub" and later returned with an officer's overcoat.[15]

While enduring severe losses as the Union line collapsed, the regiment had done all it could to save the cannons and prevent the envelopment of the army's left wing. A veteran officer reported to the governor that the Second had "never fought more bravely" and had executed Bailey's commands "in as good order as it would have been at a battalion drill."[16] Fifty-six officers and men were killed or mortally wounded, 134 wounded, and fifty-six missing or captured.[17] Among these were seven recruits killed and ten wounded, most of them severely, from the disbanded Seventeenth New Hampshire.[18] Haynes thought that "No men bore their part more manfully than the Second Regiment's contingent from the Seventeenth."

After the battle and before Dame's arrival in Gettysburg, members of the Second returned to the ground their regiment had nearly spent itself defending. Pvt. John Burrill ventured into the Peach Orchard before the dead were buried, but soon regretted it. In the faces of the dead, he saw a fate that had spared him for no reason he could think of. "The men had turned black, their eyes swollen out of their heads and they were twice their natural size," he wrote his parents. "The stench of the field was awful." Burrill decided he would "rather go into a fight than see the effects of it afterwards for a man in the heat of battle thinks nor cares for nothing but to make the enemy run."[19] Albert Whipple, a musician who had come over from the Seventeenth, took a similar walk on July 5. "Every soldier lying on the battlefield has been robbed by the sharks who follow the army for that purpose," he observed. Near one corpse, he found a letter from a mother and sister congratulating their soldier boy "on his success in escaping with his life thus far, and saying they should look forward for the time when he would return home and that that would be the happiest day of their lives."[20]

Colonel Bailey and Col. Benjamin Carr led groups of men to search for the regiment's wounded. At Abraham Trostle's farm, Carr's party walked through the dead horses lying about the yard and entered the barn. There they saw Maj. Samuel Sayles and a few others and brought them in. Sayles had a severe thigh wound. Men who had lain in the field near him when a Confederate thief pulled the boot from his lame leg had never heard "a more complete and comprehensive gospel of damnation." In the Peach Orchard, Bailey and his orderly "found the regimental line marked plainly by our dead: here, Capt. Metcalf, to the left, Captain Roberts, and from right to left each company's station." When the men formed, Henry Metcalf had said to a comrade, "A good line, that." Seconds later, a bullet crashed through his skull. Bailey observed years later that the sight of these dead officers and the battle line they had anchored remained "as gallant and glorious an offering of discipline and devotion as ever was laid on the altar of our country." After finding twenty-one wounded men of the Second at a nearby farm, Bailey and his orderly called for ambulances to move them to the Third Corps hospital.[21] Most would come under the care of Harriet Dame.

Some of the walking wounded departed Gettysburg on their own. Capt. George Gordon, who had been hit in the arm, neck, and side, hiked ten miles to Littleton. He wrote home from a hotel there that his wounds were painful but minor. Later, at a Washington hospital, he concluded that even though Robert E. Lee probably wished he had skipped his trip to Pennsylvania, the newspapers were making too much of the Union victory: "There is more fighting to be done and hard fighting too, and many lives will be lost." Gordon's company had been a hundred men strong in 1861. Now, he told his wife after returning to the regiment, "eleven guns" remained.[22]

When the armies left after the battle, they abandoned their wounded. Desperation and chaos suddenly reigned. Nearly twenty-one thousand wounded men, a third of them Confederates, remained on the field amid the thousands of dead. Pennsylvania newspapers soon carried brief pleas like this one: "Any person at Gettysburg, who can give information of the exact burial place of Lieut. Humpherville, of the 24th Michigan Inf., will confer a favor on his sister."[23] As strangers filled the town, residents opened homes, churches, and buildings to the wounded. Sallie Broadhead and her family had spent much of the battle in their cellar. On July 6, when she brought food to a makeshift hospital, it bothered her to see so many men lying untreated. She offered to help even though she had never dressed a wound. One man she attended was near death, his leg "all covered with worms." She wrote to the soldier's wife but feared the woman would never again see him alive. Broadhead soon took three more wounded men into her house. After the man with the wormy leg died, she sent his wife a lock of his hair.[24]

Gettysburg people were as curious as anyone about the battlefield, which had so recently been a ring of sylvan slopes around their prosperous town. Young Daniel Skelly explored the rich farmland near the Round Tops not far from where Dame would soon nurse wounded men. Heavy rain had swamped the roads, but by destroying the fences, the armies had opened the fields to pedestrians. Crossing them, Skelly saw huge trees "knocked off and splintered in every imaginable way." At the Trostle house, near the barn where some of the Second New Hampshire wounded had been rescued, he found the kitchen table "still set with all the dishes from the meal, and fragments of food remained, indicating that the family had gotten up from their meal and made a hurried getaway." At another farm, dead rebels lay "on their backs, their faces toward the heavens, and burned as black as coal from exposure to the hot sun."[25] In fifteen-year-old Tillie Pierce's wanderings, she saw "dead horses, swollen to almost twice their natural size." The landscape made her feel "as though we were in a strange and blighted land." At home she stared out her window at men being laid on a bench one after another as surgeons lopped off their arms and legs. They were given chloroform from a cattle horn, but some screamed and writhed under knife and saw. Pierce soon beheld "a pile of limbs higher than the fence."[26]

While townspeople and visitors could turn away from such sights, soldiers sent out to bury the dead lacked this option. One of them observed bodies "with glassy eyes staring up at the blazing summer sun; others with faces downward and hands filled with grass or earth," a historian wrote. "Here a headless trunk, there a severed limb, in all the grotesque positions that unbearable pain and intense suffering contorts the human form, they lay. Upon the faces of some death had frozen a smile, while upon others was indelibly set the firm stamp of determination."[27] As a Philadelphia man traversed pastures that had been "almost ground to a jelly," he discovered "something impressive about a dead man on the battle-field. To see him lying there, with his hands clenched, his teeth set, and his limbs drawn up, with ramrod of musket firmly held—lying just as he was standing then the fatal bullet struck him—teaches a sad lesson."[28]

As soon as possible after the battle, Dame left the work of the New Hampshire Soldiers' Aid Association in Washington to Miranda Swain, her deputy, and set out for Gettysburg. She had known the town might be her destination since mid-June when newspapers began reporting that it lay in the path of Lee's invasion.[29] On June 23, with the rebel army eight miles away, the *New York Herald* reported townspeople "flying in crowds from Gettysburg, literally blocking up the roads."[30] Travelers faced similar obstacles after July 3, but Dame soon made it to the town.

For her, what was new about Gettysburg was precisely what was new about it for the soldiers, the armies, and the country: the scale of the battle. Three days of savage fighting by seasoned soldiers on both sides had taken a human toll unequaled in the war so far. Union and Confederate soldiers had clashed on many fields, but Gettysburg had been a three-act bloodbath whose stakes for the nation rose with the body count. The horror of the battle did not escape the fighting men. As they departed, they looked out upon a wasteland of green swards and craggy hills strewn with destruction and mangled corpses lying in shallow graves or no graves at all. Reclaiming the land and recasting it as hallowed ground would have to wait. The armies also left a sprawling village of field hospitals, busy, overpopulated enterprises where limbs piled up, moans and howls resounded, and men died by the hundreds. In the days after the battle the number of men fighting for their lives far exceeded Gettysburg's population of twenty-four hundred. For Dame, the chaos of military field hospitals was familiar, but the ever-growing mass of wounded men here was overwhelming. After previous battles, she had nursed in a large house at Yorktown, a bloody field at Oak Grove, and a church and a house in Centreville, near Bull Run. Never had she faced endless days of mending bodies and easing the anguish of doomed men on such a grand stage.

What she witnessed on the way to the field hospital went unrecorded, but she could only have cringed at the gore and desolation. A worker for the US Christian Commission who arrived at the same time as Dame described a field that looked as though "an army of men, with every kind of material, had started up in the night, leaving everything but what was fastened to their bodies." At the field hospitals, he discovered that the wagonload of food and supplies he had brought was a piffling offering amid "such a multitude" of gravely wounded men. Rain had drowned some of them "for want of help to move them from low to flat places."[31] In the eyes of a Philadelphia reporter, Gettysburg and its environs became "literally one vast and overcrowded *hospital.*" Even after days of frantic medical care, "several thousand are lying, with arms and legs amputated, and every other kind of conceivable wound, in tents, on the open fields, in the woods, in stables and barns, and some of them even on the bare ground, *without cover or shelter.*" Anyone who came to Gettysburg to feed or help the wounded would be welcome, the reporter advised, "but let all mere sightseers *stay at home.*"[32]

Larkin Mason, the state agent whom Dame had met in November on her way to Falmouth, arrived just after she did. He came from Concord after speaking at a celebration of the Union victories at Gettysburg and Vicksburg. On the way he toured a Philadelphia hospital, where he found "a liberal sprinkling of Gettysburg wounded" from his state. Mason estimated that more than two hundred of them lay in that city's hospitals. "You would be pleased to see the patriotism and loyalty of our wounded soldiers, even while suffering pain," he informed Gov. Joseph Gilmore. "Not one has been heard to say, 'stop the needless war,' but all say, 'let us put down this rebellion.'" He left Philadelphia the next day to join Dame in her efforts to help the state's wounded men still at Gettysburg.[33]

Charles Jewett of the Sixteenth Massachusetts served as surgeon-in-chief of one of the brigades whose wounded were delivered to Dame's hospital. He and Hadley Fowler of the Twelfth New Hampshire were two of the three "operators," as amputating surgeons were called. The other three members of the team were assistant surgeons who kept records, supervised burials, and managed the provision of straw and shelter for the patients. Earlier, during the battle, the Third Corps hospital had been sited "on the brow of Round Top Mountain," where balls and shells struck terror in both the wounded who poured in from the battle and their caretakers. Jewett described July 2 as "a black day for the 3d Corps." By this point in the war, two rules governed the operators' decisions: act fast and take off too much of a limb rather than too little. On July 2 and 3, they performed fifty-three amputations. Twenty-four men died soon after their operations, including nineteen who had their legs sawed off at the thigh. Fifteen hundred men reached the hospital before it was moved to safer ground.[34]

When Dame arrived, the Third Corps hospital sat well behind the Round Tops on a high bank above White Run, which provided a good water supply. One medical team served each of Sickles's two divisions, which included thirty-five infantry regiments, two sharpshooter regiments, and five artillery batteries.[35] Although the patient count fluctuated as men came and went and died, a mid-July estimate put occupancy at twenty-four hundred.[36] As more and more men were brought in, Dame cleaned and bandaged filthy wounds and handled an endless parade of alarming postoperative cases. She fed the men, wrote letters home for them, and dispensed brandy, whiskey, and other spirits to soothe and calm them. Her boys from the Second had missed her during her time in Washington but found her "back in season for Gettysburg."[37]

She was not the only woman at the hospital. Helen Gilson of Chelsea, Massachusetts, also found her way there.[38] Dorothea Dix had rejected Gilson for a nursing job in 1861, when she was just twenty-six, nine years younger than Dix's minimum age for nurses. The US Sanitary Commission hired Gilson after she learned to dress wounds by attending surgical lectures. In September 1862, Gilson had nursed scores of wounded men in barns near the Antietam battlefield, preparing "gallons of cornstarch and liquors to feed the poor fellows shot through the mouth and throat."[39] She visited several field hospitals at Gettysburg. At Dame's, she tended to men from her home state and informed their families of their condition. She and Henry Bellows, the Sanitary Commission's president, happened upon a barn where more than two hundred rebel wounded lay in stinking straw.[40] After they handed out their supplies to these men, a soldier asked Gilson to sing a hymn. "I'll sing you a song that will do for either side," she responded. The tone and clarity of her voice as she sang "When This Cruel War Is Over" inspired Bellows to remove his hat. After the rebels applauded, a man raised his left arm and apologized for not joining in. His right arm had been amputated.[41]

The efficiency of Civil War weaponry and the limits of medical knowledge worked against the wounded and complicated the work of Dame, Gilson, and other attendants. A minié ball, the standard Civil War bullet, consisted of a one-ounce sphere of soft lead that could be fired accurately from up to four hundred yards. It caused gaping wounds, ripped tissue, and fractured or shattered bones. Before trying to repair the damage, surgeons probed wounds with dirty tools and fingers. Even if handwashing had been a practice, most field hospitals lacked clean water. After a light rinsing in a pail of murky, bloody water, a cloth or sponge that had cleansed the days-old wound of one patient was used on the next. Like the rest of the medical staff, Dame spent her days plodding through bloody mud. Doctors knew little about the causes and treatment of the infections that killed many of their patients.[42]

Sgt. Richard Musgrove of the Twelfth New Hampshire had a harrowing experience at Dame's hospital. His regiment had fought along the Emmitsburg Road near the Peach Orchard and lost as heavily as the Second. A few days later, Musgrove learned that a wounded tentmate wished to see him at the Sixth Corps hospital. He found Pvt. Jonathan Leavitt on a stretcher under an apple tree. A shell had crushed both feet and ankles, and Leavitt had lain

Left: Like Dame, the self-taught Helen Gilson treated soldiers of both armies. (Library of Congress, LC-DIG-ppmsca-57123); *right:* Surgeon Hadley Fowler of the Twelfth New Hampshire (from the Twelfth's regimental 1897 history)

untreated for a day and a half. Musgrove and three comrades carried him to the Third Corps Hospital, where Fowler, the Twelfth's surgeon, amputated Leavitt's feet. Musgrove toured the hospital during the operation. "Men were mutilated in all conceivable ways and piles of legs and arms told of the work of the surgeons," he wrote. Some had been buried, but the rains had swelled White Run and washed away the earth that covered the rotting limbs. Musgrove visited Charles Drake, a private who had lost a leg. Later he asked what had become of the leg. "The hogs ate it up," Drake replied. Leavitt, meanwhile, died during his double amputation.[43]

Fowler and his mates were among the few surgeons at the hospital, as most had left with their regiments to chase Lee's army. Just 106 of them remained on the field amid thousands of casualties.[44] On hearing of the army's departure, a Christian Commission member exclaimed: "What! take away surgeons here where . . . if the men have not immediate help, hundreds must die for want of that attention."[45] A native of Bristol, thirty-six miles north of Concord, Fowler was a graduate of Dartmouth Medical School.[46] He had run the field operating hospital at Chancellorsville, where his regiment had been mauled. The Twelfth's historian called him "the hero of the amputating table, few, if any, severing more limbs and saving more lives by his courage, alertness and skill."[47] Fowler met Dame at the hospital, quickly came to admire her work, and would later hire her to help him run a much larger enterprise.

To reduce the patient count, men were sent to hospitals in Baltimore, Philadelphia, New York, or Washington as soon as they were fit to travel. Many hobbled on their own to the depot. The road was "thronged with wounded men, here on canes, there on crutches, not seldom with amputated arms, and heads still bleeding, making their way on foot from the corps hospitals two, three, four miles to the depot," wrote Henry Bellows of the Sanitary Commission. His group set up a shelter near the depot where nurses cared for these men as they awaited their trains.[48] One of them, Georgeanna Woolsey, noted that the nurses "couldn't help being good to them when they were in our hands," often becoming so attached that they hated to see them go. They changed bandages and treated the men to bread with jelly and butter and a boiled drink that combined milk, whiskey, and sugar. Nearly sixteen thousand Union and Confederate soldiers passed through the station in three weeks. Woolsey was not alone in disparaging local "Dutch farmers" who charged wounded men three or four dollars each to take them from field hospitals to the depot in "wagons as hard as the farmers' fists." It also outraged her when a farmer who had fled town during the battle wandered into the waiting station in hopes of laying eyes on a wounded rebel. Asked why he had not stuck around to help drive the invaders out of town, he answered: "Why, a feller mighta got hit."[49]

Pennsylvanian William Watson was one of the operators at the Third Corps' First Division hospital adjacent to Fowler and Dame's. As was customary, he made the Union wounded his priority, leaving rebels to await care "in the most distressing condition." No slouch with the tools of his trade, Watson amputated fourteen limbs in a single session and fifty during his first three days at the operating table. These included six legs above the knee from a single infantry company. He relished the opportunity to tie off major arteries and "amputated every bone in the body." Many of his patients died of gangrene, tetanus, or postoperative hemorrhaging. Few whose amputations caused infection survived second operations.[50]

The war was a learning experience for surgeons, and treatment for amputees had evolved in ways that affected Dame's care of her patients. Lint, the used linen that women at home had prepared and sent to the front early in the war, had fallen out of favor with surgeons because it irritated wounds. Ideally, as Jewett described it, the stump was first treated with coal oil, which acted as both a disinfectant and a deodorant. It cleansed the wound, sometimes killing larvae already present, and kept flies and other vermin at bay. Then a lighter cloth manufactured for the purpose was cut into the shape of a Maltese cross and pressed gently onto the stump.[51] Jewett reported that as far as he knew, every man who underwent an amputation at his hospital received chloroform beforehand and was given whiskey as the effects of the anesthesia waned. Jewett's postsurgery dietary recommendation called for a dozen eggs a day for two days, but it is unlikely that Dame, well versed in feeding sick and wounded men, followed this odd course.

Although she left no known account of nursing at the Third Corps hospital, only the volume of the suffering might have shocked her. At the time she arrived, Bellows described conditions as "intensely wretched. Men with both legs shot off—shot in the eye, the mouth, both hands gone, or one arm lost, were laying in rows." The state of the wounded rebels was "too horrible for recital."[52] Dame had no time to write friends, and she spoke little about Gettysburg after the war. Fortunately, two sources bearing on her efforts there have survived and will be deployed here: the recollections of those she treated and letters from civilians from New Hampshire who saw her in action at Gettysburg and sent accounts of her labors to the governor.

New to life as a Northern war governor, Gilmore had no plan for a catastrophe like the aftermath of Gettysburg. Nor was it the only crisis he faced during his first full month in office. On the Fourth of July, Democrats who favored making peace with the Confederacy, known as Copperheads, jammed the State House lawn and Main Street in Concord to cheer former president Franklin Pierce's denunciation of the war. Their timing was off, as news of the Union victory circulated in the crowd before it dispersed, but the event was boisterous.[53] Then came fury over the draft, especially in Portsmouth, where a mob confronted the police, leading to gunfire and a bayonet charge.[54] "These demonstrations should be taken by the forelock and not allowed to acquire momentum," warned Oliver Pillsbury, a member of Gilmore's Executive Council.[55] In light of the draft disturbances, Secretary of War Edwin Stanton approved Gilmore's request to raise a second artillery regiment for Fort Constitution on the Seacoast. When a "mob spirit" put Manchester "in great danger of falling into the hands of the enemy," its mayor requested six hundred cartridges for the smoothbore Springfield muskets in the city's arsenal.[56] At Gilmore's request, President Lincoln arranged for the remnant of the Fifth New Hampshire to be sent home in case the riots worsened. In the meantime, Gilmore learned in mid-July that while attacking Fort Wagner near Charleston, the Seventh New Hampshire had suffered more than two hundred casualties, including seventy-seven dead and mortally wounded. Haldimand Putnam, the regiment's colonel, was among those killed.[57] As if he did not have enough challenges, Gilmore nearly inflicted another on himself, inviting Abraham Lincoln to Concord. He knew Mary Lincoln planned to tour the White Mountains and wanted the president to come, too.[58] Lincoln declined, writing: "I am by no means certain that I can leave Washington at all this summer. The exacting nature of my official duties renders it exceedingly improbable."[59]

Gettysburg commanded Gilmore's attention not as a military triumph but as a human tragedy that had struck home. Appeals from the families of wounded soldiers filled his mailbox. George Francis, a South Sutton farmer, had sent two sons to war but was too proud to accept the state aid offered to families whose soldier-sons had worked on their farms. He had used his cows as collateral for a loan to keep the farm going while counting on his boys to return. "We have nothing to look for but the labor of their hands," he told the governor. Now his son Daniel, a Second New Hampshire private, had been shot. While asking for financial help to bring Daniel home, Francis shared a frank appraisal of his family's prospects: "To speak plain, we are poor and the war has made us more so."[60] Augusta Edgerly's brother Charles had lost both legs at Gettysburg. "i told him to goe & fite four our Country & be brave & he did & now he is wher he is," she wrote Gilmore. Neighbors would help pay to bring Charles home if the governor approved of the idea.[61]

Gilmore reacted swiftly and effectively to the fate of the three battered New Hampshire infantry regiments at Gettysburg. He dispatched five merchants and professional men to the battlefield hospitals. Other men, some encouraged by the governor, also set out to aid the state's wounded. A few proved to be enterprising, others less so. At the Second Corps hospital, where the Fifth New Hampshire's wounded were being treated, the physician Thomas Wheat took charge of four wards.[62] Because many patients at Dame's hospital lay on the ground, a volunteer traveled four miles to a farm to buy straw to fill their mattress covers, known as "ticks." While scribbling a note to Gilmore during the return trip, he ended abruptly: "Can't write any more. Men are calling for help. I am writing this from ambulance and perhaps you cannot read it."[63] The Dover merchant Oliver Wyatt, by contrast, decided soon after reaching Gettysburg that there was little for him to do.[64] He led Gilmore's official delegation, and as another member would soon complain, his mantra quickly became "The crisis is passed."[65] Wyatt appreciated hearing broken men welcome him with "glistening tears," but he departed for home after a single night in a tent at Dame's hospital. The wounded, he reported, were in capable hands:

"Miss Dame, Mr. Mason and others from our state are unwearied in their efforts to do them good."[66]

Indeed, although wet weather complicated their task, Mason and Dame became the core of the state's effort on its Third Corps soldiers' behalf. As they searched for wounded New Hampshire men, Mason told Gilmore, they "found between one and two hundred men wallowing almost in the mud on the battlefield."[67] According to Samuel Clark, a New Hampshire court clerk who helped out, these men were "scattered about in various parts of the field and in different hospitals [and only] slightly protected from rain with little or no straw underneath them."[68] They had lain for days, most of them maimed, drenched, and spent. "We soon displayed our Yankee genius by getting beds &c., and taking them out of the mud," Mason wrote. Dame settled in at the hospital, bathing and clothing them and dressing their wounds. "There is no other such hospital camp as that of the 3d Army Corps," Mason assured the governor. A nurse who visited two nearby corps hospitals lamented: "Language fails to depict the misery that was present." She pitied the rebels who lay hungry and idle in pelting rain outside one; in the other, gravediggers fell behind, and the dead lay unburied at tent doors. Reflecting on these scenes, she asked: "Is it not well sometimes to pause and think at what an awful cost our country was then and there redeemed?"[69] While Dame toiled day and night, Mason ran a long-distance relay to gather information and supplies. He checked on the New Hampshire wounded in Baltimore and Philadelphia hospitals, asking the state agent in Pennsylvania to send Dame shorts, drawers, bed ticks, and soap. After moving on to the Soldiers' Aid Association's rooms in Washington, he collected whatever Dame requested. As Mason described the operation to Gilmore, "Miss Dame remains with the soldiers on the battlefield and we forward supplies from this place."[70]

The conditions of the Second New Hampshire wounded at Dame's hospital speak to the challenges she faced. When Pvt. Aaron Goodwin was shot through the thigh, the bullet struck no bone but damaged his femoral artery. To stanch the bleeding, a surgeon tied the artery shut above and below the wound with dental silk or silver wire. Goodwin died after nearly a month of suffering. Cpl. William Mix, struck in the rib cage by a cannon ball, bled copiously from the lungs for five days. Then the bleeding suddenly stopped, and Mix recovered.[71] Pvt. Edwin Parker remained in the corps hospital until July 13 with gunshot wounds to his elbow and thigh. Doctors in Baltimore later removed twenty-nine fragments of his ulna and radius. Pvt. Thomas Severance, hit in the head by a piece of shell, seemed to be responding to treatment until his caregivers in Philadelphia noticed telltale inflammation at the edges of the wound. Severance complained of stiffness in his jaw. The treatment included ammonia, back rubs, a diet of whiskey-laced milk punch, and a liquid concoction of boiled-down meat and bones known as beef tea. As usually happened after lockjaw symptoms appeared, a tetanus infection killed the patient.[72] Dame tended to officers, too, treating Major Sayles's thigh wound and the stumps of Albert Perkins and Levi Converse, newly promoted captains who had each lost an arm. All three credited Dame with saving their lives. Maj. John D. Cooper often heard sick and wounded men say: "What should we have done without Miss Dame?" He added: "It is *not* for notoriety that she so untiringly devotes herself to the cause. The poorest and most humble private receives her attention as readily as the officer highest in rank. She always goes where her services are the most needed. Shot and shell strike no terror to her."[73]

One of the most gruesome cases to reach Dame's hospital was that of Cpl. John Barker, who had worked in the Manchester fabric mills before the war. After the First Battle of Bull Run, he had spent nearly a year in three rebel prisons. At Gettysburg, he was leaning against a peach tree when an artillery shell fractured the top of his skull, exposing his brain. Comrades carried him away from the orchard but dropped him when the man holding one of his legs was suddenly killed. Alert but with a terrible headache, Barker crawled on. Finally, someone guided him to the corps hospital.[74] He was later transferred to Satterlee Hospital in Philadelphia, where surgeons sawed off the largest piece of depressed skull bone and another two-inch chunk. An infection swelled Barker's brain, but he survived it.[75] Eleven months after the battle, the army decided that vertigo and incessant head pain disqualified him from further service. Barker would marry, father children, lead a light artillery company back home, and live till 1907.[76]

For a few days at least, Dame had company from home at her hospital. The homeopath Ezra Abbott of Concord arrived, and the corps medical director put him to work. Among others, he began treating the enemy wounded and men from the New Hampshire sharpshooter companies. There is "much suffering and a willing hand can find enough to do, especially among the wounded rebels," he reported to the governor.[77] Severe diarrhea sidelined Abbott after a few days, but he and Dame would meet again on other bloody fields.

Another visitor, D. K. Foster, took special interest in wounded Twelfth New Hampshire soldiers from in and around Pittsfield, where he ran a school so slight that even he referred to it as "a one-horse Academy." Dame cared for most of the wounded from this regiment. On July 19, on her advice, Foster informed Isaac Carr that if his son Asa were sent home, the jostling of wagons and train cars might kill him on the way. A minié ball had struck Asa in the shoulder and passed through his left lung. He had lain on the field all night before comrades carried him to the Third Corps hospital. Foster promised Isaac Carr he would do his best for Asa and the "other New Hampshire boys who are here on all sides with legs off and holes through them in all places and directions."[78] Dame watched over Private Carr for nearly a month before he was sent to a Baltimore hospital and then home for good. As souvenirs, he kept his Bible, cap, canteen, and bones from his shattered shoulder and ribs.[79]

Foster also made excursions on the battlefield. A guide took him to the area along the Emmitsburg Road where the Twelfth had fought to search for the body of Lt. Henry French of Pittsfield, who had been shot in the head. The only possible trace they found was a burial trench near where he died. A board above it read, "Here lie seventeen bodies." Foster and half a dozen wounded "Granite boys," as he called them, went blackberry-picking the next day and delivered a bushel to Dame for her patients. He also brought her milk for which he had paid "an avaricious Dutchwoman" seven cents a pint.[80]

In a cranky account written after his return home, Foster described his experience as a member of the governor's delegation. While praising Dame and her work, he condemned Wyatt, the group's leader, as a profligate do-nothing. At a Philadelphia hospital on the way down, Foster had tried to comfort Pvt. Henry Emery, a former student at his academy who had been shot in the head. Foster and Wyatt left the rest of the delegation in Baltimore to move on to the battlefield on July 16. The train from Hanover Junction to Gettysburg took seven hours to cover seventy miles with "heat, dirt and baggage cars jerking and jostling Sisters of Charity and brothers of the bottle all down together in laughing piles as the stupid Dutch *ass* engineered his iron *mule*." After walking from the station to the Third Corps hospital, Foster and Wyatt found Dame hard at work. Foster, who stayed for two weeks after Wyatt's hasty departure, called her "a mother and sister to our soldiers, desolate and dying in the camp, the first and the last to cheer and bless them in all their sufferings." Dying men entrusted "the memorials of their loves" to her, and she was "ever near to bestow her parting blessing and catch their last words and treasure them up for the comforting of the dear ones at home." He worried that she was "doing more labor and encountering more hardship than *any* one person could endure." Foster felt protective toward her, seeing it as his duty "to guard Miss Dame while in the midst of her ceaseless labors of love [from] these gentlemen-commissioners who visit the hospitals and the battle fields with a morbid curiosity to gratify."[81]

Nineteen days after Dame reached Gettysburg, thirty men still needed help at her hospital. "I keep her supplied with everything necessary for the comfort of our wounded men," Mason wrote the governor. He predicted the mortality rate among the last of the wounded would be "unusually large on account of the unfavorable season and the severity of their wounds." With Dame at their sides, he assured Gilmore that they would not die for want of care. A few days later, several men had indeed died.[82]

What to do with the dead remained a challenge. Three-man burial teams patrolled the field in the first days after the battle. Two carried a stretcher, the other a pole to prod the corpse onto it. Later, the dead were lined up along the ground and buried in trenches.[83] Things had improved by late July, when Joseph Greeley, one of the governor's men, noted that all three New Hampshire infantry regiments had fought on the Union left, the most exposed place on the second day, and that all three were mauled. Greeley found men from the state in several field hospitals, but "most in the 3d Corps hospital where Miss Dame is in attendance who is doing good work for our soldiers." He saw a dozen patients die in a few days. Unlike the anonymous burials just after the battle, bodies not sent home received "appropriate services. There is a slab set up at the head of each grave giving the name, Co. and Rigm't so that their friends can find the grave." Because of the heat, he advised friends at home to let the bodies lie.[84] Silas Sylvester, a Concord seller of crockery and mirrors, came anyway for his son George, a Fifth New Hampshire corporal who had been killed. He informed a local newspaper that many identified corpses from the state had been buried in marked graves on the land of John G. Frey. The provost marshal had ruled that their loved ones could come and claim them, but not until after October 1. Sylvester recorded the names of fourteen dead soldiers from the three New Hampshire infantry regiments.[85]

One of them was the newlywed Lt. Charles Vickery of the Second. He had lain helpless with a ball in the back after the battle as, in Haynes's words, the rebels "stripped and robbed him with their usual dexterity." The enemy held Abraham Trostle's barn at the time, and a Confederate major ordered his men to carry Vickery there and leave him a canteen of water. A search party, probably Colonel Carr's, found him on July 5, and Dame later cared for him at the hospital on White Run.[86] Vickery was "full of courage and confident he would be all right in a short time." Pvt. Samuel Oliver, who stayed behind to help Dame, spoke with him often before he died on July 11. "We got a box made and I marked a board & put [it] at the head of his grave," Oliver informed Vickery's bride.[87] The body was later unearthed and sent home.

Dame always demurred when men claimed she had saved their lives, saying that the severity of their wounds determined their fate.[88] This was certainly the case at Gettysburg. Shot in the abdomen, Lt. Charles Patch of Portsmouth initially lay among strangers in a field where the Second Corps wounded were taken. He eventually made it to Dame's hospital but lived only until July 10. Capt. Joseph Hubbard was shot in the forehead and never reached any field hospital. After he wandered senseless into enemy lines and died, fellow members of the Masonic Order buried him. Late in July, Larkin Mason reported that Hubbard's body had been found and would be sent home when "a proper case can be prepared." He informed the governor that several Union states were reserving lots on Gettysburg's Cemetery Hill for men buried on the field. He would have telegraphed Gilmore "if the case had seemed to justify it. But our 5th and 12th regiments were so decimated no details for burial service were made for them." Their dead were "buried by strangers and their graves not marked, consequently cannot be recognized. A few of the 2d are marked and they are so well made they can be opened any time."[89]

In early August the Third Corps hospital began sending the last of its wounded to Camp Letterman east of town, where the army was consolidating medical care.[90] The hospital was named after Jonathan Letterman, medical director of the Army of the Potomac, who had reformed medical care since taking the job a year earlier. At Gettysburg, perhaps his most significant achievement had been an independent ambulance team for each corps, improving efficiency in transporting the wounded from the battlefield to corps hospitals.[91] The exhausted Larkin Mason had decided to leave Gettysburg. Dame would see to the few remaining men. Most soldiers left behind by the armies were gone, to their homes, to their graves, to hospitals on the East Coast.[92] Army Medical Inspector Edward Vollum, Dame's colleague at the Second Bull Run battle, advised his superiors that 15,425 wounded Union and Confederate soldiers had been sent to east-coast hospitals. Including men left behind by the enemy in towns, barns, and houses along their march route, he estimated there were 15,000 wounded rebels.[93] The Third Corps hospital closed on August 8, about a month after Dame arrived there. The medical staff had treated 2,600 Union and 259 Confederate wounded.[94]

Sophronia Bucklin, one of the first volunteer nurses at the new Camp Letterman, described most of the patients there as wounded rebels, "grim, gaunt, ragged men—long-haired, hollow-eyed and sallow-cheeked." The wards stood in four parallel rows, each with nine wide tents. To Bucklin, the tents "looked like they had white wings." She had nursed in Washington hospitals, but nothing

Sophronia Bucklin, who would cross paths with Dame again later in the war (from *In Hospital and Camp,* Bucklin's 1869 memoir)

prepared her for Gettysburg. "Boots, with a foot and leg putrefying within, lay beside the pathway, and ghastly heads, too—over the exposed skulls on which insects crawled—while great worms bored through the rotting eyeballs." She saw birds pecking at a headless, limbless soldier in a tree and arms rising from shallow graves "as though pleading to be assigned enough earth to keep them from the glare of day." At Camp Letterman she washed faces, untangled matted hair, bandaged wounds, and served drinks flavored with raspberry vinegar and lemon syrup.[95] Dame had remained at the Third Corps hospital until August 7, when the last patients departed for Letterman.

The cost of victory at Gettysburg would long hang over the Second New Hampshire. In an age when physical labor was the norm for men, many returned home unable to work. Jonathan Merrill and his brother Simon, whom Dame had treated, remained in a Baltimore hospital for more than five months. An artillery shell had blasted away Jonathan's thigh as he stood beside Private Haynes. He informed a cousin in January that he and Simon, whose left leg had been amputated below the knee, were nearly healed.[96] The dozens of captives carried south to wither away in prison camps fared worse. At least seven from the Second survived long enough to be transferred to Andersonville, Georgia.[97] Two died shortly after reaching this patch of disease and starvation, and only Pvt. John W. Jones was still alive by September 1864. He succumbed two months later.[98]

After the battle General Marston used his influence to guide the remnant of his old regiment to a safe posting while it recruited new troops. "Suddenly and unexpectedly, after all our troubles and tribulations, the Second Regiment finds itself in clover," Haynes exulted. On the chase after Lee's army, the men were "marching through Warrenton, sweating and puffing, when we saw General Marston standing in front of one of the houses and looking mighty pleasant and smiling."[99] General-in-Chief Henry Halleck had ordered Marston to establish a prison camp at Point Lookout, Maryland. This was the resort at the mouth of the Potomac where the Second New Hampshire had sat out the worst of the storm during its passage to the Peninsula in the spring of 1862. Halleck noted that the state's Second, Fifth, and Twelfth regiments, all devastated at Gettysburg, now totaled about three hundred men, just the number needed as guards. Atop freight cars filled with Confederate prisoners from Gettysburg, the Second and the Twelfth rode from Warrenton to Washington on July 27. They boarded a ship to Point Lookout three days later, arriving at around the same time as 136 of the prisoners.[100] "The boys, as you may imagine after the long marches and hard fighting they were 'put through,' were not a little pleased with the operation," one man remarked. In addition to guard duty, the soldiers would train draftees and volunteers.[101] The Fifth, the smallest of the three regiments, would come later, after standing by in Concord in case of further draft riots. "They are gallant fellows," Marston wired the governor. "Treat them well."[102]

One man Dame had cared for after the battle was Edmund Dascomb, a lieutenant known for his way with words. The previous winter, with the Second at home to rest, vote, and recruit, Dascomb's speech at a reception for the troops had "carried the audience by storm."[103] The lieutenant then campaigned for Gilmore and the Republican ticket.[104] At Gettysburg, he was among the wounded men rescued by Colonel Bailey. Neither Surgeon Fowler nor Dame could save him, and he died on July 13. Eventually he was one of forty-nine soldiers from the state buried in the National Cemetery at Gettysburg, but his friends at home held a service for him, too. One of them read a poem by Dascomb, beginning with these words:

I am dying, brother, dying,
'Mid the wounded and the slain,
And around me forms are lying

Which will never strive again:
Much I would but cannot tell thee,
Of a home I cherished dear,
Of the friends I've left behind me,
Who will shed the silent tear.[105]

9

Bound for Dixie

Shortly after leaving the toils and sorrows of Gettysburg, Harriet Dame finally went home. She had been at war for more than two years without a break, but her trip to Concord from the Soldiers' Aid Association offices in Washington was no vacation. George Dame, her fifty-five-year-old brother, had died on August 24, 1863, of dysentery.[1] For years, George and Harriet had operated boarding establishments a few blocks apart on North Main Street, both just a short walk from the home of their sister, Mary Ellen Shackford, and her family. George had helped Harriet manage her affairs at home during her army service. The few days she spent in Concord for his funeral would be her only break in more than four years with the army.[2]

The visit came during a distressing summer in New Hampshire. Gazing out the window of the *Statesman* office in Concord on the morning of August 3, Editor Asa McFarland was shocked by "a spectacle of truly affecting character." Marching up Main Street was the proud remnant of the Fifth New Hampshire Volunteers, just home from Gettysburg. A one-armed lieutenant caught McFarland's eye amid the hundred or so men in the formation. Less than two years after their festive departure, the men of the Fifth looked as ragged as their battle flags.[3] The regiment had come home to suppress any further anti-draft violence before reporting to Point Lookout to join the Second and the Twelfth regiments as prison guards. In Portsmouth, a hotbed of draft resistance, Capt. John Godfrey, the quartermaster who had spent an anxious night with Dame during the Peninsula retreat, now served as provost marshal, the head of the military police in the city's congressional district. In mid-August, after receiving orders to use force, if necessary, he dispatched soldiers to hunt down draftees who were fleeing to Canada.[4]

Tragic scenes played out in Concord when trains carrying survivors of two nine-month infantry regiments pulled into the railroad station early that month. Many women in the crowd awaiting the Sixteenth New Hampshire burst into tears upon learning that soldiers they had gathered to welcome had died on the way home. Louisiana bayou fevers still afflicted many of the living aboard the train. Carts and carriages carried some of them to a sixty-bed hospital at city hall, which stood between the boardinghouse and the inn that Harriet and her late brother had run. Even with the women of the local aid society nursing them, seventeen more soldiers soon died.[5] By early September, when the terms of the Fifteenth and Sixteenth Volunteers expired, disease had claimed more than three hundred and fifty of these men.[6]

For Dame, who had rushed off to war during the first flush of Union feeling, the contrast between the Concord of 1861 and the Concord of 1863 must have been jarring. Many people in town went about their lives almost as if there was no war at all, but political divisions had deepened, too. In an economy that greatly limited women's workplace options by rule and by custom, scores of war widows faced poverty. Frequent calls for more troops created a backlash that even supporters of the draft understood. Congress had passed the first draft in the nation's history in March, requiring all men from twenty to forty-five of age to register. The law allowed a draftee to buy his way out of the draft for $300 or to hire a substitute. Large bounties paid to draftees and substitutes seemed unfair to soldiers and families who had received none. As the Second New Hampshire would soon learn at Point Lookout, the substitutes, many of whom were recent immigrants or homegrown ne'er-do-wells, would change the character of the regiments. New Hampshire "prides itself with filling up its quota with the cast off population of Europe and the released convicts of our numerous poor houses and State Prison," a soldier near Charleston complained.[7] Col. Mason Tappan, the man who shared the soldier's comment with the governor, had commanded the First New Hampshire Volunteers. Now he warned Gilmore that "the horror of the draft" could be avoided only by employing discerning agents to recruit men who were loyal to the state.

After seeing her brother to his grave and visiting with friends and family, Dame left Concord in September. She had considered rejoining her regiment, but because there was a good hospital at Point Lookout, she decided the troops there did not need her. Back at the rooms of the New Hampshire Soldiers' Aid Association in Washington, she looked so haggard that her col-

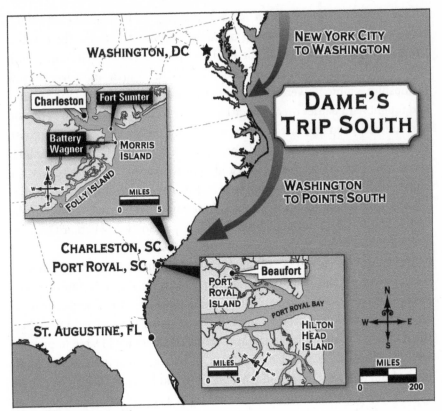

Harriet Dame's trip south

leagues thought she needed a rest.[8] They helped arrange a working trip down the Atlantic coast for her, although the notion that this would be relaxing to a woman who awoke each morning determined to be useful to others must have seemed dubious even to them.

Gov. Joseph Gilmore had proposed the mission and perhaps even mentioned it to Dame during her time in Concord. Many New Hampshire troops were serving in a military department along the south Atlantic coast between Charleston and points in Florida. Deaths from sickness ran high among these men, and Gilmore asked Dame to visit the regiments and the hospitals at their posts and report to him on the quality of their medical care.[9] Having received glowing reports about Dame from Larkin Mason and others who had seen her in action, Gilmore had confidence in her. She knew the ways of Union field hospitals and surgeons, she was a faithful advocate for the soldiers, and she spoke her mind.

The genesis of this mission is hard to track. As he had at Gettysburg, Gilmore was increasingly relying on male emissaries to assess the medical needs of the state's soldiers in the field, but thus far he had sent none south of Fredericksburg. When Dame set out, the Third, Fourth. and Seventh New Hampshire regiments were stationed in the South Carolina Sea Islands. They had fought hard battles on Morris Island and at other points near Charleston and suffered from the diseases common along the southern Atlantic coast. Perhaps the governor had heard complaints from New Hampshire families about the hospitals at Hilton Head and in Beaufort. In a later diary entry, the already well-known Clara Barton, who had spent considerable time in the Sea Islands, was certain things were amiss in the hospitals there but was equally certain she could do nothing about it.[10] One question was whether Dame, as persistent and caring as she was, could gain access to them.

Dorothea Dix warned her of the dangers of the mission and the likelihood that, as a woman, she would be barred from leaving the ship at Union-occupied ports, forts, and camps. Yet even Dix was curious about the medical care at Union hospitals in the deeper South. If Dame ignored her advice and did go, she requested a full report. In the end, an inside tip enticed Dame to proceed with the mission. "Was told in *confidence*," she wrote, "that there was to be *the* fight of the war very soon, and Charleston would be ours." With Gettysburg fresh in mind, she surely doubted the notion of a larger battle, but Charleston had been the flashpoint of the war, and, like any good Yankee, Dame longed for its downfall and jumped at the chance to witness it. Had it not been for "that yarn," she later said, "I would not have gone."[11]

She headed to New York in October 1863 to board the *Arago,* an eight-year-old sidewheel steamer that had been used before the war for transatlantic freight and passengers. The army had chartered it and now used it as a mail boat, transport, and troop ship to and from Union-occupied points along the south Atlantic coast. Dame found herself "busy all the way to Hilton Head taking care of seasick women, mostly schoolmarms that were teaching the freedmen at South Carolina and Florida."[12] Hilton Head, a shoe-shaped island tucked along the coast, was the headquarters of the Department of the South. All the regimental camps on Dame's itinerary belonged to this command.

The Third and Fourth New Hampshire regiments had been part of the expedition that passed Hilton Head on its way to capture the island of Port Royal two years earlier.[13] After the motley armada of nearly a hundred ships survived a stormy voyage, its gunships made quick work of this mission. The

Formerly enslaved people of Thomas Drayton on Hilton Head Island, photographed in 1862 by Henry Moore of Concord (Courtesy of the New Hampshire Historical Society)

soldiers found Beaufort, Port Royal's chief village, "deserted upon the arrival of our troops, except quite a number of negroes and one white postmaster," recalled Pvt. Elbridge Copp of the Third. Their presence invited a wave of freedom. Enslaved people "came flocking into our camp by the hundreds, escaping their masters." In their arms and across their backs they carried bedding, furniture, chickens, piglets, gunnysacks filled with clothing, and bags of sweet potatoes. Muscular men balanced upturned tables on their heads. "There seemed to be an underground telegraph that took the news of the arrival of the northern troops to the slave population for miles around," Copp observed, "and deserting their old masters and the plantation, they came into our camp for freedom and protection."[14] By the time Dame arrived, the Sea Islands were firmly in Union hands. The seasick women she had nursed on the *Arago* joined a legion of abolitionists who had come to educate, clothe, and feed formerly enslaved people at Port Royal and Hilton Head.

After a brief stop, the *Arago* carried Dame about ninety-five miles back north to Morris Island at the mouth of Charleston Bay, where all three regiments on her itinerary were stationed in late 1863. With Mary Marden, who had been her tentmate early in the war, Dame toured the camps of the Third, Fourth, and Seventh New Hampshire.[15] The Seventh had followed the Fifty-Fourth Massachusetts, the famous Black regiment, in the charge on Battery Wagner on July 18 and suffered its own deadly repulse. The Third and Fourth had participated in the subsequent siege, shoveling up walls of sand and filling sandbags to support them as they readied for another assault on the island's forts. This proved unnecessary when, shortly before Dame arrived, the rebels abandoned Battery Wagner.

A military escort took Dame to see the fort during her stay. A soldier on the island described the area around it as "thickly strewn with fragments of missiles as various in kind as the genius of man has invented. A collection might be made which would form a *heavy* museum of curiosities." On an excursion two days later, the same soldier counted "over 200 graves in the burying ground mostly of men died of disease on this island."[16] After Dame toured Wagner, she and her guide started for Fort Gregg but stopped when the rebels began shelling it from Fort Moultrie, near Charleston. Although Union artillery battered Fort Sumter in Charleston Bay and arced shells into the city five miles away throughout her time on Morris Island, she was disappointed to hear that there would be no campaign to capture Charleston anytime soon. Perhaps she took some consolation in seeing that Union shelling had reduced Fort Sumter to a brick pile.[17]

For the soldiers, the presence of Dame and Marden was a welcome novelty during the hot, sandy days of monotony on Morris Island. A soldier of the Third New Hampshire remarked that the regiment had not seen a woman from home for months.[18] While visiting the Seventh, Dame kept her promise to the Second New Hampshire's quartermaster to look up his father, Capt. Jeremiah Durgin. The son, Abner, relayed this news home from Point Lookout, marveling over Dame's exploits. "She has had a chance to see all there is in this war," he informed his mother.[19]

Reasonably satisfied with medical conditions among the regiments on Morris Island and nearby Folly Island, Dame boarded the *Arago* for St. Augustine, Florida, to assess the idea of building a military hospital there. It was more than an idea, in fact, as army engineers had already begun the preliminary work.[20] Union marines had captured this Florida town and its centuries-old Spanish fort in March 1862, and the Seventh New Hampshire had been among its early occupiers. Half the men of the Seventh had encamped at the old coquina-stone Fort Marion, the rest in a former Franciscan monastery. St. Augustine was a charming town with balconies overhanging its narrow streets and a New England granite promenade capping its seawall.[21] Many pro-Confederate families had left the city of their own volition after the Yankees took over. As provost marshal, Captain Durgin had banished dozens more, a task he quickly grew to loathe. It troubled Union marines and soldiers to witness how adamantly some Confederate women protested their ouster.[22] The troops who occupied St. Augustine had good food and quarters and relatively light duty.[23]

The reports of the Seventh New Hampshire's surgeon to his superiors may have advanced the idea of a hospital there. At Beaufort in the Sea Islands, where the regiment had been stationed the summer before it moved to Florida, William Brown wrote, twenty men had died of typhoid fever in the first month. When the Seventh embarked for St. Augustine six weeks later, one hundred-fifty men were unfit for duty, and a third of them were too ill to make the trip. Many of the sick died, and others were sent home. In contrast, as Brown had reported from St. Augustine in late 1862, "the health of the regiment has rapidly improved, and no sickness of any severity having its origin here, has occurred."[24]

When Dame reached the city nine months later, the Seventh was long gone, but she met another officer who knew Florida well enough to offer an educated opinion of the hospital proposal. John T. Sprague, the adjutant general of New York, had served in Florida twenty years earlier as aide-de-camp for two commanders of the US force charged with uprooting and expelling Florida's Indigenous people. During the so-called Seminole wars, he had personally led 211 men, women, and children to exile in Oklahoma.[25] Now in charge of military recruitment in New York state, Sprague was on his own journey to investigate the living conditions of his state's troops in St. Augustine. Dame spent days touring the city, talking with the sick, and watching a troop review by Sprague and Gen. Truman Seymour. The three of them then boarded the *Cosmopolitan* to steam back to South Carolina. Along the way, Sprague told her that both he and Seymour strongly opposed the hospital idea.[26]

Rather than simply endorse his views for her report to Governor Gilmore, Dame went straight to the source. She toured the big hospital at Hilton Head and moved on to Port Royal to wait for the *Arago* to carry her back north. "I visited all the hospitals at Beaufort, and these were a large number," she wrote. "Most of the houses and all the churches were filled with sick and wounded."[27] Wherever she went, she sought out sick men from New Hampshire to ask whether they would rather be treated there or at a new hospital in St. Augustine. Patients told her one after another that they preferred the Sea Islands. St. Augustine, they said, was just too far from home.

While at Hilton Head, Dame met Clara Barton, who had been a teacher in Massachusetts before moving to Washington, DC, in 1855 to work as a clerk

Clara Barton, by
Matthew Brady,
circa 1865 (Library
of Congress, LC-
USZ62-108565)

at the patent office. She had been nursing on and off since the start of the war, and her exploits were widely known. Most recently she had witnessed the July 18 charge of the Fifty-Fourth Massachusetts on Fort Wagner and ridden onto the field of battle to rescue and treat wounded men. When Dame arrived at Hilton Head, Barton had been living there for several months riding and walking along the beach, socializing, and otherwise leading a life that a biographer would later characterize as "enforced leisure." Her tendency to act on her own and her gender had led the commander and the chief medical officer of the department to banish her from the Sea Islands hospitals.[28]

Perhaps Barton's frustration over this prohibition explains why she dismissed an alarm raised to both her and Dame about the care of sick and wounded soldiers. Aware of Dame's mission, Margarette Dorman, wife of the army paymaster, urged her to "stir people in the North" to come to the aid of soldiers at the Hilton Head hospital.[29] Dorman made a similar appeal to Barton one night. During a visit to the hospital, as Barton described it in her diary, Dorman became "excited upon the subject," expressing concerns about the near-empty storeroom and the wretched diet of the sick. She suggested cir-

cumventing military leaders on the island in the hope of persuading Secretary
of War Edwin Stanton to demand a wholesome kitchen for the hospital.[30]

There is no evidence that this issue was addressed. Barton did not deny
that sick soldiers were being "oppressed by puffed-up, conceited, and self-suf-
ficient superiors," nor did she doubt that an efficient kitchen run by women
would lead to longer lives or easier deaths for the patients. She simply did not
think she could do anything about the situation or that it was her place to try.
"My *confidence* in my ability to accomplish anything of an alleviating character in this department is completely annihilated," she admitted in a rambling,
self-pitying diary entry.[31] As for Dame, it is likely that she had neither time
nor opportunity to investigate the problems raised by Dorman. In similar circumstances when she did have firsthand knowledge, she had been sharp and
candid in her criticisms of Washington hospitals.

Good care and nutritious diet were at the heart of all her efforts, and she
soon had a chance to further those causes. Faced with the neglect of sick and
wounded men during her journey north to New York from Dixie, she acted
with diplomacy and determination to correct an alarming discovery. She
could not stand seeing these men crowded out in the open on the deck of the
Arago. When she tried to give up her cabin to a feeble private, she was told that
only officers, who wore shoulder straps signifying their rank, were permitted
to use the staterooms. "How I did long for a big pocket filled with shoulder
straps," Dame fumed. She shared her complaint with Sprague, the New York
adjutant general, who advised her not to blame the captain, as he was probably just obeying orders. Instead, the two of them rolled up their sleeves and
went to work. Sprague had the baggage room cleared, and they moved the
worst medical cases there. To create even more sheltered space, Dame cleaned
and refitted the ship's empty stable, which had been filled with cows for the
Sea Islands on the trip down. A steward assigned by the ship's captain to help
her often misbehaved when the boss was out of sight, but at least he provided
some assistance. Soon Dame was ushering sick and wounded soldiers from
the deck into new quarters. Chaplain Joseph Emerson of the Seventh New
Hampshire, an old friend of hers from Concord, happened to be aboard, and
they "worked all the time to make the poor fellows comfortable."[32]

When Sprague promised to back Dame up if she reported the poor conditions for the sick and wounded on the ship to Surgeon General Joseph Barnes,
she took him up on the offer. After returning to Washington, she marched into
Barnes's office to tell him what she had seen and done. She had hardly begun
when Barnes interrupted her to say he had just received letters from New York

complaining about the same thing. Sprague had followed through on his promise, and the team approach worked. Soon all hospital ships, including two that regularly served the Sea Islands, had at least one surgeon aboard and wards for enlisted patients. Dame also advised Barnes against building a general hospital at St. Augustine, and the project was abandoned.[33] Years later, a congressional report praised her efforts on behalf of "the unfortunate who were compelled to make long journeys to reach suitable hospitals."[34] Shoddy treatment of the sick and wounded on hospital ships would remain a problem, especially after major battles, but Dame had spoken up and done her best to correct it.

Her regiment, the Second New Hampshire, remained at Point Lookout, which was rapidly growing into the Union's largest prisoner-of-war camp. As bitter winter weather arrived in December, nine thousand Confederate prisoners crowded into a motley and tattered array of tents on its grounds. Many were ragged, and blankets and firewood were scarce. By the end of February 1864, seven months after the prison was established, five hundred and forty prisoners had died.[35]

The ranks of the battered Second New Hampshire, meanwhile, were slowly restored to their original size. Unfortunately, most of the new men had been brought to New Hampshire by brokers to fill the state's draft quota. Cities, town, and the state had promised these substitutes big bonuses, but the brokers siphoned off much of the money. Echoing the disgust of many of the original members of the regiment, the musician Simon Fifield called the new draftees "the hardest men I ever saw. They are all the time fighting, gambling, getting drunk." There were so many desertions, most of them unsuccessful, that Fifield correctly predicted that some deserters would be executed as a warning to the rest. Each day, in the meantime, several deserters were "strung up to the flag pole by their wrists and thumbs, to stand for 2 to 4 hours, just touching their toes."[36] On the positive side, Capt. George Gordon set up a recruitment office in late December to reenlist original members of the regiment for a second three-year term. With the help of $900 bonuses offered by the state of New Hampshire, he signed up Fifield and seventy-eight others within three weeks.

The regiment's new chaplain arrived at Point Lookout that month and recorded another phenomenon. An outspoken man, John W. Adams would soon begin chronicling the Second's fortunes for newspapers back home. He would also come to appreciate Dame and her efforts on the men's behalf. Shortly after arriving, Adams witnessed the plight of the enslaved people of Maryland who had boldly seized their freedom. Thousands of them had "left their kindred and the graves of their fathers behind them" to enter the haven of the Union Army. "At dead of night in midwinter," Adams wrote, "they have made their way to the Virginia side of the Potomac, and with their wives and children thinly clad, have committed their fortunes to a small open boat. In this way they have crossed the broad Potomac, near its mouth, and have landed in the morning at Point Lookout. Scores of them found the soil of freedom within a few feet of my tent."[37] It had been vital for the enslaved people to cross into Virginia first and pose as Virginians; otherwise, they might be returned to their owners in Maryland, a Union state. General Marston allowed their former enslavers to enter the camp to look for missing slaves, but he also took the Black people's word for it when they inevitably claimed they were from Virginia and had never seen the white men in question.

Harriet Dame promptly reported to the governor on what she had seen and learned during her tour of the South.[38] Afterward, she returned to the New Hampshire Soldiers' Aid Association to work alongside Miranda Swain, although the organization's rooms proved to be only a waystation in her journey. She had spent the last six months toiling at a field hospital and visiting soldiers in distant camps, but she knew her place was near the fighting. Soon enough, thanks to events already in motion, she would be drawn back into the orbit of her beloved Second New Hampshire.

10

Cold Harbor

Sgt. Richard W. Musgrove of the Twelfth New Hampshire boarded a steamer at Point Lookout in late 1863 to deliver two smugglers to the provost martial in Washington. It was Christmastime, and Musgrove and a comrade had secured five-day passes. They arrived as darkness fell, handed over their prisoners, and headed up Seventh Street to the New Hampshire Soldiers' Aid Association. There they were greeted by "that distinguished nurse, Harriet P. Dame, and her associate, Miss Swain."[1] The women were working late, as usual. To Musgrove's delight, Dame told him that during her recent southern tour, she had spoken with his brother Abbott, a hospital steward at Beaufort, South Carolina. Musgrove and his friend took a room in a nearby hotel. On Christmas night, after two days of sightseeing, they went to Ford's Theatre to see *The Drunkard,* with the acclaimed actor John Wilkes Booth playing the title role.

On the trip back to Point Lookout, they were shooting ducks from the deck when ice on the Potomac punctured the ship's bow. The captain steered for the riverbank, but the vessel hit bottom before reaching land, leaving only the upper deck above water. Hours later, another ship rescued Musgrove, his pal, and the other passengers and carried them back to Washington. The next ship they boarded at the wharf there nearly vanished in a fog and narrowly avoided colliding with a boat carrying President Lincoln toward the capital. At Point Lookout, where the two men worked at the prisoner-of-war camp, they heard that Lincoln and Gen. Benjamin Butler had just stopped in to inform the troops of the Second and the Twelfth New Hampshire that they were being assigned to Butler's Eighteenth Corps.[2] This development

Sgt. Richard W. Musgrove (from
the Twelfth New Hampshire's 1897
regimental history)

reshaped Dame's future. Before long, the newly formed corps would become
the principal realm of her endeavors.

While she remained faithful to the Second New Hampshire, a larger field
had opened to her. Nursing at the Third Corps hospital in Gettysburg and
investigating medical conditions in the South for the governor had broadened
her sense of what needed to be done and what she had to offer. In December
she traveled to Portsmouth, Virginia, to visit the camps of the Tenth and Thirteenth New Hampshire regiments. In her generally approving report to Governor Gilmore on medical care for these men, she suggested that she return
to the south Atlantic coast soon to deliver supplies. "As I have promised many
times before," she assured Gilmore, "every article sent me shall be given to our
soldiers." She also requested $300 to $500 for apples. If she received enough
donations, she intended to leave for the South in January.[3]

Changes at the Soldiers' Aid Association gave Dame the freedom to take up
such new challenges. Swain had settled in as chief administrator, and Larkin Mason, Dame's Gettysburg supplier, worked regularly out of the office.[4] Although
the agency had struggled the previous spring to keep up with the multitude of

wounded and sick from the state who poured into the capital, just thirty New Hampshire soldiers lay in hospitals in Washington by early 1864. It was normal to have fewer men to look after in winter, but the war was evolving, too.

To command the Union Army in the East, Lincoln had plucked Ulysses S. Grant from the war's Western theater. Promoted to lieutenant general, Grant succeeded a string of top generals whose mistakes could have filled a manual on how not to fight the war. McClellan had been slow to move except during his army's flight from the Peninsula. Lee had outmaneuvered Pope at the Second Battle of Bull Run, Burnside at Fredericksburg, and Hooker at Chancellorsville. Gen. George Meade had won a colossal victory at Gettysburg only to allow Lee's beaten army to slip away yet again. Grant, by contrast, was a master strategist and a relentless warrior. He envisioned a campaign of ceaseless battle well south of Washington. By putting constant pressure on Richmond and Petersburg, he would keep the enemy in front of him and disrupt rebel supply lines. Grant trusted his subordinate generals to apply similar pressure in the deeper South and the Shenandoah Valley, robbing Lee's army in Virginia of mobility and denying him reinforcements.[5]

Although men wounded in major battles in the East would still be sent to Washington and other major coastal cities, the scale of Grant's campaigning and the concentration of his troops in Virginia would require bigger and better field hospitals nearer the front. By late spring, eleven of New Hampshire's thirteen active infantry regiments would be fighting on the Virginia Peninsula, along the James River, and around Petersburg. This would become Dame's theater of operations for the rest of the war. While her state's Soldiers' Aid Association in Washington maintained its core role, tending to the wounded in the capital and helping families find loved ones, it also undertook a broader effort. Men sent by Gilmore delivered the agency's donated food supplies and material goods to Dame and others well south of the capital to sustain New Hampshire soldiers closer to the fighting. These good Samaritans included Ezra Abbott and others whom Dame had first met at Gettysburg.

After she returned from her southern mission, she and Mason picked up where they had left off. From his home in northern New Hampshire, he informed Gilmore that he was collecting "liberal contributions of flannels, sacks, &c." to add to the supplies Dame had gathered for the men at the front.[6] As he began his journey south, he stopped in Concord to inspect a temporary military hospital. He cringed at the conditions there. The men's diet was wretched. Even though many sick soldiers were too feeble to venture into the wintry nights to relieve themselves, there was "not a single vessel under their

Chaplain John Adams, who had many encounters with Dame during and just after the war ("Chaplain John Adams," MOLLUS-Mass Civil War Photograph Collection Volume 107, U.S. Army Heritage and Education Center, Carlisle, PA)

beds for night use." Like many others, Mason strongly favored building a full-service federal military hospital in New Hampshire so that sick and wounded soldiers could recuperate closer to home, but what he saw discouraged him. "We can never get a hospital established in Concord NH if the one we have remains in such disrepute even with a NH surgeon for medical director," he complained to Gilmore.[7]

As the army reorganized for Grant's spring campaign, Dame made a short visit to Point Lookout, where her old regiment had been stationed since shortly after Gettysburg. There, for the first time, she met the affable John Adams, who had left a wife and five children at home to become the Second's chaplain.[8] He wore civilian clothes under a jaunty military cape that swallowed his slight frame. Dame never arrived empty-handed. On this trip she delivered food and clothing and greeted many men she had known since the start of the war. As Adams soon learned, she was "a general better than McClellan, for she always managed to have a good stock of supplies, and was ready to move at a moment's notice.... She was an obsessive worker and kept everybody around her at work." Her can-do habits inspired him to compose a prayer: "From empty titles and hollow pretensions—Good Lord, deliver us. From kid-gloved nurses who stand by the bedside of human suffering, merely simpering, 'My good fellow, I pity you'—Good Lord, deliver us."[9]

Adams described Point Lookout as "a long narrow tongue of land" where the Potomac emptied into Chesapeake Bay. On it stood Hammond General Hospital, a wooden complex with long wards radiating from the chapel like the points of a star. General Marston lived in a hotel on the grounds while his troops took turns patrolling a walkway along a twelve-foot fence that gave them a view of the prison inside. The Confederate prisoner count varied from eight thousand to thirteen thousand that winter. With so many foreigners among the Second New Hampshire's new recruits, Adams ordered Bibles in seven languages: English, French, German, Russian, Italian, Norwegian, and Spanish.[10]

The veterans who had known Dame since the start of the war were enjoying their sojourn on the outskirts of war after many months in the thick of it.[11] Pvt. Martin Haynes's letters to his wife, Cornelia, captured their leisurely life. "I have an ocean of waste time," he wrote. In exchange for butter and other provisions, he assisted Atherton Quint, a Manchester merchant who now, as a sutler, ran the prison's authorized private store. While looking out over the water one day, Haynes saw seven boatloads of freed Black people carrying everything they owned. The sight made him imagine a "misguided rebel somewhere mourning the loss of several thousand dollars' worth of live stock." He noted that at least a few of the rebels in the prison swore allegiance to the US Constitution and joined the Union Army or Navy. As the new regimental postmaster, Haynes fixed up one of the new cone-shaped Sibley tents as his post office. He installed a box for outgoing mail outside and nailed ten cigar boxes inside, one for each company's incoming letters. "By the time I am discharged I will have an office that will rival Boston or New York," he assured Cornelia. A surprise snowstorm struck on March 23, and the Second and the Twelfth squared off in an hours-long snowball fight that resulted in much laughter and a few black eyes and bruised limbs.[12]

Even in such relative peace, a fateful question hung over the "old men," as Haynes called the original volunteers who were still with the regiment. Their three-year hitch was scheduled to end in June, and they could either reenlist or accept their discharges. Haynes had told Cornelia he would come home, but events beyond his control caused him to waver.[13] George Gordon, the captain of his company, oversaw the challenge of turning the new recruits into soldiers. Many were foreigners, many tried to desert, some were criminals. Most of the old men, including Haynes, despised them.[14] After Gordon suggested that he might order Haynes to assist him in training them, Haynes decided to apply for a commission to escape such a fate. This was a serious about-face for a man who, on principle, had spent three years resisting promotion to corporal. A commission would also keep him in the army longer. After filling out the application to become a lieutenant, he immediately changed his mind. "I have a little piece of news which I know will make your heart glad," he wrote Cornelia. He promised to return home soon and settle into married life as a civilian. To Haynes's relief, Gordon found another training assistant.

The captain did sometimes offer encouragement rather than tough criticism in his efforts to bring the recruits into line, but he was no less dubious about their prospects than Haynes and the other old men were. After the regiment left Point Lookout to return to the Virginia Peninsula, Gordon headed courts-martial that sentenced four of the seventy deserters among the new men to death.[15] He then oversaw their executions by firing squad.[16] "What an awful moment it must have been for them when they heard the click of the gun-locks as the executioners cocked their pieces," wrote Haynes, who witnessed the executions with the rest of the regiment. "The next instant they fell back across their coffins, each pierced by five bullets."[17] One of them raised his hands several times before death stilled him. Although Haynes disliked Gordon, he approved of the executions, which were carried out under an army-wide policy. "These measures were harsh," Haynes observed, "but they had a most salutary effect and the desertions were immediately checked."[18] Even though Captain Gordon had taken charge of reenlisting many of his original comrades, he, like Haynes, promised his wife he would leave the army when his term was up in early June. "I have gone so far and got honorable scores enough and now I can go home and live contented in relating the adventures of camp life while in the army," he told Angeline Gordon.[19]

In May, the opening of Grant's campaign in the East drew both Dame and her friend Larkin Mason to Virginia, but they took different routes. Mason rushed to the front during the battle of the Wilderness, where several New Hampshire regiments were fighting. His telegram to the governor from there on May 10 crackled with urgency: "Direct from battle field—Loss of both armies appalling. N. H. suffered severely."[20] Dame's move came a short time later. She cast her lot with her old regiment, joining the men of the Second just before they left Point Lookout for Yorktown.[21]

As Chaplain Adams pointedly reminded the public in an open letter to a New Hampshire editor, it was not the regiment Dame had known earlier in the war. If the Second failed to live up to its reputation, he scolded, "the people at home may blame themselves and not us." Had men with pride in their state refilled its ranks, the regiment "should have been spared the painful and mortifying specter of the execution of four of our number." At least the veteran soldiers who remained in the Second had confidence in Grant. "He ought to succeed—we believe he will," Adams said.[22] Dame and these veterans began their new journey on familiar ground. From Yorktown, they moved on to Williamsburg, where the Second had fought two years earlier. The regiment was in the Army of the James now, where its new corps, the Eighteenth, included the Twelfth New Hampshire. Hadley Fowler, the Twelfth's surgeon, had toiled with Dame at Gettysburg, and other joint ventures lay just ahead.[23]

For all the familiarity of the surroundings, these movements occurred during a transformative moment for the Union Army. Black men had enlisted in droves since Lincoln's Emancipation Proclamation took effect the previous year. Black infantry regiments replaced the Second and the Twelfth as prison guards at Point Lookout, and Dame would soon work at a corps hospital for troops of both races. Two Black regiments camped near the Second at Williamsburg. One day, as Haynes mounted his "great, stout, rawboned Buckskin" to pick up the mail in Yorktown, two Black cavalrymen rode along and kept him "in a roar of laughter relating their experiences in the army."[24]

Like the civilian population of the North, Union soldiers held a wide a range of opinions about race and slavery. Most knew that the slavery question had divided the country but viewed abolition as a radical idea. As one historian later put it, some believed that Black people "by their existence as slaves, had brought on the troubles that tore the soldier from his home." Many who had come around to accepting the Emancipation Proclamation took pains to point out that they did so not for the sake of abolition but for practical reasons. Slavery had to go, they argued, because slaveholders had destroyed the Union specifically to protect the institution.[25] As had occurred with the Second New Hampshire in Maryland in 1862, exposure to slavery's brutality increased support for emancipation in the Union Army. Naturally, most Northern soldiers also welcomed the recruitment of Black men to fight the war, especially now that their personal freedom was at stake.[26]

The Second broke camp as General Butler's Army of the James started up the river of the same name in "monitors, gunboats, ironclads, & transports of every conceivable plan and capacity." Black troops led this armada. As the *Grey-*

hound, Butler's command ship, pulled alongside theirs, the colonel of a Black brigade saw the general standing on deck, hat in hand, with "the fresh wind streaming his long thin hair behind him."[27] They were all bound for several posts between Richmond and Petersburg. On May 6, the Second camped on the Appomattox River at Point of Rocks, which would soon become Dame's headquarters.[28]

First, there was fighting to be done. "Seven days out of the eight just past, our Regiment has been under fire in battle," John Cooper, the Second's adjutant, reported on May 17. To the surprise of many, he added, the new bounty soldiers "fought nobly."[29] Haynes delivered the mail to his regiment during the battle of Drewry's Bluff and hung around "to watch the sport." During his return trip, the walking wounded and ambulances "loaded with mangled humanity" crowded the road. Chaplain Adams sat in one of them beside the corpse of Capt. James Platt, one of the Second's old men, who had been shot in the head.[30]

During this stretch of fighting, the regiment began to engage in frequent and extended battles that portended the trench warfare fifty years into the future. As Cooper described it, all along the brigade line, the men erected "a breastwork as high as a man's shoulders, with big logs and dirt, and we had a row of green bushes stuck up the whole length, so that the gray-backs could not see our breastworks." The next morning, when the rebels attacked, "we reserved our fire until they came within thirty yards, and then poured it into them. . . . Such slaughter I have never witnessed before. The ground was covered with the dead." Cooper credited Col. Edward Bailey of the Second with the idea of holding fire until the enemy drew near the Union lines. He might be a Democrat, the adjutant acknowledged, but he was also "a true, loyal soldier who has heroically performed his whole duty to his country."[31]

The wounded from this fighting joined the sick men in Dame's care. Luther Locke, a Nashua doctor who worked for the US Christian Commission, saw her in action two days after the battle at Drewry's Bluff. "I do not see how anyone could well do more," he wrote to a New Hampshire editor. After he watched her give strawberries to all the sick and wounded, the men assured Locke that "she was always doing anything she can, but no more important service than writing letters to loved ones at home."[32] As a signal corps man from Massachusetts experienced firsthand, Dame's generosity extended to men from states other than New Hampshire. Lt. Andrew Holbrook, who worked near the Second's camp, described the regiment as "continually in the front and under fire." One of its soldiers had helped Holbrook by climbing a tall pine to install an observatory. "With my telescope glass, we got a good view of the city of Richmond and its surrounding, *seemingly* impenetrable fortifications," Holbrook wrote. Dame and Mary Marden were working at the vast tent hospital at Point of Rocks, where Holbrook was sent with high fever. He described their tender care and felt grateful to be "a participant in their kind offices." After several days of observing Dame, he assessed her work habits as "more than would seem possible for poor humanity to stand up under."[33]

As Butler's Army of the James clashed with the Confederates defending Richmond, General Grant and Gen. George Gordon Meade pointed the Army of the Potomac south. Grant quickly proved to be the anti-McClellan. When his army made a "change of base," it was toward the rebel capital, not away from it. After the brutal fighting in the Wilderness in early May, he sent his men crashing into Lee's army again at Spotsylvania, sixty miles north of Richmond. The human cost of this fighting was staggering: thirty-two thousand Union casualties, eighteen thousand Confederate. "The world has never seen so bloody or protracted a battle as the one being fought and I hope never will again," Grant wrote to his wife Julia on May 13.[34] Next, his army moved twenty-five miles deeper into Virginia, where it clashed again with Lee's forces at the North Anna River.

Back at the camp of the Second New Hampshire on the night of May 26, twelve days before the old men of the regiment were to be discharged, all soldiers too ill to march were ordered from their regimental hospitals to Point of Rocks. Haynes knew what this meant: "We will doubtless move very soon."[35] Word spread that a large part of Butler's army would reinforce the Army of the Potomac. "I have been through the campaign here and not a scratch yet, so I am all right," a stoical Captain Gordon wrote home. After recent battles, which he considered minor, he speculated that if the Second had to join Grant's army, the men would see much tougher fighting.[36] Private Haynes relinquished his postal duties, returned to the ranks, and prepared to move out. "I have turned in my horse, and will 'frog it' with the boys," he informed his wife.

Dame left the Eighteenth Corps field hospital at Point of Rocks on May 29 and rejoined her regiment aboard the *General Lyon* for the trip down the James. It was one of many ships transporting thirty-seven infantry regiments and four artillery batteries of Butler's army to the Peninsula.[37] Adams held a Sunday service aboard the *General Lyon*. "The deck is my church, a box is my pulpit," he declared.[38] After rounding Fortress Monroe and anchoring at Yorktown, the ship traveled up the York the next day and swung onto the Pamunkey, which Haynes considered "the most crooked river we ever traversed." The ship ran aground on the river's muddy shoals well short of White House Landing, its

White House Landing (Library of Congress, LC-DIG-ppmsca-33269)

destination, and a rescue boat had to ferry Dame and the men to the landing. Such delays in the arrival of reinforcements seemed like petty nuisances, but in fact they gave General Lee's army time to complete a web of trenches and log parapets in the marshes between Richmond and the expanding armies under Grant.[39] On dry land again, Captain Gordon wrote his wife: "All are well as usual and the old men are expecting to go home in four or five days. Love to you and babies and Kiss them for me."[40] Etta and George Jr. were nine and six but still babies to a father who had rarely seen them during the last three years.

Dame knew White House Landing well, having visited the Lee mansion there in 1862 and later seen the smoke rise from the fire that consumed it during her retreat across the Peninsula. Now only its brick chimneys rose from the grounds, which sloped down to the log huts of the Black people who lived and labored along the riverfront. All manner of boats crowded the river's edge with a maze of planks laid between them to create walkways to and from the shore. A hundred hospital tents had been pitched on the lawn to shelter men of the Army of the Potomac who had been wounded during Grant's Overland Campaign.[41] Dame made her way to the field that would soon be the site of the Eighteenth Corps hospital. As well as any of the men, she understood that the armies were preparing for a major collision and that she must brace for the consequences. She knew from experience, especially at the Second Battle of Bull Run and Gettysburg, that her work during the aftermath of this new clash would be a trial. To make matters worse, the Eighteenth Corps had arrived without ambulances, hospital tents, or medical supplies.[42]

The soldiers of the Second and Twelfth New Hampshire regiments, who served in the same brigade, removed their backpacks to lighten their load and marched seventeen miles east toward Richmond through dust, stifling heat, and the stench of dead horses abandoned by the cavalry.[43] They stopped near Cold Harbor, a place so obscure that many of them, and even General Grant and some newspapers, called it "Coal Harbor."[44] Here, they were ten miles from Richmond, the closest they had come yet to the rebel capital.

On June 3, their brigade formed for an attack with the Twelfth taking the lead and the Second at the rear. Ordered to advance, the brigade charged toward the very center of a bow-shaped segment of the rebel infantry line, which was well supported by artillery. As the Union soldiers moved into close range, the rebels fired volley after volley into the leading Twelfth New Hampshire and assaulted both flanks of the brigade. After advancing just two hundred yards, the Twelfth buckled and disintegrated in the torrent of fire. The veteran Lt. Asa Bartlett described the moment as "more like a volcanic blast than a battle."[45] So many dead and wounded men dropped at once that some unhurt soldiers hit the ground, too, thinking they had missed an order to lie down. Many of the wounded lay still on the field, afraid to move lest they be shot again. A soldier mangled by an artillery shell pulled out his jackknife and cut his own throat. Sixty-three men of the Twelfth were killed or mortally wounded.

With four regiments in front of them to absorb the brunt of the barrage, the soldiers of the Second fared well enough to regroup. Lying on their bellies, the men clawed the ground with bayonets, knives, and fingers in a desperate effort to carve out rifle pits.[46] Sylvanus Bunton, their fifty-two-year-old assistant surgeon, did some digging of his own behind the Union battle line. He bandaged many wounded men in the hole he had dug and sent them on to a makeshift hospital on a hillside half a mile from the battlefield. Chaplain Adams toiled at Bunton's side. He later wrote that he had feared this battle so much that only shame propelled him "into the carnival of death."[47] Staying busy took the edge off his fright.

The open field before the rebel riflemen became a shooting gallery. They killed several old men of the Second who, had they survived, would have been discharged a few days later. A bullet in the neck felled Capt. Harry Hayward, and Sgt. Maj. Moses Smith died in agony after being shot through both thighs.[48] After a ball struck George Gordon in the top of the head, Adams did what he could for him at his post behind the lines. "Here is Captain Gordon," he wrote, "fatally wounded. . . . He never thought much of chaplains, but never mind, let us lay him carefully into the ambulance." Gordon lived just an hour.[49] Months later, Angeline Gordon would ask Surgeon Fowler for help in having her husband's body sent home to Suncook. "I am sorry to say that the remains of your dear husband and my brother cannot possibly be got at the present time," Fowler responded.[50] Angeline Gordon joined thousands of war widows who were denied this small comfort.

Even the bodies retrieved from the field shortly after the battle would not be going home. At great peril, Capt. William H. H. Fernal of the Twelfth New Hampshire crept out onto the field with a detail of forty men during the night of June 3 to bring in as many of the dead and wounded as they could. One they found was Gorham Dunn, one of Fernal's lieutenants. A man who had lain at Dunn's side had shared his last words with Fernal. Moments after acknowledging that he was badly wounded, Dunn had gasped: "O dear." It was dusk when he uttered these two words, and his comrade believed a second rebel bullet might have struck him at that moment. Crawling on their hands and knees, Fernal and others managed to carry Dunn's body in on a stretcher or blanket. The captain emptied the lieutenant's pockets and sent seventy dollars and his other belongings to his widow in Laconia. He shared with her the news that he had found a wound between Dunn's breast and shoulder and blood on one of his boots. After one of Fernal's men dug a grave, the captain placed boughs in the bottom, wrapped the lieutenant in a blanket, spread his handkerchief over Dunn's face, and helped to lower his body into the earth. "I think he looked very pleasant and did not look as if he suffered severely," Fernal informed the widow. He added that the lieutenant was "a man of good principle free from all those vices so common to officers. . . . You have the consolation of knowing that he fell bravely at his post in defence of his country." Dunn was one of twenty men of the regiment brought in and buried that night.[51]

Back at White House Landing, one of many nurses who had arrived to care for the wounded described the scene. "On the ground men and mules lay together asleep—the mules still in the harness, lying forward on their knees—the soldiers with their trusty guns beside them," wrote Sophronia Bucklin. "They had been walked over till the dust half-covered them, some so deeply that their heads only were visible, and they crawled up upon the legs of the animals to keep from being earthed alive." While some men slept beneath hitched and loaded army wagons, others ran errands, carrying slabs of meat or firewood, boiling coffee, or pitching tents. Hundreds of enslaved people who had escaped to the Union Army gathered nearby. Whenever Bucklin passed them, they grinned at her and proclaimed their freedom. By the time the fighting was done, 13,656 men wounded at Cold Harbor would be loaded onto ships at the landing and transported to hospitals in Washington.[52]

Dame had reached the Eighteenth Corps hospital with little time to prepare for a medical catastrophe that rivaled the aftermath of Gettysburg. Some of the corps' hospital equipment and medical supplies finally arrived the same day the Second and Twelfth New Hampshire regiments fought. Men hung forty tent flies end to end, quickly creating decent hospital wards with openings at the bottom to provide fresh air. By June 4, seventeen hundred wounded men of the corps had arrived on foot, in ambulances, and in commissary wagons. After the tents filled, men lay on the ground anywhere they could find room. Hadley Fowler, James Merrow, and other surgeons amputated one limb after another. Men prayed to die, and many got their wish before even seeing a surgeon. Their bodies were wrapped in blankets and rolled into a pit.

Pvt. George Place of the Twelfth had been wounded three times during his regiment's ordeal. Because of the battle smoke arising from the Confederate line, he had not even been able to see the enemy soldiers, but they had had no trouble locating him. A chunk of shrapnel penetrated the skin below his eye. A bullet through the arm knocked his rifle to ground, and another hit him in the back. Eventually he made his way back to Dame's hospital. As he waited to have his wounds dressed, he suddenly realized he was sitting near an amputating table. He tried to get up to leave but grew faint from a loss of blood. "Twice during the time I was there, a load of arms, legs, hands, and feet was carried off on a shelter tent and dumped into a ravine," he wrote. Place finally made his escape.[53]

Late during the day of the battle, Chaplain Adams reached the field hospital in an ambulance with a wounded man from the Second New Hampshire. Like Private Place, hundreds of other soldiers had already been unloaded on the ground. Men begged Adams for water, for something, anything, to protect them from the burning sun, and for help in seeing a surgeon. Moved by the horror of their wounds and the misery of their appeals, Adams did what he could for them. He stopped last at the spot where men had gathered after their limbs were amputated or their wounds dressed. "I shall never forget the proud smile of satisfaction that lit up their pale faces as I complimented them on what they had done and suffered for their country," the chaplain remarked. He saw a sergeant who had had his left arm amputated trade his left glove for the right glove of a sergeant who had lost his right arm. He described the field hospital's grimmest landmarks: the trench for severed limbs that Place had seen and the much larger trench filled with the dead. "It was a privilege to represent the dying soldier's sister, wife or mother at the mercy-seat as the breath was going out," Adams would later reflect. "I have no memories more sacred or satisfying than these."[54]

Dame worked day after day in the chaos that Adams described, sleepless but ever ready, cleaning and dressing wounds, scrounging up food and drink for the men, and listening to their anguished wishes and complaints. Complicating her task, men with high fever and chronic diarrhea also began to arrive from the front during the stalemate after the battle. Some medical accounts identified malaria as the chief cause, but both the sick men's symptoms and the conditions they had endured strongly suggest that dysentery, typhoid, and other deadly fevers had also struck.[55] The ambulance parade to Dame's hospital rolled on for days after the initial onslaught. Between June 5 and June 13, 904 wounded and 138 sick men of the Eighteenth Corps arrived from camp and field.[56]

Thomas McParlin, the medical director of the Army of the Potomac, described the consequences of keeping both these men and their reinforcements from Butler's Army of James in the trenches and camps at Cold Harbor after the battle. Ironically, he datelined his report "Cool Arbor," a misnomer that described the opposite of the conditions the armies found there. The region was "notoriously miasmatic and unhealthy," he wrote. Dead horses and mules and "the hides and offal of slaughtered beef cattle" lay all around the camps. With no time to dig proper latrines, the soldiers defecated wherever they could find a place to do it, and their waste washed into the streams. Decaying vegetation polluted the groundwater they drank. Meade's army had been campaigning for more than a month without a single ration of fresh vegetables. McParlin reminded Meade of the consequences that similar conditions had caused two years earlier during the Peninsula campaign. What he called "Chickahominy fever," naming it after a swampy nearby river, could in some measure be prevented, "but when it has once occurred, its subjects are lost to the army." He recommended burying the dead animals, digging proper latrines, and providing fresh vegetables. At least one of his wishes was granted immediately, as the camps and hospitals soon received a large supply of vegetables.[57]

On the battlefield, nearly all the dying and the dead lay untended for days. The stench reached both armies, but such breezes as there were blew toward the Union lines.[58] After long negotiations, General Lee allowed a two-hour truce in the early evening of June 7, six days after the first clash of arms and four days after the charge of the Second and Twelfth New Hampshire. At the appointed hours, the living ventured out to seek the wounded and bring in the bodies.

Union searchers found more than four hundred corpses but only two living men. Many of the dead, including a good number with nonlethal wounds, had starved or died of thirst or exposure. Most of their bodies had decomposed.[59] As darkness fell, a Twelfth New Hampshire sergeant who had gone looking for his brother struck a match above the face of each man he saw. He never found his brother. Lieutenant Bartlett of the same regiment decided that while some future excuse might make Grant's decision to attack at Cold Harbor seem at least plausible, no words could ever justify "the shameful and criminal negligence" of allowing the dying to rot on the field.[60] Grant himself, who had ordered many such charges into strong enemy positions during recent weeks, recognized almost immediately that the June 3 attack had been misguided. That very evening, he said: "I regret this assault more than any one I have ever ordered."[61]

Dame had one advantage over some other nurses in the hospitals at or near White House Landing: a private supply line. Larkin Mason, Ezra Abbott, and others soon arrived bearing provisions for her patients. The energetic Abbott, one of seventeen men sent by the governor to help in crises like these, came first. A homeopathic physician, he was a forty-two-year-old widower whose brother-in-law, Joab Patterson, had joined the Second as a sharpshooter at the war's outset and would soon command the regiment. In late May, Abbott had helped to close the Union hospital at Fredericksburg and to move the New Hampshire wounded north. He left the Soldiers' Aid Association in Washington on June 2 with six boxes and two barrels of food and supplies. After delivering these to Dame, he joined her in treating the wounded. "They were brought in by night and by day from the front in dreadful condition," he informed the governor, adding that about fourteen hundred men from the Eighteenth Corps were still there on June 8, five days after the Second and Twelfth had fought. With more wounded still arriving, Fowler asked Abbott to accompany eleven hundred of his patients to Washington. These men were not necessarily on the mend or fit for travel; it was just that Fowler needed space for new arrivals. When the wounded men from New Hampshire reached the capital, Miranda Swain and other workers at the Soldiers' Aid Association sought them out at the city's hospitals. "It is a great pleasure for me to be the instrument of doing something to alleviate this aggregate of human suffering," Abbott told Gilmore.[62]

During his voyage to Washington, several wounded men lodged a complaint that Dame had often heard. As Abbott summed it up, they "greatly desire to get furloughed and go home to recover. They say, 'O! that we could go to Hospitals in our own state!'"[63] Luther Locke, the Nashua physician,

Formerly enslaved people unearth dead soldiers' skeletal remains at Cold Harbor in this 1865 photo by John Reekie. (Library of Congress, LC-DIG-ppmsca-35035)

also heard such pleas. He brought Dame potatoes, dried apples, sauerkraut, lemon, cocoa, and farina and gathered news of the battered New Hampshire regiments at Cold Harbor to relay to the home front.[64] Even though Gilmore's effort to build an approved military hospital in his state had failed, Locke sought and received the governor's permission to pursue the idea of sending the wounded home. Many Northern states, including neighboring Vermont, had created military hospitals for this purpose.[65] Locke met with Charles McCormick, the medical director of the Army of the James, but McCormick turned down his request to send the New Hampshire wounded home. The federal government, he said, could not "rely on the integrity of the medical profession so fully as to put its patients into the hands of private practitioners or guarantee to pay all bills as presented." On the way to Washington with another load of Eighteenth Corps men, Locke stopped at Point Lookout, where several sick and wounded men he met at Hammond Hospital on the prison grounds also begged to recuperate at home.[66]

Abbott returned to the New Hampshire Soldiers' Aid offices to prepare for a second mission of mercy. He gathered thick, round Boston crackers, pickles, cheese, dried apples, butter, and eggs along with barrels of ale, woolen shirts, cotton drawers, and bandages to take to White House Landing. After giving Dame most of his thirty-seven parcels, he got passes for himself and the Portsmouth pastor A. J. Patterson to proceed to the front at Cold Harbor. He assured soldiers there "that altho they were far from their homes they were not forgotten by their friends." To prove his point, Abbott had saved some ale, cheese, and apples for them. After returning to White House Landing, he reported to Gilmore that the Eighteenth Corps would probably depart the next day.[67]

The scale of the Union disaster at Cold Harbor moved another of Gilmore's emissaries to compare the battle to an earlier military debacle. The dead and wounded had yet to be counted, but Union casualties would exceed twelve thousand, Confederate five thousand.[68] Charles Hackett, a prosperous farmer from Upper Gilmanton, described the carnage at Fowler's hospital as "a second Fredericksburg affair." At Fowler's urging, Hackett took six hundred more wounded men to Washington. "I have left Miss Dame and Mr. Patterson of Portsmouth at Whitehouse, who will move as the base moves, probably in a couple of days," he informed the governor. While he had admired Fowler and Dame's efforts in the field, he railed at the behavior of surgeons on the ship during his return trip to the capital. They did as little as possible for the wounded while "seeking their own comfort more than to relieve the suffering of others." The arrival of yet more New Hampshire wounded in Washington hospitals taxed Dame's former sidekick. "The Association here is doing all in their power," Hackett reported. "Mrs. Swain's work is almost incessant."[69]

Dame would later characterize the Eighteenth Corps hospital at Cold Harbor as "the most dreadful scene she ever saw" during the war. To an interviewer, she described her days there as though they had just happened: "I have worked over the wounded till my clothes and arms were covered with blood, and I have gone so long without sleep that I nearly tumbled into the fire from sheer exhaustion."[70]

Less than a week after the battle, most of the remaining Second New Hampshire men who had gone to war with Dame in 1861 had packed their gear and prepared to go home. These included Col. Edward Bailey, who had commanded the Second at Gettysburg and Cold Harbor, and Surgeon James Merrow, at whose side Dame had so often worked. More than a year after Private Haynes, the regiment's chief chronicler, married Cornelia Lane, he kept his vow to leave the war and join her in Manchester. As much as these men longed for home and counted themselves lucky to have survived, there was also sadness in parting. "I will tell you what it is, boys," one of them declared to the veterans who had signed up for a new hitch. "When I think what we have been through together, and all about the last three years, it makes me almost decide that I'll not go home till you do."[71] One of the reenlistees was Pvt. James Gammon, who had returned to the regiment despite having had buckshot removed from his fractured skull after the Second Battle of Bull Run. Now his hand had been mangled by a gunshot at Cold Harbor. He would spend months in hospitals in Washington and Connecticut.[72] At White House Landing on the morning of June 9, the old men of the Second who had chosen to go home departed on a ship called *Young America*.

It was left to Gilman Marston, who had brought them south, led them bravely, and looked after them even after his promotion to general, to give meaning to the moment. His chief concern was the regiment's future, but he reminded the governor that the seventy or so homebound veterans had "faithfully fulfilled their contract and deserved well of the country." They had taken the Second's banners and records with them, leaving two hundred and fifty men of their regiment behind in the trenches at Cold Harbor without these essentials. Hearing of the Second's bereft state, Maj. Gen. William F. "Baldy" Smith pulled the regiment out of the line to guard his corps headquarters. Marston lauded two of the old men, Joab Patterson and John Cooper, for staying on to lead the Second. "There is no braver man in the army," he said of the twice-wounded Cooper. He closed with a hope and an appeal to Gilmore. "The 2nd NH Reg. is not yet to be blotted out," he wrote. "Its record, although glorious, is not yet full. Fill up its thinned ranks and it will still carry its honored flag as heretofore in the front of battle until the rebellion is finally quelled and the authority of the government reestablished over all the land."[73]

Chaplain Adams reported that Dame "remained with us, caring for our sick and wounded, until we all swung round in front of Petersburg."[74] In postwar interviews and statements, she counted Gettysburg and Cold Harbor as her most trying ordeals and marveled at the spirit of the old men of the Second as they entered their last battle. "They went into the night willingly," she said, "and so many poor fellows, that in less than a week expected to be at home, were either killed or wounded."[75] At Cold Harbor she had again saved those she could and comforted those she could not. Now the war in the East had concentrated in the stretch of Virginia between Richmond and Petersburg. She would soon have a chance to work daily within the sound of gunfire from this front.

Point of Rocks

Harriet Dame left White House Landing by steamer in mid-June 1864 and headed back the way she had come. A special transport had been ordered to return the Eighteenth Corps, including its tents, supplies, medical personnel, and sick and wounded, to the area it had occupied before heading east to reinforce the Army of the Potomac. Dorothea Dix sent two nurses from Washington to accompany Dame and her patients to hospitals near the front at Petersburg. The ship delivered them all to Broadway Landing on the Appomattox River, but they found little shelter there. Dame and the other nurses helped their patients to a church, which quickly filled, and laid the rest of the men outside. The next morning, Chaplain Adams asked Dame where she had slept. "In the room with you," she responded. He told her he had slept outside under a tree, not in a room. "So did we," she said, "on the other side."[1]

The Second New Hampshire left the sick and wounded men with Dame and marched toward the Union trenches before Petersburg. As the chaplain rode at the regiment's rear, a large camp of Black soldiers beside the road caught his eye. Farther along, Adams spotted Abraham Lincoln coming the other way. The president was on a brief trip to see General Grant at City Point and visit the troops. Curious about what would happen when Lincoln reached the Black encampment, Adams turned around and followed the presidential party. Hundreds of men rushed to the roadside to cheer "their great-hearted emancipator," their voices rising as their number grew. When Lincoln raised his hat and bowed, they shouted louder. Especially after the ordeal Adams had endured at Cold Harbor, witnessing the "joys of freedom's golden days" lifted his spirits. He was "proud to occupy even the background of such a historic picture as that."[2] The Second marched on until it was near enough to Petersburg to see the city's spires while enemy shells rained into the new camp.

From Broadway Landing, a ship carried Dame and her party in another direction. They passed between the low bluffs and sparse foliage along the

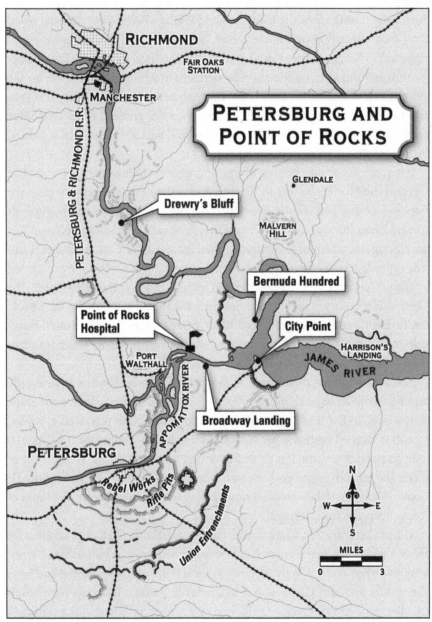

Petersburg and Point of Rocks

banks of the Appomattox River on their way to their destination. Tents for the sick and wounded stood just beyond the sixty-foot sandstone cliff that gave the place its name: Point of Rocks. Although Dame had no way of knowing it, she would spend the rest of the war on this large estate, which had been abandoned by its owner and confiscated by the Union Army.[3] Little had changed during the month since she left it for Cold Harbor. Behind the hospital stood a 125-foot tower that one nurse called "one of General Butler's great signal stations."[4] The signal corps used it to gather intelligence about Confederate movements and relay information by signal flags. Alongside the tower lay the Tenth Corps hospital, whose wards consisted of ten tents, each fifty feet long and held in place by wooden pins driven into the ground. Forty cots lined each side for patients. When the cots were full, patients slept on the ground on bags of straw or hay.

After the ferocious battles of spring, whose endless casualty lists had stunned the North, the war in Virginia had settled into a deadly siege in the trenches around Petersburg, less than ten miles away.[5] Occasionally, generals tried to break the stalemate. The most disastrous attempt would occur on July 30. Having dug a tunnel to the enemy line, forces under Gen. Ambrose Burnside exploded a mine beneath it on that day. Seeking to exploit the gap caused by the explosion, Union troops charged around and into the mine crater. The Confederates quickly recovered from their shock and slaughtered the attackers, including many inexperienced Black troops trapped in the crater. Burnside's men suffered nearly four thousand casualties, the enemy fewer than two thousand. The stalemate resumed.[6]

Sick and wounded men from the Tenth and Eighteenth corps were usually sent first to field hospitals near the fighting. After preliminary treatment, most were moved to Point of Rocks, whose two corps hospitals provided extended care. If it seemed certain a patient would not return to duty, or if he faced a long convalescence, the hospitals forwarded him to Fortress Monroe. From there, the soldier might go home or to another hospital along the Atlantic Coast. With many Black soldiers now serving in the Union Army, the Point of Rocks hospitals were segregated.

When Dame arrived, Clara Barton had been at the Tenth Corps hospital for about a week. The two women had briefly crossed paths at Hilton Head seven months earlier, and it is likely they met again at Point of Rocks. Barton had been almost idle in South Carolina, but in a letter to a friend from her new hospital, she sounded like Dame. At the end of a scorching July day, she wrote: "I have cooked ten dozen eggs, made cracker toast, corn starch blanc mange, milk punch, arrow-root, washed faces and hands, put ice on hot heads, mustard on cold feet, written six soldiers' letters home, stood beside three death-beds—and now, at this hour, midnight, I am too sleepy to write even you a tolerably readable scrap."[7] She went to the hospital's Fourth of July celebration but failed to catch the holiday spirit. "Here is the dust and toil and confusion of camp life," she began, "the mercury above a hundred, the atmosphere and everything about one black with flies, the dust rolling away in clouds as far as the eye can penetrate, the ashy ground covered with scores of hospital tents shielding nearly all conceivable maladies that soldier flesh is heir to, and stretching on beyond the miles of bristling fortifications, entrenchments and batteries encircling Petersburg."[8] Although Barton was initially charged with overseeing the diets of the hospital's nurses and the patients, she soon began splitting time between Point of Rocks and the so-called "flying hospital" where wounded men of the Tenth Corps arrived from the trenches for preliminary treatment.

Dame resumed her care of the Eighteenth Corps' sick and wounded and used her connections to supplement their diet. There was good news in this respect for New Hampshire soldiers. A. J. Patterson, the Portsmouth Universalist preacher who had stayed with Dame until she left Cold Harbor, emerged as a major contributor to the state's soldiers in the field. Aided by his church's ladies' society, he collected enough food and clothing to fill seven wagons, each pulled by a six-horse team. Ezra Abbott, the Concord homeopath, helped him distribute this largesse. After stopping at Point of Rocks to supply Dame, the two men began a marathon of visits to most of the eleven New Hampshire regiments in the field, finishing their deliveries after three in the morning. The soldiers, Abbott wrote, accepted their gifts as "a token of remembrance of their friends in N.H." The journey took the two men perilously close to the rebel pickets near Petersburg. The next morning at breakfast in the Tenth New Hampshire camp, Abbott heard trains rumbling in and out of the city. "The bullets are flying very thick & they fire at everyone who shows himself above the breastworks," he informed Governor Gilmore. "I am writing under a tree in a ravine, the bullets and shells firing above our heads." Not far from where he sat, a ball passed through a private's shoulder and struck a second man in the head.[9]

As Abbott had promised Gilmore, he and Patterson soon made another trip to visit the three New Hampshire regiments in Simon G. Griffin's brigade. Griffin, a Concord lawyer when the war began, had moved steadily up the ranks to brigadier general after captaining the Second New Hampshire's Goodwin Rifles at the outset of the war. Arriving just before the Sixth, Ninth, and Eleventh were to enter the trenches, Abbott and Patterson dispensed goods from their two wagonloads of canned beef, mutton soup, black beans, strawberries, farina, paper, and pencils. It was the first such delivery to these men. While Abbott understood that his mission entailed "hard labor & some personal danger," he believed the gifts helped to keep soldiers on duty and out of hospitals. By then, he and Patterson had been shuttling between Washington and the front for seven weeks and needed a break. In addition to supplying Dame, they had given each state regiment more than one hundred dollars worth of goods. Though not a huge delivery, at least it was something from home, Abbott told the governor, closing his report with a kernel of optimism: "Genl Grant says we will take Petersburg and Richmond, and Lee knows that our army will do it."[10]

Back at the Soldiers' Aid Association, Miranda Swain had little time to sleep as the wounded poured into Washington from Grant's campaign. In mid-July, she described to a friend the chaos of doing Dame's old job. A heat wave gripped the city, and Confederate Gen. Jubal Early threatened to invade it, causing panic in the streets. Early's force of fifteen thousand men had swept down the Shenandoah Valley, crossed the Potomac, and brushed aside a small federal force in Maryland. By July 11, the invaders camped just beyond the capital's defenses five miles north of the White House.[11] Residents and invalid soldiers began standing watch in the city. Members of Swain's association "did regular guard duty—two hours on, two off, for some days," she reported. "The music of cannon and bursting shell I never expected to hear, yet the reports were quite distinct above the noise of the city, and one night we sat upon the top of the house watching the flashes following every discharge." With Early pressing in from the northwest, hospital ships carrying the wounded from Grant's battles continued to reach Washington from the South. "We never have had such terribly wounded men as during this campaign," Swain wrote. "It would astonish the good people of New Hampshire did they know the deaths from any one hospital for a day." In the worst of them, the daily toll reached seventy-five to a hundred men. Even after Grant sent a corps north to drive Early off, Swain's labors increased. While overseeing hospital visits, she campaigned for more provisions for Abbott, Patterson, and Larkin Mason to transport to the front. Some of these she directed straight to Dame, whom she knew as "a faithful laborer for the soldiers." Swain trusted her to use the supplies wisely or pass them on to someone who needed them more than she did.[12]

Mason reached Swain's office during Early's invasion threat. "A sanguinary battle was being fought almost within shelling distance of the N. H. rooms," he informed the governor. The state's regiments had begun the war with a thousand men each. After the first few months under Grant, Mason estimated that "of the eleven regiments before Petersburg, not three thousand are left to do duty." Five hundred wounded men from the state had come to the capital by that point in Grant's campaign, and more than half of them had been sent on to other hospitals or home on furlough.[13] In New Hampshire, the prospects of the severely wounded were uncertain, as the state still lacked a federal military hospital, a problem Mason again urged Gilmore to address.

During Dame's first weeks back at the Eighteenth Corps hospital, she was the only woman nurse. Surgeons' wives pitched in as needed, but the surgeons were careful to distinguish between their work and Dame's. The doctors referred to the wives as her assistants and Dame as the "boss woman."[14] She was chiefly responsible for feeding her hospital's large, ever-changing population, but she always made time to care for patients. Among the first of many she treated from the Petersburg trenches was Pvt. George Sanborn of Pittsfield.[15] When Pastor Joseph Harvey arrived to take Sanborn home, Dame advised him that the wound was too dangerous for travel. Harvey persisted. He was a resourceful and patriotic man. On the Sunday in 1861 when the first troops from the area set off for Concord, he had marched his congregation out the church door to cheer them on. In the months and years since, he had comforted many families grieving over lost soldiers and journeyed south to retrieve several wounded men from Pittsfield. Ignoring Dame's warning, he bought a sheet, folded it sixteen times, wrapped it around Sanborn's wound, and took him to New Hampshire. Although blood soaked through every layer of the sheet, Private Sanborn survived.

A grumpy but good-humored Massachusetts private began his account of life at Dame's hospital on a sour note. "Thus far I have been unable to discover any charms in hospital life," wrote Pvt. David Day, who had been sent there with hemorrhoids, a fever, and chills. He was assigned to the convalescent camp, one of three divisions of the hospital.[16] Another housed the wounded and the perilously ill, and officers had a ward of their own. Day was one of six hundred men who bedded down under small shelter tents while all the others had cots in the long tents.

He had improved enough after a few weeks that a doctor asked him to take charge of the ward next to his, where seventy Black soldiers had been "pretty much on their own hook."[17] Day called roll, arranged visits with surgeons, and recorded arrivals, discharges, desertions, and deaths. While supervising a ward cleanup, he took note of the conditions of as many men as he could.

He got along with his charges even though he often made fun of them and considered most of them malingerers.

One exception was Ned Carter, an older Black man who was near death. Day, who referred to Dame as "an angel of mercy" in his diary, turned to her for help in shepherding Carter through his final days. Hadley Fowler, whom Dame had met at Gettysburg and worked with near two battlefields, ran the corps hospital. Only with his permission could men in the convalescent camp receive food or drink beyond the authorized diet. Carter, a blacksmith by trade, was eating so little that Day asked him what he might be able to keep down. When he requested crackers and milk, Day went straight to Dame, who, without asking Fowler, provided sustenance to the dying man. She filled Carter's cup with condensed milk and sent him soda crackers. "I have often carried Ned a cup of tea and a slice of toast with some peach or some kind of jelly on it, and the poor fellow could express his gratitude only with his tears," Day wrote.[18] Then one morning, after Carter failed to answer at roll call, Day found him dead in his bed.

When a good Samaritan with New Hampshire ties visited the Point of Rocks hospitals in the fall, he met Dame for the first time. Robert Stubbs had graduated from the Methodist General Biblical Institute not far from her Concord boardinghouse and later presided over a congregation in Claremont, New Hampshire. He now worked for the US Christian Commission, a large wartime charity devoted to soldiers. His priority was to check on the state's regiments of the Tenth Corps in the Petersburg trenches. For this mission, he brought along Clara Barton, who was still working at that corps' hospital, and Mary Marden, who assisted Barton by preparing wounded men for transfer to the hospital at Fortress Monroe. Stubbs found the Fourth New Hampshire "a mere skeleton," able to muster just sixteen men in some companies after losing seventy in recent weeks. The Seventh had suffered thirty recent casualties, and the rebels had killed the lieutenant colonels of both the Third and the Seventh.[19]

When Stubbs returned to Point of Rocks, Dame impressed on him the need for more supplies. Among her recent patients, he learned, had been Thomas Ambrose, chaplain of the Twelfth New Hampshire, who was shot while ministering to men in the Petersburg trenches and "died the death of the righteous." Stubbs called on people of New Hampshire to send more quilts, socks, and other necessities, arguing that such gifts were "eloquent preachers to the weary and burdened and suffering inmates of these wards." He reminded them of Dame's many virtues, describing her as "almost ubiquitous. She is a ceaseless and tireless worker, ever studying how to advance the highest interests of this large hospital. She is fertile in devices to minister to the desires of the poor convalescents and to turn to best account the stores at her disposal."[20]

With cooler weather coming and the Petersburg siege at a stalemate, the army decided to expand and solidify the hospital. Overseeing the task fell to Fowler, who had earned the trust of the generals through his amputating skills and leadership both at Point of Rocks and in the field. Dame considered him "a smart man, and an effective surgeon," and they were close colleagues. Even though he generally shunned women nurses, she thought he liked her because she was a veteran of the Second New Hampshire, which had fought alongside the Twelfth for more than a year.[21] For all his competence, Fowler struck many people as aloof and difficult. In a thumbnail biography, a fellow surgeon called him "not one of those who was 'all things unto all men.'" Quick to judge others, the surgeon wrote, Fowler had few close friends, and even these were often put off by "his strange odd ways and moods."[22] These quirks did not hinder him in carrying out General Butler's order to turn the Eighteenth Corps hospital into a larger and more comfortable setting for sick and wounded soldiers in winter.

Fowler delegated the building of one section of the expansion to Moses Parker, an assistant surgeon fresh out of Harvard. Parker chose land overlooking the Appomattox from which the breastworks before Petersburg were faintly visible. He had a water tower constructed on the highest point and ordered the wards built in a semicircle around it. Soldiers hacked down pine trees for log cabins and wood siding on the hospital tents. When General Grant and General Butler inspected the work, they asked why the smaller log huts had canvas roofs. Parker told them that much of the cut pine had been requisitioned for mule sheds elsewhere. Butler rescinded the order, and the log cabins soon had sturdy wooden roofs.[23]

The men also built Dame a log house near the mess tent, and it became her headquarters. For more than three years, she had lived in tents, on the ground, in field hospitals, and on the move. She had slept among bodies on a battlefield, against a telegraph pole within earshot of gunfire, and under an India rubber blanket in the rain. The cabin at Point of Rocks must have seemed like a castle. For her own needs, she used only enough room for bedding, her wardrobe, and a stove. The rest she reserved for the food, clothing, and niceties delivered by Mason, Abbott, Patterson, and others. During a short break from her toil, the Second's Chaplain Adams photographed her sitting in a chair in her doorway. She had by then acquired a hound named Whisky.

Harriet Dame and her dog Whisky in this watercolor painted by David Sullivan from a small photo in the 1896 Second New Hampshire history.

Another dog from the same litter, "his twin" by Dame's reckoning, was called Quinine. Both were common medicines then in use. In the picture, Whisky rested on his haunches at Dame's side.[24]

After making his rounds at Point of Rocks, Adams also painted a word picture of Dame in action. She stood at her post, "one moment distributing garments, comfort-bags, cordials, &c., from her private tent, at another moving under the large cooking tent, surrounded with delicate and substantial articles of diet, and the large kettles steaming with wholesome and palatable food in a state of preparation." This tent "was her throne, but she did not sit upon it." As she and her helpers distributed "luxuries to thousands," she "not only ruled with system, but with sleeves rolled up, toiled harder than any of her assistants." Dame always asked Adams about the men of the Second at the front: "Are any of them sick? When are they going to get their pay? Is there anything I can send them that will do them good?" She gave the chaplain food and clothing for "the feeble ones who did not wish to leave the front, and who had not seen the paymaster for six or eight months." Dame also instructed Adams to pester the men to write home and sent along stamps so they could not use the expense of postage as an excuse for not doing so.[25]

In late October, the few remaining original members of the Second returned to yet another old battleground, where their lieutenant colonel, an original member himself, saved them from disaster. The regiment had joined a special brigade to conduct raids north of the James River. Joab Patterson of the Second led the brigade that day under Gen. Godfrey Weitzel, the corps commander. When Weitzel and his staff lost their way, they asked Patterson for help. Recognizing that they had just reached the site of the Second's 1862 battle at Oak Grove, Patterson identified Hooker's entrenchments and the Second's campground from that campaign. Pointing ahead, he said, "You will find the rebel works there, just behind those woods." When Weitzel reached the works, he dallied long enough to allow the enemy to bring up a strong force. Then, according to Patterson, he made an unusual gesture. He asked Patterson if he would volunteer to lead his men in a charge on the works. "No, sir," Patterson answered, adding that if Weitzel ordered him, of course he would do so. Weitzel found another brigadier more willing to undertake the task. Patterson's reading of the situation saved his men from slaughter. The rebels inflicted sixteen hundred casualties while suffering only one hundred themselves. Just one man in Patterson's brigade was wounded.[26]

William Stark, Dame's former helpmate as a steward in the regiment and now the Second's assistant surgeon, rode away from the battle with Adams.

As shells burst around them, they stopped to help wounded men struggling along the road. "In my more than three years' service, I have never been so frightened before," Stark observed.[27] Shortly after the men turned in, Weitzel ordered a full retreat in a torrential rain. The night was pitch-black, the storm unrelenting, and Adams and Stark carried on a shouted conversation the whole way back so "that we might not be separated."

Under a new state law allowing soldiers in the field to vote, the New Hampshire men of the Eighteenth Corps cast ballots in the November presidential election.[28] The result attested to both the shrinkage of the four regiments and the number of recruits who had either failed to register or were noncitizens and thus ineligible to vote. Of the four regiments, only the Tenth favored the Democrat George McClellan, giving him forty-six votes to fourteen for Lincoln. The Second favored the president sixty-five to four.[29] In late August, after the endless waves of lost lives during Grant's stalled campaign, Lincoln had expected to lose. Then, on September 2, Union forces under Gen. William T. Sherman captured Atlanta. With the South now teetering, Lincoln coasted to reelection with 221 of 243 electoral votes. He lost only Kentucky, New Jersey, Delaware, and one of Nevada's two votes.[30] Shortly after the election, the Eighteenth Corps was dissolved, its white regiments going to the new Twenty-Fourth Corps, the Black to the Twenty-Fifth. For Dame and the Second New Hampshire, it was the third corps assignment of the war.

The hospital at Point of Rocks had grown by then. It housed thirty-five hundred beds for enlisted men and five hundred for officers and caregivers. It employed thirty-four surgeons, three hundred mostly male nurses, five hospital stewards, seventy-five cooks, a quartermaster, a commissary officer, and an eighty-five-man guard.[31] For months, Fowler turned away women, using Dame as his foil. When women showed up, she later wrote, "he would always send them off saying he had one woman and it was all he could get along with, then come and tell me how he got rid of them." They sometimes glared at her with scorn as they passed on the way out. Fowler gave up his crusade in late fall when Dix sent several women nurses to the hospital at a point when he needed them. Although Dame relished being the only woman in any camp, she befriended a nurse from New Jersey even after the woman "turned up her nose at our butter." The nurse promised to bring back real butter from her next trip home, but Dame never got a taste. The woman's trunk sat in the heat during the return voyage, and by the time she reached Point of Rocks, the New Jersey butter had saturated all her clothing, including her new woolen dresses.[32]

Point of Rocks General Hospital, circa 1864 (Library of Congress, LC-DIG-ppmsca-33640)

Sophronia Bucklin was one of several nurses who later circumvented Fowler's aversion to employing women. She left a lively, detailed account of her time in Dame's hospital. A year younger than Dix's minimum age for nurses, she had been hired at thirty-four in the fall of 1862 to work in Washington hospitals. Dix's hiring qualifications allowed for only industrious women between thirty-five and fifty who were sober, moral, plain, and well dressed. Before coming to Point of Rocks, Bucklin had also nursed at Gettysburg, White House Landing, and City Point, near Grant's headquarters. Though kind to her patients and especially solicitous of sick and wounded Black soldiers, she had a querulous streak that annoyed some other nurses and her bosses. Her supervisors invariably wrote kind but brief letters commending her to her next employer.[33]

Bucklin began work in a long log stockade with a canvas roof where soldiers arrived daily in bloody uniforms. Because it had no chimney, the smoke from the fire that warmed it seeped out wherever it found an opening. She and the other eight new women nurses slept three to a tent, but she noticed that, as matron of the general kitchen, Dame had a log hut of her own. Bucklin found the food supply ample. Cows on the grounds provided milk for patients, a bakehouse made hot rolls, and in late fall apples arrived by the barrel. Black and white soldiers alike partook of this bounty, including ginger tea with sugar twice a day. Although Dame ran the kitchen and the storehouses, Bucklin credited Fowler for a "regime of plenty which men enjoyed regardless of color or state."[34]

When Bucklin was not nursing or feeding patients, she spent hours teaching Black soldiers to read. The Christian Commission provided books, and men bought newspapers so she could read them the war news. Many had recently been enslaved and "were fighting to retain for themselves and children the newly acquired boon of liberty. They were universally polite and deferential to me, again and again expressing their gratitude for the good care Northern women gave them, by the remark, 'Jest as if we had white faces, missus.'" One man asked Bucklin to help him get a furlough to visit his pregnant wife at Fortress Monroe. Although she knew of no Black soldier who had been furloughed, Bucklin stopped at Dame's cottage and found Fowler there with her. He approved the leave. The soldier wrote Bucklin from home that his wife had borne a girl and they had named her Sophronia.[35]

Dame treated the corps hospital as an enlarged version of a Second New Hampshire camp, and one day her efforts won her plaudits from the top. Nearly everyone who saw her marveled at her stamina. In her hut, she stored the provisions delivered by her New Hampshire friends. When admissions were heavy, she treated patients before and after they saw a surgeon. Nearly every day, she visited soldiers, sewed for them, and wrote letters for them. But the main kitchen ruled her day. She was a stickler about diet but also a delegator, pitching in where necessary while relying on the kitchen staff to do most of the work. With his wife Julia, General Grant set out from City Point one day to visit the hospital and assess its operation. The Grants stayed at the plantation house on the hospital grounds. Pvt. Edwin R. Jones, a Tenth New Hampshire steward working at Point of Rocks, described the general as so casually dressed that the bars on his shoulders were the only sign of his rank. Jones accompanied Grant on his inspection tour, learning to his surprise that the general judged hospitals not only by operating tables and conditions in the wards but also by their kitchens. Grant visited Dame in her log hut and then inspected her kitchen, which was feeding six hundred patients at the time. "He complimented Miss Dame and expressed himself as well-pleased with her management," Jones later said.[36]

Among the patients, David Proctor became one of Dame's projects. All the Black regiments had white officers, many of them from the ranks of white regiments. At the age of twenty, Proctor had left a New Hampshire regiment for a captaincy in one of them. Shot in the hip while leading Union pickets in late November near a creek that flowed into the Appomattox, he arrived at Point of Rocks wracked with pain and expecting to die. As he later described his care, he lay on a couch among strangers, but before he knew it, Dame sat down beside him "as your own mother would." Proctor considered her a ray of sunshine that never dimmed.[37] A few weeks later, he went home to New Hampshire to convalesce.

Dame turned fifty years old on January 5, 1865. She had already exceeded the average life expectancy for women in her time. If there was a celebration of her milestone, any account of it is well concealed. Given contemporary customs regarding women's ages, it is possible she did not wish to be reminded of it. She had by then survived three and a half years of war, often spending her days in the company of men suffering from typhoid, dysentery, and malaria. She had soldiered on through a few bad colds and sore throats but contracted none of these perilous diseases. So long as there were mouths to feed and soldiers to comfort, she had no intention of quitting. She had even softened to the idea of sharing her labors with Dix's nurses, characterizing them as good workers, even if they did chew gum.[38]

In some ways, the cause that Dame served seemed more urgent than ever. The hospital's floorless, canvas-topped structures were so cold that patients lost toes to frostbite. Convalescents were regularly shipped to Fortress Monroe, but as soon as they departed, incoming sick and wounded filled their beds. Crews built sturdier structures throughout the winter, giving the impression that whatever military progress was being made, the army was preparing for a longer war. The building project remained unfinished at winter's end. The Christian Commission had better luck in expanding its presence at Point of Rocks. It had already created what one pastor called "quite an attractive village," consisting of a chapel, a reading room and library, and a schoolhouse for Black children and adults.[39] In February, carpenters were still assembling the last few pews when commission members, soldiers of both races, surgeon's wives, and a few officers gathered to dedicate a new chapel. It was forty-by-sixty feet and cost $300.[40]

Meanwhile, boatloads of Union captives released from Southern prisons arrived at Point of Rocks. "Wrecks of men," Sophronia Bucklin called them, "with ghastly countenances, with bones protruding through the sallow skin, and great hollow eyes." These "unfortunate heroes with shattered minds and skeleton frames" required special diets and extra care.[41] These were Dame's specialties. If their conditions improved sufficiently, former prisoners were sent to a hospital at Annapolis for further doctoring and discharge.

Although it was hard to tell at the hospital, Grant's strategy for winning the war had begun to work. After taking Atlanta, Gen. William T. Sherman's army had marched to Georgia's Atlantic coast. On Christmas day, Sherman telegraphed Lincoln that it had captured Savannah. In February, his men burned Columbia, the capital of the first state to leave the Union. The Confederates decided it was time to pull their troops out of Charleston. Five days later, on February 22, Union forces retook Fort Sumter. After a string of Union victories in the Shenandoah Valley, meanwhile, Gen. Philip Sheridan's cavalry headed south from Winchester, Virginia, to destroy railroads and occupy Charlottesville. Grant's army before Petersburg extended its lines by four miles, leaving Lee to defend a wider expanse with a shrinking force.[42] President Lincoln came from Washington in late March to consult his military leaders about the war's final moves. Shortly after he arrived, a telegram from Secretary of War Edwin Stanton sought approval for a victory celebration at Fort Sumter on April 12, the fourth anniversary of the start of the war.[43]

The day before Lincoln's parlay with Grant, Sherman, and David Porter, the acting rear admiral, the president and his wife Mary boarded the *River Queen* for the brief cruise to Point of Rocks. They walked from the landing to the hospital, where they were met by Moses Parker, the officer of the day, who had led a major building project at the hospital. To Parker, Mary looked fashionable in black silk, but the president seemed carelessly dressed. Wearing his customary top hat, he towered over the officers he met. He spoke little, seemed careworn, and entered none of the buildings during his tour. He "evidently wanted to be alone," Parker speculated, "for he soon left us, walking to the Point of Rocks some twenty rods away." Lincoln sat near the cliff's edge under a tree known as the Pocahontas Oak, which supposedly marked the spot where the Pamunkey woman of that name saved the English colonizer John Smith. The president gazed out toward the Union breastworks in the far distance. "Sometimes he placed his elbow on his knee and rested his head on his hand," Parker wrote. "He was thinking of something we knew not of." In the meantime, officers' wives had taken the "large, stout and dignified" Mary Lincoln to see a few wards. As the first couple headed for the landing, convalescent soldiers emerged to watch. Lincoln tipped his hat and bowed to them.[44]

Lee's army abandoned the trenches before Petersburg on April 2, 1865. Union troops quickly captured both that city and Richmond, where Confederate forces had also decamped along with the government. On their way out, the rebels torched both their capital and the fleet on the James River.[45] The Thirteenth New Hampshire drummer Charlie Washburn, who marched at the head of the first Union troops to enter Richmond, pilfered a pencil from the Capitol to record the moment. He was, he wrote, "*perfectly astonished* at our *bloodless victory*."[46] About two hours after the fires began, Dame's Second New Hampshire also "marched triumphantly into the capital of the fugitive oligarchs," as Chaplain Adams put it. It seemed like a dream to behold Union soldiers guarding enemy soldiers in Libby Prison, a former warehouse known from shortly after the start of the war as an overcrowded and unsanitary hellhole.[47] Martin Haynes later wrote that the men found Richmond attired "in the sackcloth and ashes of defeat." It might be aflame, "but it was Richmond, the goal of four years' desires."[48]

Three and a half years earlier, when McClellan's army had lain idle for months, Dame had divined what defeating the Confederacy would require. Only when the army's leaders were prepared to sacrifice tens of thousands of men in battle, she had written to young Anna Berry, might the Union begin its march to victory.[49] Her sanguinary foresight had found its champions in generals like Grant and Sherman, and in Lincoln, whose decision to enlist Black soldiers had replenished the ranks with eager warriors. She had experienced firsthand the consequences of all-out war at some of the bloodiest fields of battle. And now the war was won.

On April 10, the day after Lee surrendered, Dame's hometown of Concord joined the Union victory celebration. The grand processions through the streets included fire engine companies, wounded soldiers, a company of relieved re-cruits, and residents in festooned carriages. Bells pealed, crowds cheered, fireworks lit the night sky. Among those making short patriotic speeches at Eagle Hall was Dame's friend Henry Parker, the chaplain who had gone home in 1862 to resume his ministry at South Congregational Church. Lizzie Corn-ing, a teenager from a prosperous local family, went serenading that night with her friends. Up till nearly midnight, they "celebrated in a glorious way."[50] In reporting on the occasion, a local newspaper observed: "The events of the last ten days are incomprehensible, and the mind staggers in contemplation. The rebel army in great numbers in an impregnable city, as they thought, defended by seven distinctive lines of fortifications, evacuated without previous arrange-ment, the army fleeing and pursued to its surrender by out gallant troops. Who can comprehend it, and not stand amazed?" The editor blessed President Lin-coln, "who has never failed or taken a retrograde step."[51]

In Washington on the day after this report was published, Dame's helpmate from Concord, Ezra Abbott, also set out to celebrate. He secured a ticket to *Our American Cousin*, the play at Ford's Theatre a few blocks from the New Hamp-shire rooms. During the third act, he heard the pop of John Wilkes Booth's derringer, saw the flash of his blade, and watched the assassin spring from the presidential box and land awkwardly on the stage.[52] Booth had shot Abraham Lincoln in the back of the head with a .44-caliber ball. After soldiers carried the comatose president to the Petersen house across the street, Abbott entered the small room where Lincoln lay. When the doctor in charge cleared it of all but medical personnel, Abbott remained.[53] He was, after all, a homeopath who in one letter to Governor Gilmore had signed himself as "assistant surgeon." He took a seat on the edge of the president's bed. Beginning at eleven o'clock, forty-five minutes after the shooting, he regularly checked Lincoln's vital signs. Ab-bott's notes were released to reporters throughout the night "as a grief-stricken nation waited for the next 'extra edition of their town newspapers.'"[54]

Abbott's spare account tracked what the physicians knew was a death watch. He took Lincoln's pulse nine times during the first hour as it fluctu-ated between forty-two and forty-eight beats a minute. Just after midnight, he counted twenty-two breaths a minute and noticed the bruising and swelling of Lincoln's right eye and a "struggling motion" in his arms. Mary Lincoln entered the room shortly after two o'clock and left with her son Robert after half an hour. She returned at three. By six, the president's pulse had begun to weaken, and an hour later, Abbott noted "symptoms of immediate dissolution."[55] Several times, the doctors thought he was dead only to hear him draw another breath.[56] When Lincoln's breathing finally stopped, Abbott checked his watch. The time was 7:22 A.M.

Whether in Concord or at the Second New Hampshire's camp just outside Richmond, the shock of the assassination registered in the same key. In her diary Lizzie Corning, the teenager who had gone serenading the night after Lee's surrender, captured the mood of the North at this cruel reversal of fortune. "This is the darkest day the people ever passed," she wrote. "All is gloomy." Residents packed Eagle Hall, where six days earlier they had listened to a run of victory speeches, "to mourn the nation's greatest man, Abraham Lincoln."[57] Near Richmond, Chaplain John Adams described a similar turnabout: "The booming cannon that so recently belched forth in the exultant tones of victory have in sad and measured cadence announced the nation's loss."[58]

The war had changed Dame's life, as it had many others. While Union soldiers at Point of Rocks began their mass departure, Confederate veterans from nearby towns streamed into the hospital, many suffering major wounds infested with insects. The exodus began in earnest after the government ordered the hospitals vacated by June 1. Shiploads of Union men left each day.[59] The last several hundred were sent to City Point Hospital, where a Christian Commission agent described a parade of lame and sickly men struggling through the rain to the landing each day to wait in vain for ships to carry them north. At night they slept on the floors of muddy sheds. At Point of Rocks, as the patient count dwindled, so did the nursing staff.[60] Having seen so much of the war, Dame would have been surprised by the summation of one of Dix's departing nurses. "It would be impossible for me to describe what I passed through," wrote Clara Hoyt. "Nothing but the strongest devotion to country and flag could have enabled me to endure it."[61] Dame, who had endured far worse, reflected on her experience in matter-of-fact terms. Soon after the rebel surrender, she observed, "Our hospital was all cleared away."[62]

The dismantling of the Point of Rocks hospital ended Dame's most successful partnership of the war. She and Hadley Fowler had toiled together in hastily pitched hospital tents at Gettysburg and near White House Landing after Cold Harbor. At Point of Rocks, they had created a medical regime to meet the needs of an army in constant battle. At the close of the war, when the hospital was turned over to the Freedmen's Bureau, Fowler declined an offer to stay and returned home to his family. Walter Libby, a private who knew both the doctor and Dame, paid them an unusual tribute. Libby had joined the Twelfth New Hampshire in 1862 as a musician and become beloved by his comrades as "the left-handed drummer" and a superior wrestler despite his slight size. He had left the trenches before Petersburg in 1864 to work at the Point of Rocks hospital, where he met and married Annie Stowe, a local girl. The couple named their daughter Hadley Dame Libby.[63]

The end of the war also cut Dame's ties with the New Hampshire Soldiers' Aid Association, which had been renamed the New Hampshire State Military Agency. The Washington agency's work was nearly finished. "I was never more anxious for the accomplishment of any object than I am to return to my home," Larkin Mason informed Governor-elect Frederick Smyth in mid-May. Only the continued needs of the soldiers delayed his departure. As they closed down, Point of Rocks and other hospitals in Virginia sent more New Hampshire invalids to Washington. A regiment still in the field asked the agency for vegetables, a request that Mason deemed reasonable. He expected more such entreaties and figured they could easily cost the agency $1,000. With men from the state expected to stay in Virginia for several months, he advised Smyth to keep Miranda Swain on after he left to provide information to troops in the field and their families at home.[64]

Like the old men of the Second New Hampshire, Dame had "compassed the rebel capital on all sides" during the war, and they arranged for her to see the vanquished city. She took a boat to Petersburg and a train from there to Richmond. In Adams's words, she "right well enjoyed" her visit.[65] "On to Richmond," an early rallying cry of the war, remained lodged in the Union vocabulary long after the soldiers realized how grueling the war would be. While Dame may have reveled in the triumph of being there, the charred skeletons of buildings and the hunger and poverty at every turn surely gave her no joy. Outside charities were feeding and clothing throngs of poor people abandoned in the ruins.

For many Northerners who had left home to put down the rebellion, a tour of Libby Prison, the view of the destruction from the Confederate capitol's cupola, and the other sights of Richmond served as a farewell to war. Harriet Dame's life took a different course. When she heard that the regiment she had joined four years earlier was not going home, she decided she was staying, too. If the Second New Hampshire's war was not over, neither was hers.

12

Till Death Did Them Part

The war was over, but Harriet Dame kept moving. After squaring away her kitchen at Point of Rocks and packing her meager belongings, she returned to Richmond to rejoin the Second New Hampshire in its postwar peacekeeping mission. In a letter to a newspaper editor in mid-June 1865, Chaplain John Adams informed her neighbors in Concord that Dame, "so generally and favorably known by the sick and wounded of all our N. H. regiments, is with us scattering comforts and sunshine as usual."[1] Adams also felt the need to remind New Hampshire readers that while other regiments had departed and dispersed, the Second was still on duty and eager to hear from home. "The mail for the whole brigade was last night brought up in the coat pockets of the carrier," he complained.

Dame and the regiment encamped across the James River in Manchester, a town that would later become a neighborhood of the Virginia capital. On July 10, when she and the men took a freight train to Fredericksburg, Adams and Surgeon William Stone rode in one car, the sick occupied a second, and Dame made room for herself in the baggage car. "She seemed to think she was highly favored to have a rude freight car so much to herself," Adams remarked, "and was only anxious to make the sick ones as comfortable as possible." At dusk, when damaged tracks halted the train short of the city, she got her chance. She dispatched men who could walk to local farms for milk and vegetables to prepare a meal and turned the sick car into a working hospital. Soon after the train reached Fredericksburg, she rushed to Washington for more supplies.[2]

The regiment split up and moved to three outposts during her absence, and she settled in at its headquarters in Warsaw upon her return. This small town

lay fifty miles northeast of Richmond on the northern neck of Virginia between the Rappahannock and Potomac rivers. The Second's mission there was
to restore order and authority amid a bitter, dispirited populace and to connect
with the Freedmen's Bureau as it strove to usher in a new era in race relations.
Winning the peace would soon seem as elusive as winning the war had been.

Although Adams had encountered Dame at Cold Harbor and Point of
Rocks, this was the first time they had worked shoulder to shoulder. Their
proximity settled two questions that had bothered him: "Was there not something indelicate in such familiar association with society composed entirely of
men? And did she not subject herself to insult from the rude soldiery?" He
quickly concluded that he and the regiment's other officers need not worry
about her. "Her devoted spirit, discreet bearing, and holy mission were all the
protection she needed," he wrote. "A mother could be no safer with her children, nor a sister safer with her brothers than was Miss Dame among the New
Hampshire soldiers." Had she needed help, "a single word from her would have
put every sword and bayonet of the command between her and the offender."[3]

In one way, Dame had come full circle. The Second was again nine hundred men strong, as it had been at the First Battle of Bull Run. Its expansion
had come about after three other New Hampshire regiments mustered out in
June. The 267 recent recruits in these regiments who still had time to serve
joined the Second, raising its strength to a level that required three top staff
officers.[4] Dame knew them all well. Joab Patterson, who had begun the war as
a first lieutenant in the regiment, became its colonel. As for John Cooper, the
new lieutenant colonel, Dame had twice nursed his battle wounds, including
a bullet through the lung at the Second Battle of Bull Run. She had also cared
for and comforted Maj. Levi Converse after he lost an arm at Gettysburg.

A sad reality soon reminded Dame of her early days at war. With all these
men thrown together in the heat and humidity of summer in a ruined Virginia
landscape, infection and fever ran wild. "When the excitement of war had
passed away and no longer quickened the pulse or braced the nerve, many of
our men found themselves victims of chronic diseases and broken-down con-
stitutions," Adams observed. Their chief complaints were diarrhea, dysentery,
pneumonia, and diphtheria.[5] Dame found it more taxing to nurse sick men
than those wounded in battle "because they were so long in getting up." Dysentery often immobilized even its survivors for a week to ten days, but many
never rose from their sickbeds.[6] In all her time with the regiment, Dame later
said, the men's suffering never distressed her more than after the Confederate surrender. She found it unconscionable that men who should have been

Joab Patterson, last colonel of the Second New Hampshire, in dress uniform (undated) ("BG Joab Patterson," MOLLUS-Mass Civil War Photograph Collection, U.S. Army Heritage and Education Center, Carlisle, PA)

home with their families instead "heard and answered the last roll-call. God is good and gracious and I will put my trust in him, but if they only could have gone home."[7] In August, the men built a field hospital under Surgeon Stone's supervision so that he and Dame could better care for these suffering souls.[8]

One of the first to die after the war was an original member of the Second, but it was not illness that killed him. Samuel Gillespie had joined the Concord sharpshooter company in 1861, but he deserted seventeen months later. Unlike some of the bounty men who had been executed for desertion at Point Look-out, Gillespie returned to the ranks after his arrest and made sergeant within a year. He still had time left to serve when the war ended. In early June 1865, he and a comrade took a swim in the James River. They set out from an island for a flotilla of pontoon boats anchored in the distance. Upon reaching them, Gillespie's friend looked back but saw no sign of him. The body was never found.[9]

The mission in Warsaw and at the regiment's other outposts faltered from the start. A month into the occupation, a remarkable report from Chaplain

Adams exposed the local frictions that consumed the time and energy of the occupying force. The exercise left him deeply pessimistic about the prospects of the South.[10] The Warsaw Court House, where he preached each Sunday, served during the week as the venue for resolving disputes throughout the county. With Colonel Patterson on leave, Cooper oversaw the court. "Many of the inhabitants being as intensely disloyal as ever," Adams began,

> there being but little law except the military—the social relation of the dominant and servile classes being broken up, and the ignorant blacks, and especially the passionate whites, being predisposed to redress their real or fancied grievances, I do not need to tell you that Colonel Cooper's duties have been extremely varied.... All sorts of imaginable and unimaginable cases are brought up to our headquarters for settlement. The parties are summoned, the witnesses are required to appear, and a speedy verdict rendered, from which very few seem disposed to appeal.

Nearly every case involved an angry, arrogant white man. After planting a farmer's crop, a Black man was "told that he is no longer wanted, and that the former master has nothing to pay him with," wrote Adams. He continued,

> Another slave has worked nights to buy a horse, and has used the horse on the master's plantation, while the latter has been in the rebel army, and now the master claims the horse. A white woman complains that her husband, who married her for her money, is doing nothing for her support, but is selling horses, cows, beds, and everything belonging to her, while she is reduced to a coarse and meagre fare, with the prospect of soon being robbed of both "bed and board." A white man turns out one of the "white trash" who has worked for him for four and a half months, with only one half a month's pay, and threatens to shoot him with a borrowed pistol if he don't keep away. A "white gentleman" complains that another white man, who is "too worthless to challenge," and whom he seriously thought about shooting, has charged him with stealing a plow, and he demands that the Colonel shall cause his wounded honor to be satisfied, for he "will have revenge." A bachelor, who has illustrated the beauties of the system of cohabiting with a yellow piece of property until the paler chips of the parent block are multiplied by three or four, proposes to set the whole party adrift, without a day's rations, simply because "Eliza" has begun to put on airs.[11]

The racism and hubris that Adams witnessed convinced him that even the Union military triumph would not usher in an era of change in the South.[12]

"The equal weight which is given to the colored man's testimony is very humiliating to these bred-in-the-bone tyrants," he wrote. "This is the most disloyal portion of the State we have been in. Nothing will develop the symptoms of hysterics among the ladies as to intimate that Jeff. Davis is a wicked man, and may possibly be hanged." Adams believed that holding the defeated South to high standards was crucial to the nation's reunion, but he suspected that white Southerners' belligerence would prevail in the end, especially on race. "They are still disposed to suppress the negro, to vent upon him the pent up indignation of a humiliating defeat, and to so shape the future policy of the Government, that tens of thousands of loyal men shall forever be denied the franchise."[13]

The actions of Andrew Johnson, the new president, encouraged the erstwhile rebels. To the chagrin of Southerners loyal to the Union who had been persecuted for their beliefs during the war, he moved swiftly to restore full political rights to nearly all secessionists.[14] He sided with the planter class, not the Freedmen's Bureau.[15] As Southern white leaders yoked formerly enslaved people into a legal status as close to slavery as possible, Johnson's silence signaled consent. Despite his efforts as governor to keep Tennessee in the Union in 1861, he reverted to his racist roots in his postwar policies.

By October 1865, many other occupying regiments had departed, and Chaplain Adams wondered why the Second New Hampshire was still in Virginia. His opinion of local race relations had softened to match his longing for the regiment to go home. With baseless optimism, he wrote: "The prices paid for labor are far too small, but will probably be raised after the planters have had a little time to recover from their prostration."[16]

Death in the ranks continued to cause anxiety. Disease had killed four soldiers that month, including Henry Johnson, a private from Denmark who had probably been given that name after joining the regiment as a bounty soldier. A bigger blow to the old men came shortly after Colonel Cooper headed home on leave. He had been Dame's compatriot in the regiment since mustering in as a corporal in Concord. On his way to New Hampshire Cooper stopped for a night at the Maltby House, a fashionable five-story hotel in Baltimore. When he failed to come down the next morning, a man sent to check on him found Cooper incoherent, and he soon died. Instead of welcoming him home, his wife and daughter put on mourning black.[17] He was buried in Concord's Old North Cemetery seven months after hostilities ended.

Cooper was not long in the ground when the Second at last received orders to muster out. After reuniting his scattered regiment in Richmond, Colonel Patterson arranged for the men to spend December 4, their final night in the former Confederate capital, at the old Libby Prison. It was no longer the hell on earth of wartime legend, but the men must have smiled at the irony of the choice. After two weeks at City Point, Grant's old headquarters, where their officers made out the muster rolls, they officially left the army and headed north. On Christmas Day they paraded through the streets of Concord to the cheers of their neighbors, the first New Hampshire regiment to go off to war for three years and the last to return. Perhaps some men might have skipped the festivities and headed straight home, but the powers-that-be had wisely scheduled payday for December 26. Money in hand, Martin Haynes wrote, the old soldiers "went their several ways."[18]

Harriet Dame had said her good-byes in Virginia. For the rest of her life, when anyone asked her when she mustered out, she would respond: "I enlisted at the beginning of the war, and I can't say that I have ever been mustered out."[19] She was a modest, forward-thinking person, but surely the departure of the Second caused her to reflect. She had nursed the men of her regiment and many others in the field after six battles, including two of the bloodiest of the war. She had gone wherever she was needed for four and a half years without a furlough. She had been captured twice, stood fearlessly amid shelling, and trudged long distances in fierce heat. She had saved the sick and led them across the Peninsula in the summer of 1862. In Washington, she had been the linchpin of an organization that connected the sick and wounded of New Hampshire with their families at home. As the governor's emissary, she had traveled to far-flung posts to check on the medical care of other regiments. When the war ended, she was overseeing the feeding of hundreds of sick and wounded men at a large hospital near the front. Wherever and whenever possible, she had used connections with Good Samaritans to provide sustenance to the men.

Dame did not go home to Concord because she no longer had a home there. Her boardinghouse had been emptied and sold after her brother George died in 1863. She did have a house in Washington from her time running the New Hampshire Soldiers' Aid Association, and it was there that she returned.[20] Then, between her work as a war nurse and whatever came next, she decided to hit the road again. She was a seasoned traveler whose wartime journeys had encompassed many points between her native New England and Florida's Atlantic coast. Her destination now was the Midwest. She had two older brothers, both born in the 1790s, who had gone west decades earlier to make new lives. Joseph Dame, the older of the two, had worked in the lumber business in Maine and upstate New York before becoming a trader of lumber and clocks in Wisconsin and Michigan. He settled in Grand Traverse Bay in the latter state, where he gave the village of Northport its name, drew the first map of the place, and taught local Ottawa and Chippewa people to farm. John Dame, who was sixteen years older than Harriet, had moved with his wife and five children to Spring Prairie, Wisconsin. During the summer of 1866, Harriet set out to reconnect with this extended family. Her war service impressed at least one member of a rising generation of the Dame family. Her nephew Eusebius, a carpenter, and his wife had a son that year and named him Gilman Marston Dame after Aunt Harriet's first colonel.[21]

Back in Washington, Dame had plenty of help finding her way forward. The well-connected J. A. Prescott solicited letters recommending that Congress provide her with a sum of cash for her efforts during the war. He asked Colonel Patterson to write to Rep. Marston "stating what you know in regard to her services while under your observation."[22] Although Marston took up her cause, in the end it was a younger politician from Concord who provided Dame with a steady job. In early 1867, William E. Chandler, a Republican campaign operative and party leader who had been appointed first assistant secretary of the US Treasury, offered Dame a clerkship in Treasury's loans and currency division.[23] Dame would hold the job for nearly thirty years while traveling each summer to New Hampshire to visit her sister, Mary Shackford, and attend veterans' reunions. Washington also became her base for charitable work and activism on behalf of former war nurses.[24]

The New Hampshire Legislature honored Dame for her service the same year. Its joint resolution expressed the state's "grateful recognition of her devoted, self-sacrificing and distinguished services rendered during the whole period of the late war of the rebellion, amid the exposures, dangers and fatigues of the march, the battle-field and hospital, in taking care of the sick and wounded soldiers of New Hampshire." The kind words came with a check for $500.[25] To put that amount in perspective, Dame had signed on for six dollars a month in 1861. Long after the war, she told the writer Frances Abbott: "The most they ever pretended to pay me was ten dollars a month, near the close of the war, and some of that is owing to me now. But no matter, I didn't want the money for myself." Much of her pay, which never reached the level of a private's monthly wage, she had given to needy soldiers.[26]

For her work at the Treasury Department, Dame earned $75 a month, or $900 a year. A government report several years into her service exposed the gaping salary gap between the fourteen male clerks and the nineteen female clerks in her division. The six higher-ups, all men, received $2,500 to $2,900 a year. Among the clerks, nine men but no women earned $1,600 to $1,800. The average salary for a male clerk was $1,571 compared with $947 for a woman.[27]

When Dame attended the first reunion of the New Hampshire Veterans Association in 1875 in Manchester, the welcome she received set the pattern for her appearances at such events for nearly a quarter century. At that inaugural gathering in Riding Park, held in October, the nights were chilly, the campfires toasty and jolly. Nine hundred strong, including fifty veterans of the Second New Hampshire, the old soldiers took "more pleasure in the renewing of old associations than of observing the routine of military life," a reporter noted.[28] Gen. Simon G. Griffin, who had risen from the Second to command a division during Grant's Overland Campaign in 1864, led the veterans in a rousing rendition of "Tramp, tramp, the boys are marching." Griffin was one of a half dozen generals on hand, and four governors addressed the crowd. To the reporter's eye, "One of the most touching features of the day was the presentation to the audience of Miss Harriet P. Dame, one of the Florence Nightingales of the war, who was received with the heartiest applause."

In early 1881, Dame, Dorothea Dix, and Susan Edson formed an association to promote the interests of former war nurses and became its top officers.[29] Although Edson had nursed during the war, she was, in fact, a medical doctor and a close friend of President Garfield's family. After an assassin shot Garfield in the back on July 2 of that year, Lucretia Garfield demanded that Edson be given a seat at the president's bedside. Dr. Willard Bliss, the chief physician, grudgingly allowed her in but then ignored Edson's advice as well as proper sanitation. Garfield died after two and a half months of having his wound probed with unclean tools and fingers.[30] The Ex-Nurses Association of Washington, DC, as the organization was initially known, helped members find work and medical care. To that end, its leaders began to appear at events in the capital, including a Union Veterans Corps fair where Gen. William T. Sherman and Gen. Philip Sheridan spoke. A reporter who covered the fair made

especial mention [of] the table of army nurses. For the first time since the war have the nurses been publicly recognized as part of the great army of the Union. So silent and unassuming have they each one been that although nearly two score of them are resident in this city, not even the soldiers knew until lately that Harriet P. Dame, than whom no other woman of the war did more, if as much, or "Gentle" Annie Etheridge, or any of the rest of them were here.[31]

As the nurses' group expanded throughout the North, Dix remained its president even after she became too ill to participate in its meetings. Dame took over just as the organization began to push to make all war nurses eligible for pensions.

Harriet Dame in early 1886, shortly before her seventy-first birthday (Courtesy of the New Hampshire Historical Society)

As Dame learned through experience, women who nursed during the Civil War could receive pensions, but only through individual acts of Congress. New Hampshire's congressional delegation proposed a bill on her behalf in 1883, collecting testimonials to her war record and shepherding the pension through both houses. "Miss Dame was the bravest woman I ever knew," wrote Marston. The process also required her to testify to her own service. When Rep. Ossian Ray, who managed the bill in the House, asked her to submit her wartime story, Dame turned him down. She later had second thoughts and sent a rambling letter about her service to Louise Bryant, the recording secretary of the nurses' association. Bryant gave it to Ray, who attached it to the bill seeing a pension for Dame. "An artless statement," he called it, adding that anyone who told her full story "would perpetuate an example worthy of emulation to the latest times." Even without a more elegant accounting of Dame's wartime exploits, Ray argued that she deserved "the help of a nation she did so much to save."[32]

In addition to her modesty and reticence, the circumstances under which Dame had composed her war history affected the outcome. After the veterans' reunion in New Hampshire in 1883, she had gone to Concord, as usual, to visit Shackford, her blind sister, intending to read to her and tell her stories. "Last Saturday she fell down stairs, breaking one arm and otherwise seriously injuring herself," Dame informed Louise Bryant in the letter. "My days and nights will now be all taken up nursing, until I leave for Washington." Knowing she would sleep little, she decided to write her account late at night. She used lined stationery, then complained when fatigue caused her hand to stray outside the lines. As she finished the five-thousand-word letter, the clock struck three in the morning. Although Dame scarcely mentioned Gettysburg and Cold Harbor, the letter had its virtues. Her chronological narrative touched on many experiences in the field, and from the opening sentence, her prose was clear and direct: "When the war first broke out, or was talked of, even, I began to look about me to see what a woman could do, should there ever be real fighting." The text included many details and clues that helped fill out her war story.[33]

Dame also placed her thoughts about a pension on record. "My soldier friends are determined to make a grand effort to have me pensioned," she began. "They have been talking about it for years, but I have always said get the soldiers pensioned; let me take care of myself." The soldiers ignored her, and over time she warmed to the idea. "Now they have risen in their wrath and say if I don't keep quiet, they will put a real army sticking-plaster over my mouth," she wrote. "Well, to tell the truth, I am tired of hard work, and would not object to living without toiling for my daily bread." She knew her letter's faults, and writing it had given her a headache. "'Rest for the weary, no rest for me,' not in this world, I fear," she lamented before joking that perhaps her case could be handled as a federal public works project. "If my soldier friends would only allow me to make one suggestion it would be this: Call me the Dame River, or harbor, a *flat* even; get an appropriation to have me repaired. My feet are lame, hands swollen, head aches, &c, &c. Think I need repairs and will sleep."[34]

Rep. Ray made the closing case for Dame's pension with just one change, and not a slight one, from the original bill. "Miss Dame is nearly 70 years of age, very feeble, and much of the time afflicted with rheumatism, sometimes necessitating the use of crutches," he argued. "Your committee are clearly of the opinion that her services should be recognized by allowing her a pension to aid in her support during the remainder of her life." The original bill had called for a monthly stipend of seventy-five dollars, the same amount Dame received as a Treasury Department clerk. In the version that passed,

Miss Blanche M. Gerrish sits on Miss Harriet Dame Rock near Second New Hampshire house at the Weirs. Gerrish's late father Hiram was a corporal in the regiment. She named her dog Phil Sheridan. (Courtesy of the New Hampshire Historical Society)

the amount was reduced to twenty-five dollars.[35] It was something, but not enough to allow her to retire at seventy, despite the crutches.

Dame set aside much of this extra income with a purpose. New Hampshire veterans had been meeting since 1876 at Weirs Beach on Lake Winnipesaukee, where the Boston, Concord & Montreal Railroad had donated an ample hillside tract along Lakeside Avenue for annual reunions. With a train depot across the street and spectacular weather and views, it was a pleasant place to gather in late summer. The regiments began erecting Queen Anne–style houses, but until 1886, the Second New Hampshire Volunteers had none.[36] Dame remedied that, donating $1,000 to her old comrades to build their house. Frederick Smyth, the state's last wartime governor, paid for the furniture. As Martin Haynes described the place, "From the piazza one enters directly the great reception room, occupying the entire floor, with the exception of a space at one end which is fitted and furnished for a kitchen. The walls are hung with portraits and pictures and mementoes of especial interest to the Second, and a big fireplace, with andirons of a special military design, is a token of cheer and comfort of a cold evening."[37] The men's sleeping room and Dame's apartment were upstairs. For the next decade, she never missed a reunion. A large boulder near the house became known as Harriet Dame Rock.

In gratitude for her generosity, Enoch Adams, one of the regiment's prolific letter writers, celebrated her military career with "Harriet Dame and Stonewall,"[38] which included this quatrain:

> She followed us close to the battle's brink,
> And never was known to flee or shrink;
> Mid danger and death, mid sickness and pain,
> We never looked for her face in vain.

Earlier that year, a photographer had made a portrait of Dame that both pleased her and reminded her of the governor's refusal to sanction her going to war. She sent the picture to a veterans' organization with a note proclaiming: "Tomorrow I turn seventy-one, and serving four years and eight months in the army in the field would wrinkle and fade many people more than it did me." She had, in fact, served slightly less time at or near the front, but she counted her nearly two months of caring for sick soldiers before she left Concord as part of her service, dating her war as having begun on May 3, 1861. Her note continued: "We did not go to the war for money or praise. When I went it was a horrid affair, even dear old Governor Berry opposed me, and would not give me transportation, but I fought them all and went!"[39]

A journalist who saw Dame a year later found her a "well-preserved woman for her age. She wears a plain black dress, has well formed, expressive features, dark eyes and hair only partially turned to gray. Her nose and forehead are sharply and yet becomingly outlined."[40] Dame's account, and the reporter's, omitted a new reality in her life, one that Ray had alluded to when he told Congress that she sometimes used crutches. She had slipped on the ice during the winter of 1885 and sprained her wrist and injured her spine.[41] At the Weirs that summer, she fell while alighting from a carriage and fractured her other arm.[42] Though still active, she had begun to suffer from osteoporosis and the balance issues of old age.

As president of the Army Nurses Association, Dame became a leader in the struggle for federal pensions for women who had served as war nurses.[43] Under a system requiring that each former nurse apply individually to Congress for a pension, she believed many deserving women would go without

Harriet Dame, on stairs at left, with Manchester veterans at a reunion, 1890s
(Courtesy of the New Hampshire Historical Society)

them.[44] Her colleague Dix was eighty-four years old and slowly dying in New Jersey.[45] Dame kept her apprised of the association's struggle as it made its case for pensions in an atmosphere of suspicion and opposition. She told Dix that she and others would fight on despite "the system of spies that are in the halls to watch our going out and coming in. We intend to do our duty now as we did twenty years ago and throughout all the war." Because so many former nurses had no jobs and the association lacked the resources to help them all, its meetings became contentious. "There are several of the nurses very poor but too proud to ask assistance from any one," Dame wrote. "All they want is a chance to take care of themselves. Then others are continually borrowing money. One had pawned her watch. I redeemed that for her. Forty dollars." Impoverished members constantly begged Dame and her colleague Caroline Burghardt to bail them out. "They think we are alone and full of money, but I have many others to help besides myself," Dame complained to Dix. "We often wonder who they called on before they knew us. I am always glad to do all I can for Soldiers and the noble women who done their part and done it well to put down the Rebellion." She wanted Congress to act so that all the former nurses would be "provided for, as a few of us are."[46]

In response to pressure from the Grand Army of the Republic, the largest Union veterans' organization, Congress had by then expanded pension eligibility for soldiers and their families into a mammoth welfare program.[47] In 1890, when widows of men who had served at least three months were added to the rolls, military pensions cost the country $106 million, 40 percent of the federal budget. War nurses still lingered behind the long line of pensioners. Dame and her group supported a monthly pension of twenty-five dollars, the amount she was receiving, but the Grand Army objected to giving all nurses more than some soldiers received. Dame and her association eventually compromised, and in 1892, President Benjamin Harrison signed a bill granting a monthly pension of twelve dollars to qualified Civil War nurses. Applicants had to prove they had served for six months or more under a medical officer with the proper authority to employ them. Spotty records of the nurses' service made this difficult. Under the new law, 2,448 women would seek pensions. A later examination of a sample of their cases suggested that 65 percent of applicants, nearly all of them old and broke, received pensions.[48]

On the Fourth of July in the year the bill became law, the largest gathering of soldiers in Concord since the war assembled in front of the State House for the dedication of the Soldiers and Sailors Memorial Arch. "The veterans owned the town," one reporter wrote. As they marched to fife and drum, he noted the changes time had wrought. "Then young and enthusiastic: today nearly everyone middle-aged or past, many stooped and gray, others lame and almost incapacitated by disease." He singled out Dame and Berry, the wartime governor who had tried to keep her home, as the "most conspicuous of the guests." The Florentine arch rose thirty-three feet, six inches, near the spot where Edward Sturtevant had pitched the capital's first recruiting tent in 1861. The arch served as the gateway to State House Park. A statue of Winged Victory was planned for the top, and panels were left blank for bas-relief scenes of glory, but these features were never added.[49] The ceremony began a long stay in Concord for Dame, who attended the John Hale statue festivities and the Veterans Association reunion later that summer.

She was back in Washington when tragedy struck on a late spring day in 1893. The old Ford's Theatre, site of the Lincoln assassination, had been re-fitted as office space for the hundreds of clerks who handled the paperwork for all those military pensions. Shortly after nine thirty on the morning of June 9, the top floor collapsed into the second, and those two crashed onto the basement floor. Scores of clerks fell, too, or were crushed at their desks. Twenty-two died and more than a hundred were injured. Newspaper coverage was vivid and damning. The next day's *Wheeling Intelligencer* of West Virginia opened its story this way: "Hundreds of men carried down by the falling walls of a building which was notoriously insecure. Human lives crushed out by tons of bricks and iron, and sent unheralded to the throne of their Maker. Men by the score maimed and disfigured for life. Happy families buried in the depths of despair; women calling for their husbands; mothers calling for their sons; not an answer to the cry!"[50]

Inquiries lasted for months. Negligence charges were brought, including one against the pension bureau chief, but the courts found the evidence too flimsy to try them. Congress eventually paid off the victims' families.[51] Public donations poured in, including one from Dame on the day of the tragedy. As a government clerk, she had reason to empathize with the victims, but she gave to all manner of causes in Washington. She also joined Clara Barton, the Red Cross president, in leading the charity work of the Grand Army of the Republic.[52]

Dame had long traded in real estate, possibly beginning with the proceeds of the sale of her boardinghouse in Concord. In addition to what one reporter called the "little cottage" she lived in, she bought several lots in Washington.[53] A newspaper listed her transactions and reported her net property worth as $14,800 ($442,000 in 2021 dollars).[54] At least one purchase benefited her church. In 1889, she had become an incorporator of the Society of All Saints, a group seeking to build a Protestant Episcopal cathedral on the city's northern heights. At some point, Dame transferred ownership of a tract of her land to the project. The National Cathedral later rose on this and surrounding property.[55]

Dame's opposition to one nurse's pension application in the mid-1890s turned ugly for reasons that available records do not fully explain. A former officer testified on Sarah Warren's behalf that she had been recruited as a nurse by one of the Second New Hampshire's companies but had fallen ill and departed after two or three months at Bladensburg. He had recently learned that she was in "very poor health which she has attributed to the exposure of Camp life." Two other officers vouched for her, but Dame took an opposing view. She may have doubted Warren's claim to have nursed with the Second or fixed on Warren's failure to serve the minimum six months required by the pension law. Warren responded to Dame's opposition with a scathing letter to Joab Patterson, who had supported the application. She attributed Dame's "ruinous slander" to senility and blamed her for the pension office's threat to investigate and possibly prosecute her. Warren had recently attended a Weirs reunion, and she speculated that her presence had made Dame jealous, writing: "Thank God I never wanted to build myself up on the wreck of others nor did I embark in '61 for glory." She wanted Patterson to have Dame's testimony stricken from the pension record. Although Warren's letter wound up in Dame's possession, Dame's response to it seems not to have survived.[56] Yet there is evidence that Dame liked being the lone woman among her soldier friends. She had criticized and even ridiculed Mary Marden, who tented with her briefly at the start of the war. Much later, she complained to Patterson when Congress granted $15,000 to a woman who had acknowledged doing little actual nursing during the war. This was almost certainly Barton, who was awarded that amount for efforts to locate missing men and identify the unknown dead after the war.[57] Although Dame had championed nurses' pensions, she also held sharp opinions and did not hesitate to share them.

As she aged, injuries shrank her world. While walking in Lafayette Square in Washington shortly after her eightieth birthday in 1895, she fell on an icy sidewalk and fractured her leg.[58] She vowed to recover in time to see her comrades at the New Hampshire summer reunion, and she made good on the promise. Nine months after that fracture, as Dame was walking to visit a sick friend, a bicyclist struck her and broke the thigh of her other leg.[59] When she exhausted her leave and could not return to her job at the Treasury Department, her boss terminated her employment, causing widespread indignation. Dame had recently told a reporter: "I want to keep my position to the end, for if I have to give it up, I may as well count my life's work as ended."[60] Senator Chandler intervened. He had gotten her the job in 1867, but the best he could do was to exact a commitment that Dame would be rehired when she could work again.[61]

Nearly a year after the first fracture, she could walk only short distances. In writing to Patterson, her last wartime commander, she vacillated between upbeat and discouraged. He was helping her sell off parcels of land, and she enjoyed their correspondence. "What shall I do for letters from you when the land sales are done?" she fretted. She quoted Job to Joab, telling him that at night, "I am full of tossings to and fro unto the dawning of the day." A doctor recommended another operation for a misplaced bone, but she was finished with surgery. "Think I am getting stronger but the same ugly leg is here," she wrote.[62] Eventually she moved back to Concord.

That Dame now used crutches at all times and needed help at the Weirs reunions only made her more popular. For the 1896 meeting, she stayed at the Hotel Weirs and brought the veterans a war memento for their collection: the medical tools of James Merrow, one of the Second's surgeons. Failing in body, she remained nimble in wit.[63] On governors' day, the highlight of the meetings, "tender hands carried her chair to the speakers' stand in the grove," a friend wrote. The loudest applause was always for her, and "at the close of the exercises, she it was who was the center of the largest crowd in a court of her own . . . where she received the grateful homage of her subjects."[64]

Dame turned eighty-five on January 5, 1900. She had moved into a rest home on Park Street in Concord a few blocks from where she had first cared for sick soldiers in her boardinghouse nearly forty years earlier. When the veterans encamped in Concord that spring, she could not attend. Those present voted to request an increase in her pension, sent their good wishes, and expressed hope that she would live for years to come.[65]

It was not to be. Charles Corning, a probate judge who lived in her neighborhood, saw Dame standing in her doorway in mid-April. "I found her very feeble & I was obliged to tell her my name," he wrote in his diary.[66] She died a few days later, at seven o'clock in the evening on April 24, 1900.

Dame's last home was a short walk from St. Paul's Episcopal Church, where she worshipped. On the morning of April 28, a Saturday, she lay in state there for two hours with a small American flag draped over her breast and a larger one upon her casket. Hundreds of people paraded through the church to "gaze upon the face so well known in life and now composed as if in peaceful sleep," the local newspaper reported. It was to be a full military funeral, and the National Guard squad that watched over her consisted of a corporal and four privates.[67] When the funeral began at one o'clock, a reporter counted forty members of "the old Second Regiment, New Hampshire Volunteers" seated in the packed congregation. This contingent was led by Maj. Frank Wasley, wounded at Gettysburg, now a factory inspector in Massachusetts.[68]

A long procession accompanied Dame's casket to the burial plot she had bought for her family in Blossom Hill Cemetery. A pastor who attended the funeral noted that after a rainy morning, the "rather lowering clouds" parted just as the graveside service began, allowing the sun to burst through. It also struck him as "richly suggestive" that at the first volley of the salute fired near Dame's grave, a flight of white doves rose into the sky and circled until the final volley echoed in the distance.[69] David Proctor, whose wounds Dame had treated at Point of Rocks, dropped an evergreen sprig on her casket.[70] Corning, who had watched the troops leave Concord in 1861 when he was five years old, was pleased that she had been laid to rest with military honors. "No officer would have received fuller ritual," he wrote. "She deserved it & more."[71] Using veterans' donations from thirteen states and Cuba, her comrades from the Second would soon purchase and install a granite gravestone topped with the diamond-shaped symbol of the Third Corps, in which Dame had served for much of the war.[72]

"My boys," as Dame often called the men, paid her the ultimate posthumous tribute in 1901. The state's veterans had a tradition of naming each reunion after a New Hampshire hero of the war. When the state department of the Grand Army of the Republic held its thirty-fourth annual meeting in Concord in the spring, the badges distributed to attendees bore a likeness of her. Camp Harriet Dame opened under a blue sky, and praises to her echoed throughout the grounds that week.[73] Reflecting on her presence at past reunions, John G. B. Adams, the Grand Army's national commander, recalled how the old veterans inevitably teared up when the presiding officer introduced her. "For a moment," he said, "the distinguished officers present are forgotten, and they gather around the dear old lady, eager to grasp her hand and say some kind and loving word in appreciation of her services." Martin Haynes, by now a newspaper editor and former congressman, cited Dame's endurance while on campaign with the regiment. "While this manner of living was not a pleasant one," he said, "yet no one ever heard a word of complaint but rather she was always cheerful and had a kind word for everybody. . . . It mattered not whether the soldier was rich or poor, she had no especial favors to give, but used every sufferer alike."[74] Haynes had recently captured her essence in his second history of the regiment. "There were army nurses and army nurses," he wrote, "but those who, like Harriet Dame, 'roughed it' with the men, who shared their hardships, and often their dangers, whose ears were familiar with the roar of battle, and whose hands bound gaping wounds fresh from the battle line, could probably be counted upon the fingers of one hand, with fingers to spare."[75] The veterans recalled how the late Gilman Marston's initial misgivings about Dame had quickly yielded to deep admiration. In her work in the field, he had once written, "she was the pioneer American nurse, and is entitled to the credit and honor of that service, and to the renown which her heroic example and patriotic devotion confer."[76]

Dr. Granville Conn, the Grand Army's medical director, argued at the encampment for "a suitable shaft or a bronze statue in Miss Dame's honor." He favored a life-size likeness in a small park in Concord that would inspire residents on each Memorial Day and "stand as an object lesson in patriotism and self-sacrifice to every passerby." Conn knew his idea would fare better if he were suggesting a statue for a male hero, but he asked: "Shall it be said that the men and the women of the old Granite State have less respect for a woman who has performed equally noble deeds?"[77] Concord veterans later proposed a bronze statue of Dame atop the State House arch, an odd idea considering that structure's height. Eventually a cannon was mounted there, its barrel trained on the hotel across the street. Although no statue of Dame was erected, in 1904 the city named a new school after her. It remained in use until 2012, when it became a community center.[78]

Among the old veterans, Frank Wasley, who had led the Second New Hampshire men at her funeral, arranged what he hoped would be a lasting salute to her memory. Wasley had joined the regiment at the start of the war and risen from corporal to lieutenant during his three years of service. A popular soldier, he had been a singer in the Second's quartet. After the war, he helped place the regiment's monument on the correct spot in the Peach Orchard at Gettysburg. Wasley wanted Dame to rest on Blossom Hill beneath a fresh silk American flag. Before each Memorial Day, he sent a new one to Concord to be raised at her grave. Alas, in 1908, after inspecting a factory in his hometown of Lowell, Wasley dropped dead at sixty-nine. His obituary made it known that "Mr. Wasley had a great love and reverence for Harriet P. Dame."[79]

A few months after her death, the New Hampshire Legislature appropriated $250 for a portrait of her to hang in the State House.[80] To paint it, the state commissioned Caroline Ransom, who had thrown Dame a seventy-eighth birthday party in her Washington studio in 1893.[81] A native Ohioan and a close friend of Lucretia Garfield, widow of the slain president, Ransom painted Dame from a photograph, her stern, aged face staring straight ahead.[82] Her narrow shoulders were square, and like an old soldier, she proudly wore medals presented to her for valor and signifying the army corps she had served. In a building whose walls were filled with portraits of male politicians, journalists, and war heroes, Dame's was the first of a woman.[83]

She had lived long enough to create a self-portrait of her own wartime service. Women like her who had left home to serve their country harbored no thought of glory for themselves, she had told one interviewer.[84] Although she had occasionally advised public officials about medical issues, she had no ambition to involve herself in politics or lead great armies into battle. A nurse's province in wartime was among the sick in camp hospitals or just behind the lines in the aftermath of battle. If a soldier she was treating died of his wounds, she had to stifle her emotions and turn to the next man. In Dame's memory of the war, her work had been endless, and death ever present. During the worst of times, she had felt "that the sun can never shine the same, nor the voice ever ring a glad echo." The tools of her trade, she told the interviewer, were "tenderness, patience, and intelligent skill."

By all accounts, during her nation's deadliest war, Dame had become the epitome of these qualities.

Acknowledgments

This book was researched and drafted during the first year of the COVID-19 pandemic. For a writer who had the good fortune to avoid the disease until much later, this created both benefits and challenges. The total devotion of healthcare workers in treating virus victims inspired me to think more deeply about the work of Harriet Patience Dame during her more than four years under somewhat similar pressures. Quarantine in our New Hampshire hermitage kept my wife Monique and me safe and gave me more time than I have ever had to focus on a book project. We had celebrated our fiftieth wedding anniversary just before the pandemic struck, and Monique took her usual loving care of me during our fifty-first year together. Our routine during the winter of 2020–21 called for a daily walk, usually two miles, unless the wind chill sank below thirteen degrees. The first person I must acknowledge here is Monique, my lover, my third and fourth ear in shaping every story, the first reader of every first chapter draft, and my No. 1 supporter.

The main challenge caused by the pandemic was the closure of archives. Early in the project, Joan Desmarais, the vice president of the New Hampshire Historical Society, kept me going by seeking out documents I needed from the society's collections and finding relevant photographs I did not know existed. When the society's library reopened to researchers on a limited basis, Sarah Galligan, the director, allowed me to photograph the Anna D. Berry collection of Harriet Dame's wartime letters before they had been sent for conservation. She also helped me navigate the society's amazing trove of old photographs, many of which grace this book. On my later excursions to the society, Paul

Friday, a reference librarian, retrieved family papers and diaries for me and set me up for mind-numbing but productive slogs through newspaper microfilm.

The New Hampshire State Archives and Records Management closed to researchers throughout the early pandemic months, but Brian Nelson Burford, the state archivist, created a safe space for me in the building and gave me access to a remarkable collection there. It is the Executive Documents Collection, consisting mainly of the incoming mail of New Hampshire governors from the eighteenth century onward. I had used this collection before, but I found it especially helpful for this book. It included, for example, Dame's report on an 1862 medical inspection trip and many letters from government agents at camps and field hospitals describing her and her work in the aftermath of battle. The collection also helped me form a clear picture of the severe trials of the state's war governors, especially Joseph Gilmore.

The Milne Special Collections and Archives at the University of New Hampshire also closed to outside researchers in 2020. Bill Ross, the head librarian, who retired in 2021, is a longtime friend. Although he could not admit me, he looked at collections of interest and sent me images of many relevant soldier letters. These enhanced the twin stories I tell: Dame's experience and the war as seen by soldiers of her regiment, the Second New Hampshire Volunteers.

I must acknowledge a special assistant on this project. For years, Janice Brown has written *Cow Hampshire: New Hampshire's History Blog* (https://www.cowhampshireblog.com/). Her work is a carefully researched and fascinating blend of genealogy and human stories. Whenever I needed a deep dive into Dame's large and far-flung family or information about other characters in the book, Janice tracked down the relevant facts. She lives in Merrimack, but because her blog celebrates families and stories from all around New Hampshire, it has become a rich connective resource for exploring the state's past.

My close friend Robin Wagner, dean of Musselman Library at Gettysburg College, gave me access to several books from the stacks about the aftermath of the battle. Although I had visited Gettysburg more than a dozen times and read more about that battle than any other aspect of the war, I had much to learn for this book about the battle's brutal aftermath, which was, after all, Harriet Dame's realm. Robin led me to several fine works on this subject. Later, when the pandemic eased, she and her husband Michael Birkner, a history professor at Gettysburg College for more than thirty years and a friend since his days at the *Concord Monitor* in the early 1980s, hosted Monique and me as we tromped around that storied ground. During this trip, we searched for and found the site of the Third Corps hospital where Dame nursed after the battle.

As usual, I sent early drafts of chapters of *No Place for a Woman* to friends for comment and direction. Mark Travis and Felice Belman, two longtime colleagues from my newspapering days, kept me on track from start to finish. Mark is a fine writer, and nothing gets past his sharp eyes as an editor. When the manuscript was finally drafted, Felice was in the process of moving from New England to New York for her new job as an assistant national editor of the *New York Times*. She nevertheless read the entire manuscript again and offered advice about word choices, judgments, and structural issues. I took nearly every suggestion to heart. My Florida friends Tom Keyser and Linda Blalock shared their thoughts on the work in progress, as did historian John Belohlavek, who started me on my journey as a historian forty-five years ago at the University of South Florida. My worst habit in writing history is to veer off into fascinating (to me) but irrelevant tangents. This crew was not shy about calling out such sins.

David Morin, an avid hunter and scholar of New Hampshire letters, documents, and images from the Civil War, helped me solve several mysteries. Before decamping to Florida, Dave gave copies and transcriptions of his collection to the New Hampshire Historical Society. I used many of the letters in this vital resource to deepen and enrich my story.

Charlotte Thibault and David Sullivan, both friends of several decades, helped me with the visuals for this book. I persuaded Charlotte, a retired newspaper graphics artist and a fine painter, to do the maps. Her research skills led to important discoveries about the terrain traveled by Harriet Dame. Dave helped me assemble photographs for the book and painted the watercolor of Dame and her dog Whisky from a small, grainy photograph. Both have performed similar magic with some of my earlier books, and I am ever grateful for their help.

Thank you to Peter Carmichael, a professor of history at Gettysburg and director of the Civil War Institute there, for pointing me to Kent State University Press as a possible publisher. The editors I encountered there, including Professor Angela Zombek of the University of North Carolina-Wilmington, Kat Saunders, and the able and affable copy editor Valerie Ahwee, proved to be sure-handed guides through the publishing thicket. I am also grateful to Mary Young, the press's managing editor, for handling the final details of manuscript preparation. During that process, the veteran Civil War historian Matt Gallman's thorough and helpful critique of the manuscript led to many vital adjustments and additions to the text.

In closing, I wish to express my fear that the decline of daily newspapers and letter writing will diminish the ability of future historians to tell stories of our times. My notes attest to how much I relied on letters and firsthand accounts published by newspapers in small communities all across the country. Many of these old papers are now searchable online, a boon to historians. Today, there is more and faster communication than ever, but most of it vanishes soon after it is written. These societal shifts will handicap historians of the future.

Notes

FOREWORD

1.   Harriet P. Dame to Louise V. Bryant, Home of the Afflicted, Pineland, Concord, NH, Oct. 1, 1883, in US State Department, *The Statutes at Large,* vol. 33 (Washington, DC: GPO, 1885).

2. Frank Moore, *Women of the War* (Hartford, CT: S. S. Scranton & Co., 1866); Linus P. Brockett and Mary C. Vaughan, *Woman's Work in the Civil War: A Record of Heroism, Patriotism, and Patience* (Philadelphia: Ziegler, McCurdy & Co., 1867).

3. This reference also erroneously called her "Harriet B. Dame." After the war, and at the time *Women's Work in the Civil War* was being compiled, Harriet P. Dame was paying an extended visit to her brothers and their families in Michigan and Wisconsin, which may have led to the mistake in her home state.

INTRODUCTION

1. For a good summary of Douglass's career as an abolitionist, see Manisha Sinha, *The Slave's Cause: A History of Abolition* (New Haven: Yale Univ. Press, 2016), 425–28.

2. Frances M. Abbott, "Harriet Dame: Interesting Sketch of the Veteran Army Nurse," in *People and Patriot* (Concord, NH), Sept. 20, 1892. Abbott was a committed suffragist, which may have drawn her to Dame. See Francis M. Abbott, "A Comparative View of the Women's Suffrage Movement," *North American Review,* Feb. 1898, 142–51.

3. Abbott, "A Comparative View."

4. Martin A. Haynes, *A History of the Second Regiment, New Hampshire Volunteer Infantry, in the War of the Rebellion* (Lakeport, NH: Private print of Martin A. Haynes, 1896), 296.

5. *Boston Journal,* Aug. 25, 1892.

6. [William E. Chandler], *The Statue of John P. Hale Erected in Front of the Capitol and Presented to the State of New Hampshire by William E. Chandler* (Concord, NH: Republican Press Association, Railroad Square, 1892), 3–7.

7. [Chandler], *The Statue of John P. Hale,* 11–13.

8. Mary Olive Godfrey, "Strafford's First City—Dover by the Cocheco," *Granite Monthly,* Apr. 1900, 222–23.

9. Charles R. Corning diary, Aug. 4, 1892, Corning Papers, New Hampshire Historical Society.

10. Harriet P. Dame to Anna D. Berry, Hill Top, MD, Apr. 2, 1862, addition to Apr. 1 letter, Berry letter-book, NHHS.

11. D. L. Day, *My Diary of Rambles with the 25th Mass. Infantry* (Milford, MA: King and Billings Printers, Gazette Office, 1884), diaries entries for July 20, 1864, 141, and Aug. 8, 1864, 144.

12. Frederick Douglass, *The Life and Times of Frederick Douglass: From 1817–1882, Written by Himself; with an Introduction by the Right Hon. John Bright* (London: Christian Age Office, 1882; updated 1892), 551–54.

13. [Chandler], *The Statue of John P. Hale,* 16–19.

14. [Chandler], *The Statue of John P. Hale,* 10–11.

15. F. M. Abbott, "Harriet Dame."

16. *Reports of Committees of the United States Senate: First Session of the Forty-Eight Congress, 1883–'84* (Washington, DC: GPO, 1884), 1–2.

17. *Congressional Record, Containing the Proceeding and Debates of the Forty-Eighth Congress, First Session,* vol. 15 (Washington, DC: GPO, 1884), 5135.

18. *Londonderry (VT) Sifter,* June 9, 1887.

19. Dame to Louise V. Bryant, Home of the Afflicted, Pineland, Concord, NH, Oct. 1, 1883, in US State Department, *The Statutes at Large,* vol. 33 (Washington, DC: GPO, 1885). As Congress was considering a pension for Dame after the war, she sent this five-thousand-word letter detailing her wartime service to Bryant, the recording secretary of the Ex-Army Nurses Association. Bryant, whom Dame first met in 1862, passed it on to the pension committee. In further notes, it will be referred to as Dame to Bryant, Pineland, Oct. 31, 1883.

20. F. M. Abbott, "Harriet Dame."

21. Harriet Dame, 1893 *Boston Journal* interview, Anna D. Berry letter-book, NHHS. Many women who went to war would have disagreed with this notion. Some women fought during the war. Annie Etheridge, a nurse with a Michigan regiment, rode into the lines during battle bearing two pistols and her medicine kit. See Elizabeth H. Leonard, *All the Daring of the Soldier: Women of the Civil War Armies* (New York: W. W. Norton and Co., 1999), 107–9.

22. *Londonderry (VT) Sifter,* June 9, 1887.

23. "The Union Veterans Corps Fair," *Evening Star* (Washington, DC), Feb. 28, 1882.

1. DUTY CALLS

1. 1893 *Boston Journal* interview, Anna D. Berry letter-book, NHHS.

2. Dame to Louise V. Bryant, Pineland, Oct. 1, 1883.

3. 1893 *Boston Journal* interview, Berry letter-book, NHHS.

4. 1893 *Boston Journal* interview, Berry letter-book, NHHS.

5. In Reid Mitchell, *The Vacant Chair: The Northern Soldier Leaves Home* (Oxford: Oxford Univ. Press, 1993), Reid Mitchell identifies women as "the key to domesticity and its virtues" in American society in the 1860s and asserts that women nurses "above all others restored some femininity to the lives of men at war," 75–76. This observation rings true of Dame's various roles throughout the war.

6. Jeremiah Peabody Jewett, *History of Barnstead from Its First Settlement in 1727 to 1872* (Lowell, MA: Marden & Rowell [Printers], 1872), 126.

7. *Encyclopedia of Massachusetts: Biographical-Genealogical* (Chicago: American Historical Society, 1910), 8.

8. Several Boston city directories in the late 1830s and 1840s list Dame at various addresses and identify her as a dressmaker.

9. Nathaniel Bouton, *The History of Concord* (Concord, NH: B. W. Sanborn, 1856), 494; James O. Lyford, *History of Concord* (Concord, NH: Rumford Press, 1903), 2:860; Janice Brown, *The New Hampshire History Blog*, https://www.cowhampshireblog.com/.

10. 1860 US Census for Concord, NH.

11. 1860 US Census for Concord, NH.

12. "Abraham Lincoln in Phoenix Hall," *New Hampshire Statesman*, Mar. 3, 1860.

13. Elwin L. Page, *Abraham Lincoln in New Hampshire*, introduced and updated by Mike Pride (1929; Concord, NH: Monitor Publishing Co., 2009), 40–42.

14. Lyford, *History of Concord*, 2:1120–21.

15. R. Irving Merrill, *Merrill & Son's Concord City Directory for 1860–61, and Every Kind of Desirable Information for Citizens and Strangers* (Concord, NH: Rufus Merrill & Son), 78; John B. Clarke, *Sketches of Successful New Hampshire Men* (Manchester, NH: John B. Clarke, 1882), 218–19.

16. Franklin Pierce to Henry Parker, Andover, MA, Jan. 23, 1861, "The Letters of Henry Parker" [hereafter Parker Papers, NHHS]. Larry Brown, a Parker descendant, posted Parker's letters and papers online years ago. In 2021, he donated them to the New Hampshire Historical Society. Subsequently he published a handsome three-volume edition of the Parker letters.

17. 1860 census.

18. Merrill, *Merrill & Son's Concord City Directory for 1860–61*, 107, listed five newspapers on Main Street.

19. Page, *Abraham Lincoln in New Hampshire*, 42; Henry McFarland, *Sixty Years in Concord and Elsewhere: Personal Recollections of Henry McFarland* (Concord, NH: Rumford Press, 1899), 192, 224–25.

20. Lyford, *History of Concord*, 1:489, 2:1168–69.

21. 1860 census.

22. Lyford, *History of Concord*, 2:909.

23. *The Thirty-Seventh Annual Report of the American Home Missionary Society* (New York: John A. Gray & Green, Printers, 1863), 105; Union School District [Concord], "Annual Reports," 29.

24. Lyford, *History of Concord*, 1:482–83; Mike Pride and Mark Travis, *My Brave Boys: To War with Colonel Cross and the Fifth New Hampshire* (Hanover, NH: Univ. of New England Press, 2001), 34.

25. McFarland, *Sixty Years*, 227–31.

26. Robert Corning diary, Mar. 12 and Apr. 17–20, 1861, Corning Papers, NHHS.

27. Advertisements and listings from Merrill, *Merrill & Son's Concord City Directory for 1860–61*, and David Watson, *The Concord City Directory, Containing the Names, Residences and Business of the Residents in the Compact Part of the City, with a Map of the City Engraved Expressly for This Work* (Concord, NH: Steam Press of McFarland and Jenks, 1864).

28. Edwin A. Charlton, *New Hampshire as It Is* (Claremont, NH: Tracy & Co., 1856), 163–70.

29. Merrill, *Merrill & Son's Concord City Directory for 1860–61*, ix, 98, 100.

30. Bouton, *History of Concord*, 493.

31. McFarland, *Sixty Years*, 121–25, 134–44.

32. Lyford, *History of Concord*, 1:482–83.

33. Stephen G. Abbott, *The First Regiment New Hampshire Volunteers in the Great Rebellion* (Keene, NH: Sentinel Printing Co., 1890), 111–12.

34. Martin A. Haynes, *A History of the Second Regiment, New Hampshire Volunteer Infantry, in the War of the Rebellion* (Lakeport, NH: Private print of Martin A. Haynes, 1896), 1–8.

35. In her study of diseases during the war, Dr. Bonnie Brice Dorwart notes that the men's ages and primitive living conditions contributed to outbreaks of many kinds. Bonnie Brice Dorwart, MD, *Death Is in the Breeze: Disease during the American Civil War* (Frederick, MD: National Museum of Civil War Medicine Inc., 2009), 22.

36. Dame to Bryant, Pineland, Oct. 1, 1883.

37. Lyford, *History of Concord*, 2:1168–69.

38. Dame to Bryant, Pineland, Oct. 1, 1883.

39. Frances M. Abbott, "Harriet Dame: Interesting Sketch of the Veteran Army Nurse," *People and Patriot* (Concord, NH), Sept. 20, 1892.

40. Georgeanna Woolsey Bacon and Eliza Woolsey Howland, *My Heart toward Home: Letters of a Family during the Civil War*, ed. Daniel John Hoisington (Roseville, MN: Edenborough Press, 2001), 79–82.

41. Thomas J. Brown, *Dorothea Dix: New England Reformer* (Cambridge, MA: Harvard Univ. Press, 1998), 276–82, 306–9.

42. Dame to Bryant, Pineland, Oct. 1, 1883.

43. Text of Parker's June 7, 1861, sermon in Parker Papers, NHHS.

44. Order signed by Frank S. Fiske, et al., Head Quarters 2d Reg't of NH Volunteers, June 10, 1861, and Henry E. Parker to Mary Parker, Washington City, DC, June 24–25, 1861, Parker Papers, NHHS.

45. Robert Corning diary, June 20, 1861, Corning Papers, NHHS.

46. Mike Pride, *Our War: Days and Events in the Fight for the Union* (Concord, NH: Monitor Publishing Co., 2012), 15–18.

47. Dame to Anna Berry, Camp Beaufort [MD], Feb. 12, 1862, Berry letter-book, NHHS.

48. Haynes, *A History of the Second Regiment . . . in the War of the Rebellion*, 297.

49. Dame to Anna Berry, Bladensburg, MD, Apr. 1, 1862, Berry letter-book, NHHS.

2. "OH, THAT I WERE THERE"

1. Martin A. Haynes to Cornelia Lane, Camp Sullivan, Washington, DC, July 7, 1861, in *A Minor War History Compiled from a Soldier Boy's Letters to "The Girl I left Behind Me," 1861–1864* (Lakeport, NH: Private print of Martin A. Haynes, 1916), 12.

2. Thomas B. Leaver to My Dear Mother [Mary Leaver], Camp Sullivan, Washington, DC, July 6, 1861, Leaver letter-book, NHHS.

3. Henry E. Parker to Mary Parker, Washington City, June 25, 1861, Parker Papers, NHHS.

4. President Abraham Lincoln, message to Congress, July 4, 1861, Miller Center, Univ. of Virginia, https://millercenter.org/the-presidency/presidential-speeches/july-4-1861-july-4th-message-congress.

5. Dame to Anna Berry, Camp Sullivan, Washington, DC, July 7, 1861, Berry letter-book, NHHS.

6. John S. Godfrey to Horace Godfrey, Washington, DC, July 31, 1861 (Godfrey quoted Capt. Tileston Barker), Godfrey Papers, NHHS.

7. Leaver to Mary Leaver, Dec. 30, 1861, Leaver letter-book, NHHS.

8. Dame to Berry, and Ai B. Thompson to Berry, July 7, 1861, Berry letter-book, NHHS.

9. James M. McPherson, *Battle Cry of Freedom: The Civil War Era* (Oxford: Oxford Univ. Press, 1988), 339.

10. Mary Parker to Henry Parker, Concord, NH, and Henry Parker to Mary Parker, Washington, DC, both July 10, 1861, Parker Papers, NHHS.

11. Haynes to Cornelia Lane, July 11, 1861, Camp Sullivan, in Haynes, *A Minor War History*, 12–13.

12. Dame's attitude toward this snub reflects Nina Silber's assertion that women who nursed during the Civil War tended to equate their motivation and status with those of soldiers: *Daughters of the Union: Northern Women Fight the Civil War* (Cambridge, MA: Harvard Univ. Press, 2005), 195.

13. Dame to Berry, Camp Sullivan, July 21, 1861, Berry letter-book, NHHS.

14. The connections between war front and home front were close at the war's outset, especially in a highly literate regiment like the Second. Historian Peter S. Carmichael explores how companies, the one hundred–man building blocks of regiments, often consisted of men from the same small cities and towns. This familiarity created a sense that the men were fighting not only for their respective causes but also for their reputations at home. Peter S. Carmichael, *The War of the Common Soldier: How Men Fought, Thought, and Survived the Civil War* (Chapel Hill: Univ. Press of North Carolina), 121–22.

15. Mike Pride, *Our War: Days and Events in the Fight for the Union* (Concord, NH: Monitor Publishing Co., 2012), 20–25.

16. Parker to Mary Parker, Fairfax Court House, VA, July 17, 1861, Parker Papers, NHHS.

17. Pvt. Charles E. Jewett to brother John, Fairfax, VA, July 20, 1861, Jewett Letters, 1859–1864, Milne Special Collections, UNH.

18. Dame to Berry, July 21, 1861, Berry letter-book, NHHS.

19. Dame to Berry, July 21, 1861, Berry letter-book, NHHS.

20. Warren H. Cudworth, *History of the First Regiment (Massachusetts Infantry)* (Boston: Walker, Fuller & Co., 1866), 40–43, 51–53.

21. Dame to Berry, July 21, 1861, Berry letter-book, NHHS.

22. Ai B. Thompson to father, Camp Sullivan, July 24, 1861, Thompson Letters (copies), MNBP.

23. Martin A. Haynes, *History of the Second Regiment New Hampshire Volunteers: Its Camps, Marches and Battles* (Manchester, NH: Charles F. Livingston, 1865), 21.

24. Sgt. Hugh "Rennie" Richardson to "Hod," Washington, DC, July 22, 1861, *Coos Republican* (Lancaster, NH), July 30, 1861.

25. Martin A. Haynes, *A History of the Second Regiment, New Hampshire Volunteer Infantry, in the War of the Rebellion* (Lakeport, NH: Private print of Martin A. Haynes, 1896), 294–95.

26. John L. Rice to Editor, *Springfield (MA) Republican*, Nov. 6, 1896, published Nov. 9, responding to news of Parker's death.

27. Letter in *Dover (NH) Gazette*, quoted in *Farmer's Cabinet* (Amherst, NH), Sept. 6, 1861.

28. Haynes, *A History of the Second Regiment . . . in the War of the Rebellion*, 294–95.

29. Parker to Mary Parker, Washington, DC, July 22, 1861, Parker Papers, NHHS.

30. William C. Davis, *Battle at Bull Run: A History of the First Campaign of the Civil War* (Baton Rouge: Louisiana State Univ. Press, 1977; paperback ed. 1981), 186–87.

31. John B. Godfrey to Henry Parker, undated letter, Parker Papers, NHHS.

32. Thomas B. Leaver to Mother, Camp Sullivan, July 21, 1861 [with additions], Leaver letter-book, NHHS.

33. Godfrey to Parker, undated letter, Parker Papers, NHHS.

34. Parker to Mary Parker, Washington, DC, July 22, 1861, Parker Papers, NHHS.

35. Report of Surgeon John F. Foye, US Volunteers: US Surgeon General's Office, *The Medical and Surgical History of the War of the Rebellion*, 2 vols., 6 pts. (Washington, DC: Government Printing Office, 1870–88), 2:83.

36. Parker to Mary Parker, Washington, DC, July 22, 1861, Parker Papers, NHHS.

37. Charles E. Putnam to brother George, Washington, DC, July 26, 1861, in Otis F. R. Waite, *A Claremont War History: April, 1861, to April, 1865* (Concord, NH: McFarland & Jenks, Printers, 1868), 59–61.

38. Dame to Berry, July 21, 1861, Berry letter-book, NHHS.

39. Dame to Berry, July 21, 1861, Berry letter-book, NHHS.

40. Henry McFarland, *Sixty Years in Concord and Elsewhere: Personal Recollections of Henry McFarland* (Concord, NH: Rumford Press, 1899), 235, 238–39.

41. Dame to Berry, July 21, 1861, Berry letter-book, NHHS.

42. Lt. Joab A. Patterson to George Wilcox, Washington, DC, July 29, 1861, Joab Patterson Papers, UNH.

43. Richardson to "Hod," Washington, DC, July 22, 1861, *Coos Republican,* July 30.

44. John S. Godfrey to Horace Godfrey, Washington, DC, July 26, 1861, Godfrey Papers, NHHS.

45. Surgeon George H. Hubbard to John B. Clark, editor, *Manchester Daily Mirror.*

46. Jeremiah Durgin to My Sons, Fisherville, NH, July 29, 1861, Durgin Family Papers, courtesy of Marcy Fuller.

47. Augustus D. Ayling [New Hampshire adjutant general], *Revised Register of the Soldiers and Sailors of New Hampshire in the War of the Rebellion* (Concord, NH: Ira C. Evans, 1895), 24–98.

48. Otis F. R., Waite, *A Claremont War History,* 60, 70–71.

49. Capt. Leonard Drown to Molly (Mary) Drown, Bladensburg, MD, Aug. 11, 1861, Drown Family Papers, NHHS.

50. George Ladd to Carrie Deppen, Camp Union, Bladensburg, MD, Aug 25, 1862, in Richard R. Long, *Dearest Carrie: The Civil War Romance of a Myerstown Girl and a New Hampshire Boy* (Morgantown, PA: Mastoff Press, 2004), 16.

51. J. W. O. [Pvt. John W. Odlin] to editor, *Independent Democrat* (Concord, NH), Camp Sullivan, Washington, DC, Aug. 4, 1861, published Aug. 15. (Before the war, Odlin lived directly across Main Street from Dame's boardinghouse.)

3. MARYLAND

1. Dame to Anna Berry, Bladensburg, MD, Aug. 13, 1861, Berry letter-book, NHHS.

2. Dame to Anna Berry, Bladensburg, MD, Aug. 13, 1861, Berry letter-book, NHHS.

3. Dame to Berry (letter fragment), probably Aug. 20, 1861, Bladensburg, MD, Berry letter-book, NHHS.

4. Henry E. Parker to Mary Parker, Bladensburg, MD, Aug. 19, 1861, Parker Papers, NHHS.

5. Jean H. Baker: *The Politics of Continuity: Maryland Political Parties from 1858 to 1870* (Baltimore: John Hopkins Univ. Press, 1973), 53–54.

6. "Port o' Bladensburg," https://bladensburgmd.gov/about-us/bladensburg-history-and-historical-sites/port-o-bladensburg/.

7. 1893 *Boston Journal* interview, Berry letter-book, NHHS.

8. Ethan S. Rafuse, "'The Spirit Which You Have Aided to Infuse,'" *Journal of the Abraham Lincoln Association* 38, no. 2 (Summer 2017): 9–10, https://quod.lib.umich.edu/cgi/p/pod/dod-idx/spirit-which-you-have-aided-to-infuse-a-lincoln-little-mac.pdf?c=jala;idno=2629860.0038.203;format=pdf.

9. 1893 *Boston Journal* interview.

10. Parker to Mary Parker, Washington, DC, Aug. 5–7, 1861, Parker Papers, NHHS.

11. Leonard Drown to Mary (Molly) Drown, Camp Union, Bladensburg, MD, Aug. 25, 1861, Drown Family Papers, NHHS.

12. Charles Jewett to brother John, Bladensburg, MD, Sept. 6, 1861, Jewett Letters, UNH.

13. S. G. Griffin to C. M. Wyman, Camp Union, Bladensburg, MD, Aug. 18, 1861, in *New Hampshire Sentinel* (Keene), David Morin Civil War Collection, NHHS.

14. Drown to Molly Drown, Bladensburg, MD, Sept. 8, 1861, Drown Family Papers, NHHS.

15. Thomas Leaver to Henry Leaver, Bladensburg, MD, Aug. 12, 1861, and to sister Anna, Aug. 28, 1861, Leaver letter-book, NHHS.

16. Martin A. Haynes to Cornelia Lane, Camp Union, Bladensburg, MD, Aug. 25, 1861, in Martin A. Haynes, *A Minor War History Compiled from a Soldier Boy's Letters to "The Girl I Left Behind Me,"* 1861–1864 (Lakeport, NH: Private print of Martin A. Haynes, 1916), 18.

17. Historian Reid Mitchell identifies the vital connections between companies, the basic units of infantry regiments, and the cities and towns where they were recruited. Soldiers believed they were fighting for their communities (Reid Mitchell, *The Vacant Chair: The Northern Soldier Leaves Home* (New York: Oxford Univ. Press, 1993), 21. This was certainly true of Leaver, Haynes, and other members of the Second New Hampshire.

18. Leaver to Henry Leaver, Camp Union, Bladensburg, MD, Aug. 10, 1861, Leaver letter-book, NHHS.

19. *Journal of the Proceedings of the Forty-Seventh Convention of the Protestant Episcopal Church* (Manchester, NH: Manchester American Office, 1847), 8–9.

20. *Journal of the Proceedings of the Forty-Eighth Convention of the Protestant Episcopal Church* (Concord, NH: Press of Asa McFarland, 1848), 8.

21. Burns P. Hodgman, "St. Paul's Episcopal Church," *Granite Monthly* 49, no. 1 (Nov. 1893): 6.

22. 1860 US census.

23. Haynes, *A Minor War History*, "Preamble."

24. Charles Jewett to brother John, Bladensburg, MD, Sept. 6, 1861, Jewett Letters, UNH.

25. Abner Durgin to parents, Camp Beaufort, Bladensburg, MD, Aug. 29, 1861, Durgin Family Papers, courtesy of Marcy Fuller.

26. Dame to Berry (letter fragment), probably Bladensburg, MD, Aug. 20, 1861, Berry letter-book, NHHS.

27. Dame to Berry (letter fragment), probably Bladensburg, MD, Aug. 20, 1861, Berry letter-book, NHHS.

28. Robert Malesky, "The Irony behind the Statue of Freedom," *Bygone Brookland: Tales from a Storied DC Neighborhood* blog, https://bygonebrookland.com/2014/07/26/

the-irony-behind-the-statue-of-freedom/, July 20, 2014. Philip Reid's government pay stub for his Sunday work is at this Web site: https://www.socialstudies.org/sites/default /files/view-issue/m1124.pdf.

29. Dame to Berry, probably Bladensburg, MD, Aug. 20, 1861, Berry letter-book, NHHS.

30. Dame to Berry, Bladensburg, MD, Sept. 15, 1861, Berry letter-book, NHHS.

31. Donald Yacovone, ed., *A Voice of Thunder: A Black Soldier's Civil War* (Urbana: Univ. of Illinois Press, 1998), 136n.

32. Dame to Berry, Bladensburg, MD, Aug. 13, 1861, Berry letter-book, NHHS.

33. Dame to Berry, Bladensburg, MD, Sept. 3, 1861, Berry letter-book, NHHS.

34. Dame to Berry, Aug. 13, 1861, Berry letter-book, NHHS.

35. Malesky, "The Enslaved Families Who Worked This Land."

36. Haynes to Cornelia Lane, Camp Union, Bladensburg, MD, Sept. 29, 1861, in Haynes, *A Minor War History,* 21.

37. Leaver to Mary Leaver, Camp Union, Bladensburg, MD, Aug. 18, 1861, Leaver letter-book, NHHS.

38. Parker to Mary Parker, Bladensburg, MD, Aug. 26, 1861, Parker Papers, NHHS.

39. George Ladd to Carrie Deppen, Camp Union, Bladensburg, MD, Aug. 25, 1861, in Richard Long, *Dearest Carrie: The Civil War Romance of a Myerstown Girl and a New Hampshire Boy* (Morgantown, PA: Mastoff Press, 2004), 16.

40. Parker to Mary Parker, Bladensburg, MD, Aug. 26, 1861, Parker Papers, NHHS.

41. Leaver to mother, Camp Union, Bladensburg, MD, Aug. 25, 1861, Leaver letter-book, NHHS.

42. Ladd to Deppen, Camp Union, Bladensburg, MD, Aug. 25, 1861, in Long, *Dearest Carrie,* 16–19.

43. Dame to Berry, Camp Union, Bladensburg, MD, Oct. 7, 1861, Berry letter-book, NHHS.

44. Dame to Berry, Camp Union, Bladensburg, MD, Oct. 7, 1861, and letter fragment to Berry, also from October, Berry letter-book, NHHS.

45. Dame to Berry, Camp Union, Bladensburg, MD, Oct. 7, 1861, and letter fragment to Berry, also from October, Berry letter-book, NHHS.

46. Leonard Drown to Israel Drown, Camp Union, Bladensburg, MD, Oct. 21, 1861, Drown Family Papers, NHHS.

47. 1893 *Boston Journal* interview with Dame.

48. Ladd to Deppen, Camp Union, Bladensburg, MD, Nov. 5, 1862, in Long, *Dearest Carrie,* 28.

49. Dame to Berry, letter fragment, Bladensburg, MD, probably Oct. 28, 1861, Berry letter-book, NHHS.

50. Dame to Berry, letter fragment, Bladensburg, MD, probably Oct. 28, 1861, Berry letter-book, NHHS.

51. 1893 *Boston Journal* interview.

4. "MY HANDS WERE NEVER IDLE"

1. John Godfrey to Horace Godfrey, Headquarters, Hooker's Division, Taylor Camp, MD, Oct. 27, 1861, Godfrey Papers, NHHS.

2. Thomas B. Leaver to Mary Leaver, Hill Top, Old Charles Co., MD, Oct. 28, 1861, and to brother Henry, Hill Top, Camp Starvation, MD, Nov. 5, 1861, Leaver letter-book, NHHS.

3. Parker to Mary Parker, Gov't Hospital for the Insane, Washington, DC, Oct. 25, 1861, Parker Papers, NHHS.

4. Leaver to Mary Leaver, Hill Top, Old Charles Co., MD, Oct. 28, 1861.

5. Godfrey to Horace Godfrey, Headquarters, Hooker's Division, Taylor Camp, Oct. 27, 1861, Godfrey Papers, NHHS.

6. Haynes to Cornelia Lane, Hill Top, Charles Co., MD, Oct. 28 [and 29], 1861, in Martin A. Haynes, *A Minor War History Compiled from a Soldier Boy's Letters to "The Girl I Left Behind Me," 1861–1864* (Lakeport, NH: Private print of Martin A. Haynes, 1916), 24–26.

7. Martin A. Haynes, *History of the Second Regiment New Hampshire Volunteer Infantry, in the War of the Rebellion* (Lakeport, NH: Private print of Martin A. Haynes, 1896), 33.

8. Leaver to Henry Leaver, Budd's Ferry, MD, Nov. 17, 1861, and to mother, Dec. 4, 1861, Leaver letter-book, NHHS.

9. 1893 *Boston Journal* interview, Anna D. Berry letter-book, NHHS.

10. Haynes to Cornelia Lane, Camp Beaufort, near Budds Ferry, MD, Dec. 15, 1861, in Haynes, *A Minor War History*, 31.

11. Dame to Anna Berry, Budd's Ferry, MD, letter fragment, probably Dec. 11, 1861, and Jan. 12 and Apr. 1–2, 1862, Berry letter-book, NHHS.

12. Dame to Anna Berry, Budd's Ferry, MD, Dec. 11, 1861, fragment, Berry letter-book, NHHS.

13. Haynes to Lane, Camp Beaufort, Near Budds Ferry, MD, Dec. 15, 1861, in Haynes, *A Minor War History*, 31.

14. Godfrey to Horace Godfrey, Rollins's rooms, Washington, DC, Dec. 15, 1861, Godfrey Papers, NHHS. Edward H. Rollins was the congressman from Concord.

15. Leonard Allison Morrison, *The History of Windham in New Hampshire (Rockingham County), 1719–1883* (Genealogies) (Boston: Couples, Upham, & Co., 1883), 624.

16. Dame to Berry, Camp Beaufort, MD, Dec. 11, 1861, Berry letter-book, NHHS.

17. *Boston Herald*, Mar. 27, 1893.

18. Dame to Berry, Camp Beaufort, MD, Dec. 11, 1861, Berry letter-book, NHHS.

19. Dame to Berry, Camp Beaufort, MD, Dec. 11, 1861, Berry letter-book, NHHS.

20. Lt. R. H. Wyman to Secretary of the Navy Gideon Welles, U.S.S. *Steamer Harriet Lane*, Off Mattawoman Creek, Dec. 9, 1861, ser. 1, vol. 5, *ORs, Union and Confederate Navies*, "Operation on the Rappahannock and Potomac Rivers," 3.

21. Ladd to Deppen, Camp Beaufort, MD, Jan. 12, 1862, in Richard Long, *Dearest Carrie: The Civil War Romance of a Myerstown Girl and a New Hampshire Boy* (Morgantown, PA: Mastoff Press, 2004), 37.

22. Haynes, *A History of the Second Regiment . . . in the War of the Rebellion*, 46–48.

23. Dame to Berry, Dec. 11, 1861, Berry letter-book, NHHS.

24. Pvt. Abner Durgin to Caroline Durgin, Camp Beaufort, MD, Dec. 21, 1861, Durgin Family Papers, courtesy of Marcy Fuller.

25. 1893 *Boston Journal* interview, Berry letter-book, NHHS.

26. Dame to Berry, Dec. 11, 1861.

27. Haynes, *A History of the Second Regiment . . . in the War of the Rebellion*, 52; Leaver to brother Henry, Camp Beaufort, MD, Dec. 17, 1861, Leaver letter-book, NHHS; Godfrey to brother Horace, Headquarters, Hooker's Division, Camp Baker, Charles Co., MD, Dec. 21, 1861, Godfrey Papers, NHHS.

28. Dame to Berry, Camp Beaufort, MD, Jan. 2, 1862, Berry letter-book, NHHS.

29. Dame to Berry, undated but probably Dec. 10, 1861, Berry letter-book, NHHS.

30. Drown to Molly Drown, New Year's Eve, Camp Beaufort, MD, Drown Family Papers, NHHS.

31. Parker to Mary Parker, Near Hooker's Headquarters, Charles County, MD, Jan. 1, 1862, Parker Papers, NHHS.

32. Dame to Berry, Camp Beaufort, MD, Jan. 2, 1862, and Budd's Ferry, Jan. 10, 1862, Berry letter-book, NHHS.

33. Dame to Berry, Camp Beaufort, MD, Jan. 2, 1862, and Budd's Ferry, Jan. 10, 1862, Berry letter-book, NHHS.

34. Dame to Berry, Camp Beaufort, MD, Feb. 12, 1862, Berry letter-book, NHHS.

35. Dame to Berry, Camp Beaufort, MD, Feb. 12, 1862, Berry letter-book, NHHS. Granville P. Conn, *A History of the New Hampshire Surgeons in the War of Rebellion* (Concord: New Hampshire Association of Military Surgeons, Ira Evans, Printer, 1906), 14.

36. Parker to Mary Parker, Camp Beaufort, MD, Jan. 17, 1862, Parker Papers, NHHS.

37. Haynes, *A History of the Second Regiment . . . in the War of the Rebellion*, 297.

38. George Ladd to Carrie Deppen, Camp Beaufort, MD, Mar. 5, 1862, in Long, *Dearest Carrie*, 42; Haynes to Lane, Camp Beaufort, MD, Mar. 23, 1862, in Haynes, *A Minor War History*, 41; Leaver to mother, Camp Beaufort, MD, Feb. 27, 1862, Leaver letter-book. As Reid Mitchell points out, most Northern soldiers had no military experience before the war and no history of subservice (*The Vacant Chair*, 42).

39. Mary L. Schell, ed., *The Love Life of Brig. Gen. Henry M. Naglee, Consisting of a Correspondence of Love, War, and Politics* (New York: Hilton & Co., 1867), 122.

40. Leaver to mother, Camp Beaufort, MD, Feb. 27, 1862, and to brother Henry, Camp Beaufort, MD, Mar. 15, 1862, Leaver letter-book, NHHS.

41. Haynes to Cornelia Lane, Camp Beaufort, MD, Mar. 23, 1862, in Haynes, *A Minor War History*, 41.

42. Haynes, *A History of the Second Regiment . . . in the War of the Rebellion*, , 49–50.

43. Dame to Berry, undated, probably Apr. 2 addendum to Apr. 1, 1862, letter, Berry letter-book, NHHS.

44. Dame to Berry, undated, probably Apr. 2 addendum to Apr. 1, 1862, letter, Berry letter-book, NHHS.

45. Leaver to mother, Camp Beaufort, MD, Mar. 27, 1862, Leaver letter-book, NHHS.

46. Naglee's order no. 24 and George E. Stephens to *Anglo-African* (New York), Budd's Ferry, Apr. 5, 1862, in Donald Yacovone, ed., *A Voice of Thunder: A Black Soldier's Civil War* (Urbana: Univ. of Illinois Press, 1998), 196n14 and 204.

47. Dame to Berry, undated, probably Apr. 2 addendum to Apr. 1, 1862, letter, Berry letter-book, NHHS.

48. Dame to Berry, undated, probably Apr. 2 addendum to Apr. 1, 1862, letter, Berry letter-book, NHHS.

49. Maj. Gen. George B. McClellan to Soldiers of the Army of the Potomac, Headquarters of the Army of the Potomac, Fairfax Courthouse, VA, Mar. 14, 1862, in Stephen W. Sears, ed., *The Civil War Papers of George B McClellan: Selected Papers, 1860–65* (New York: DaCapo Press, 1992), 211.

50. Ladd to Deppen, Camp Beaufort, MD, Feb. 11, 1862, in Long, *Dearest Carrie,* 39.

51. Haynes to Lane, Camp Beaufort, MD, Mar. 23, 1862, in Haynes, *A Minor War History,* 41.

52. Leaver to mother, Camp Beaufort, MD, Mar. 23 and 29, 1862, Leaver letter-book, NHHS.

53. Godfrey to Horace Godfrey, Head Quarters, Mar. 27, 1862, Godfrey Papers, NHHS.

54. Parker to Mary Parker, Washington, DC, but datelined 2nd N. H. Reg't. Hooker's Division, Apr. 1, 1862, Parker Papers, NHHS.

55. Dame to Berry, Camp Beaufort, MD, Apr. 1, 1862, Berry letter-book, NHHS.

56. Parker to Mary Parker, Washington, DC, Feb. 24, 25; Mar. 4, 1862, Parker Papers, NHHS.

57. Dame to Berry, Camp Beaufort, MD, Apr. 1, 1862, Berry letter-book, NHHS.

58. Leaver to mother, Camp Lookout, MD, Apr. 8, 1862, Leaver letter-book, NHHS.

59. Haynes to Lane, before Yorktown, VA, Apr. 14, 1862, in Haynes, *A Minor War History,* 43.

60. Parker to Mary Parker, on board the *South America,* and Point Comfort, Apr. 6 and 9, 1862, Parker Papers, NHHS.

61. Haynes to Lane, in camp before Yorktown, VA, Apr. 14, 1862, in Haynes, *A Minor War History,* 43.

62. Leaver to mother, Camp Lookout, MD, Apr. 8, 1862, Leaver letter-book, NHHS.

63. Dame to Berry, Yorktown, VA, Apr. 15, 1862, Berry letter-book, NHHS.

64. Leaver to mother, Camp near Yorktown, VA, Apr. 14, 1862, Leaver letter-book, NHHS. The *Virginia* attacked a fleet of wooden Union warships at the mouth of the James River on March 8, 1862. When the *Merrimack* engaged it the next day, both ironclads were disabled.

65. Haynes to Lane, Camp near Yorktown, VA, Apr. 15, 1862, in Haynes, *A Minor War History,* 43.

5. FOURTEEN MILES TO RICHMOND

1. Dame to Berry, Camp Winfield Scott, near Yorktown, VA, Apr. 15, 1862, Berry letter-book, NHHS.

2. Dame to Berry, Camp Winfield Scott, near Yorktown, VA, Apr. 15, 1862, Berry letter-book, NHHS; 1893 *Boston Journal* interview, Berry letter-book.

3. James M. McPherson, *Battle Cry of Freedom: The Civil War Era* (New York: Oxford Univ. Press, 1988), 423–24.

4. Dame to Berry, Apr. 15, 1862, Berry letter-book, NHHS.

5. Thomas B. Leaver to mother, Camp Winfield Scott, near Yorktown, VA, May 1, 1862, Leaver letter-book, NHHS.

6. Dame to Berry, Apr. 15, 1862, Berry letter-book, NHHS.

7. George Brinton McClellan, a Pennsylvanian by birth, had graduated from West Point at the age of nineteen and served as an engineer in the American war with Mexico. During the Civil War, early military successes in west Virginia earned him a chance to lead the Union armies.

8. Dame to Berry, Apr. 15, 1862, Berry letter-book, NHHS.

9. Stephen W. Sears, ed., *The Civil War Papers of George B. McClellan: Selected Papers, 1860–65* (New York: DaCapo Press, 1992), 66n; McClellan to Mary Ellen McClellan, Washington, DC, July 30, 1861, 70; McClellan to Winfield Scott, Cmdng US Army, Washington, DC, Aug. 8, 1861, 79–80 (McClellan succeeded Scott on Oct. 31, 1861); McClellan to Lincoln, Camp at Cumberland, May 14, 1862, 264; and Sears's calculation of rebel strength, 209.

10. Dame to Berry, Apr. 15, 1862, Berry letter-book, NHHS.

11. Carol Kettenburg Dubbs, *Defend This Town: Williamsburg during the Civil War* (Baton Rouge: Louisiana State Univ. Press, 2002), 20–22, 31–33.

12. Dubbs, *Defend This Town*, 71–72.

13. Henry E. Parker to Mary Parker, Yorktown, VA, Apr. 25, 1862, Parker Papers, NHHS.

14. Leaver to mother, Camp Winfield Scott, near Yorktown, VA, May 1, 1862, Leaver letter-book, NHHS.

15. Thaddeus Lowe, born in 1832 to a farm family in Coos County, New Hampshire's northernmost, had a thirst for knowledge but little time for formal schooling. He studied medicine, chemistry, and eventually aviation. After building and flying hot-air balloons in the late 1850s, he made his first flight as a Union aeronaut at the first Bull Run battle.

16. Martin A. Haynes, *History of the Second Regiment New Hampshire Volunteers: Its Camps, Marches and Battles* (Manchester, NH: Charles F. Livingston, 1865), 42–43.

17. Enoch G. Adams to brother, Camp Winfield Scott, Yorktown, VA, May 2, 1862, Adams Papers, UNH.

18. Enoch G. Adams to brother, Camp Winfield Scott, Yorktown, VA, May 2, 1862, Adams Papers, UNH.

19. Enoch G. Adams to brother, Camp Winfield Scott, Yorktown, VA, May 2, 1862, Adams Papers, UNH.

20. Haynes, *History of the Second Regiment . . . Its Camps, Marches and Battles*, 46–47.

21. "A.W.C." [Colby] to Dear Folks, Camp Winfield Scott, before Yorktown, VA, Apr. 28, 1862, https://sparedcreative21.art.blog/2020/04/12/1862-abiel-walker-colby-to-folks -at-home/.

22. Congressional pension letter: Dame to Louise V. Bryant, Pineland, Oct. 1, 1883.

23. Charles E. Jewett to brother and sister, Camp Winfield Scott, VA, Apr. 22, 1862, Jewett Letters, UNH.

24. Undated and un-datelined Thaddeus Lowe report, and T. S. C. Lowe, chief aeronaut, to Brig. Gen. E. D. Keyes, Roper's Meeting House, May 11, 1862, both in *ORs*, ser. 3, vol. 3, Correspondence, Orders, Reports, and Returns of the Union Authorities from Jan. 1 to Dec. 31, 1863, 275–77; Heintzelman to McClellan, Third Corps Headquarters, Williamsburg, VA, May 7, 1862.

25. Leaver to brother Henry, Williamsburg, VA, May 9, 1862, Leaver letter-book, NHHS.

26. Dubbs, *Defend This Old Town*, 72, 74–76.

27. Haynes, *History of the Second . . . Its Camps, Marches and Battles*, 47–49.

28. Leaver to brother Henry, Williamsburg, VA, May 9, 1862, Leaver letter-book, NHHS.

29. Dame to Louise V. Bryant, Oct. 1, 1883.

30. Dame to Louise V. Bryant, Oct. 1, 1883.

31. Dame to Berry, Old Nelson House, Yorktown, VA, May 10, 1862 [and May 11], Berry letter-book, NHHS.

32. Dame to Berry, Old Nelson House, Yorktown, VA, May 10, 1862 [and May 11], Berry letter-book, NHHS.

33. Godfrey to brother Horace, Camp near Williamsburg, VA, May 8, 1862, Godfrey Papers, NHHS.

34. Pvt. John Dean to mother, Williamsburg, VA, May 8, 1862, in Waite, *Claremont War History*, 63–66.

35. Pvt. John Dean to mother, Williamsburg, VA, May 8, 1862, in Waite, *Claremont War History*, 63–66.

36. Pvt. Frank W. Morgan to father, Williamsburg, VA, May 11, 1862, in *Independent Democrat*, May 29.

37. Haynes to Lane, near Williamsburg, VA, May 8, 1862, in Martin A. Haynes, *A Minor War History Compiled from a Soldier Boy's Letters to "The Girl I Left Behind Me," 1861–1864* (Lakeport, NH: Private print of Martin A. Haynes, 1916), 48.

38. Marston Official Report, in Haynes, *History of the Second . . . Its Camps, Marches and Battles*, 55.

39. Dean to mother, May 8, 1862, in Major Otis F. R. Waite, *A Claremont War History: April, 1861, to April, 1865* (Concord, NH: McFarland & Jenks, Printers, 1868), 64–67.

40. Marston Official Report.

41. Haynes, *History of the Second . . . Its Camps, Marches and Battles*, 55.

42. Morgan to father, Williamsburg, VA, May 11, 1862, in *Independent Democrat*, May 29, 1862.

43. Dubbs, *Defend This Old Town*, 77–79, 186–90; McPherson, *Battle Cry of Freedom*, 427.

44. McClellan to wife, Williamsburg, VA, May 6, 1862, in Sears, *The Civil War Papers of George B. McClellan*, 257–58.

45. Hooker testimony before Committee on the Conduct of the War, Washington, DC, Mar. 11, 1863, reported in "The Peninsular Campaign: Testimony of General Hooker," *New York Times*, Apr. 25, 1863.

46. John Godfrey to brother Horace, May 8, 1862, Godfrey Papers, NHHS.

47. Haynes, *History of the Second . . . Its Camps, Marches and Battles*, 56.

48. Leaver to mother, Williamsburg, VA, May 14, 1862, Leaver letter-book, NHHS.

49. William F. Fox, *Regimental Losses in the American Civil War, 1861–1865: A Treatise on the Extent and Nature of the Mortuary Losses in the Union Regiments, with Full and Exhaustive Statistics Compiled from the Official Records on File in the State Military Bureaus and at Washington* (Albany, NY: Albany Publishing Co., 1889), 137.

50. Roster count: Augustus D. Ayling, *Revised Register of the Soldiers and Sailors of New Hampshire in the War of the Rebellion* (Concord, NH: Ira C. Evans, 1895), 29–98.

51. Leaver to brother Henry, Camp at Williamsburg, VA, May 9, 1862, Leaver letter-book, NHHS.

52. Ladd to Deppen, Camp Grover, Williamsburg, VA, May 11, 1862, in Richard Long, *Dearest Carrie: The Civil War Romance of a Myerstown Girl and a New Hampshire Boy* (Morgantown, PA: Mastoff Press, 2004), 50.

53. George W. Gordon to Angeline Gordon, Williamsburg, VA, May 13, 1862, Gordon Papers, NHHS.

54. Haynes to Lane, May 8, 1862, in *A Minor War History*, 51–52.

55. Pvt. John Dean to mother, May 8, 1862, in Waite, *Claremont War History*, 64–67.

56. Parker to Mary Parker, Williamsburg, VA, May 13, 1862, Parker Papers, NHHS.

57. Parker to Mary Parker, Williamsburg, VA, May 13, 1862, Parker Papers, NHHS.

58. Leaver to mother, Williamsburg, VA, May 14, 1862, and Near Kent Court House, May 17, 1862, Leaver letter-book, NHHS.

59. Eliza Woolsey diary, in Georgeanna Woolsey Bacon and Eliza Woolsey Howland, *My Heart Toward Home*, ed. Daniel John Hoisington (Roseville, MN: Edinborough Press, 2000), 204.

60. Dame to Berry, May 11 and 25, 1862, Berry letter-book, NHHS.

61. Leaver to mother, in Camp, on the Road to Richmond, May 26, 1862, Berry letter-book, NHHS.

62. Dame to Berry, May 11 and 25, 1862, Berry letter-book, NHHS; 1893 *Boston Journal* interview.

63. "Drown funeral" and "Burial of Captain A. C. Colby," *Statesman* (Concord, NH), May 24, 1862; David Arthur Brown, comp., *The History of Penacook, N.H., from Its First Settlement in 1734 up to 1900* (Concord, NH: Rumford Press, 1902), 52, 433.

64. Dame to Berry, May 11 and 25, 1862, Berry letter-book, NHHS.

65. Dame to Berry, May 11 and 25, 1862, Berry letter-book, NHHS.

66. Fair Oaks station on the Richmond and York River Railroad line stood just north of where the tracks intersected a major road. The area was the site of fierce fighting on May 31 and June 1, 1861.

67. Leaver to mother, in Camp, Fair Oaks, VA, Friday, June 6, 1862, Leaver letter-book, NHHS.

68. 1893 *Boston Journal* interview.

69. Casualty figures from *Encyclopedia Virginia,* https://encyclopediavirginia.org/entries/seven-pines-battle-of/.

70. George W. Gordon to Angeline Gordon, Fair Oaks, June 16, 1862, Gordon Papers, NHHS.

71. Leaver to mother, in Camp, Fair Oaks, VA, June 24, 1862, Leaver letter-book, NHHS.

6. THE KILLING SUMMER

1. Frances S. Abbott, "Harriet Dame: Interesting Sketch of the Veteran Army Nurse," *People and Patriot* (Concord, NH), Sept. 28, 1892.

2. Dame to Louise V. Bryant, Pineland, Oct. 1, 1883.

3. Abbott, "Harriet Dame."

4. Assistant Surgeon H. E. Brown, quoted in Bonnie Brice Dorwart, MD, *Death Is in the Breeze: Disease during the Civil War* (Frederick, MD: National Museum of the Civil War Inc., 2009), 25.

5. Pvt. Charles E. Jewett to brother and sister, Camp near Fair Oaks, VA, June 19, 1862, Jewett Letters, UNH.

6. McClellan to Lincoln, Head-Quarters, Army of the Potomac, Camp Winfield Scott, Apr. 20, 1862, in Stephen W. Sears, *The Civil War Papers of George B. McClellan: Selected Papers, 1860–65* (New York: DaCapo Press, 1992), 244–45.

7. Stephen W. Sears, *Lincoln's Lieutenants: The High Command of the Army of the Potomac* (Boston: Houghton Mifflin Harcourt, 2017), 241.

8. Martin A. Haynes to Cornelia Lane, Fair Oaks, near Richmond, VA, June 26, 1862, in Martin A. Haynes, *A Minor War History Compiled from a Soldier Boy's Letters to "The Girl I Left Behind Me," 1861–1864* (Lakeport, NH: Private print of Martin A. Haynes, 1916), 58.

9. Col. Gilman Marston's official report, Hdqrs, Second New Hampshire Volunteers, Camp near Fair Oaks, VA, June 1862, in Martin A. Haynes, *A History of the Second Regiment, New Hampshire Volunteer Infantry, in the War of the Rebellion* (Lakeport, NH: Private print of Martin A. Haynes, 1896), 100–101.

10. Martin A. Haynes, *History of the Second Regiment New Hampshire Volunteers: Its Camps, Marches and Battles* (Manchester, NH: Charles F. Livingston, 1865), 71.

11. Count from 2nd New Hampshire roster: Augustus D. Ayling, *Revised Register of the Soldiers and Sailors of New Hampshire in the War of the Rebellion* (Concord, NH: Ira C. Evans, 1895), 29–98.

12. Casualty figures from American Battlefield Trust Web site, https://www.nps.gov/civilwar/search-battles-detail.htm?battleCode=va015.

13. Dame to Bryant, Pineland, Oct. 1, 1883.

14. On Aug. 30, 1862, shortly after the Peninsula battles, US Surgeon General William Hammond urged Union women to produce and donate more lint; http://www.encyclopediadubuque.org/index.php?title=LINT_SOCIETIES. A brief description of a "lint society" in Pittsfield, NH, appears in the next chapter.

15. Hannah Ropes to Alice Ropes, July 6 continuation of letter begun July 3, 1862, from Union Hospital, Georgetown, in John R. Brumgardt, ed., *Civil War Nurse: The Diary and Letters of Hannah Ropes* (Knoxville: Univ. of Tennessee Press, 1980), 53.

16. Haynes, *A History of the Second Regiment . . . in the War of the Rebellion*, 96–98.

17. 1860 US census (Damon's occupation).

18. Henry E. Parker to Mary Parker, 2d NH, Reg't, "Fair Oaks," VA, June 26, 1862, Parker Papers, NHHS.

19. Concord, NH, cemetery records (with thanks to cemetery supervisor Jill McDaniel-Hutchins).

20. Lee's forces attacked entrenched Union positions in these two battles, nearly winning the battle of Gaines' Mill only to be defeated the next day at Mechanicsville. The net result was to hasten McClellan's retreat.

21. Haynes, *A History of the Second Regiment . . . in the War of the Rebellion*, 102–3.

22. Casualties from American Battlefield Trust and National Park Service Web sites, https://www.battlefields.org/learn/civil-war/battles/gaines-mill,   https://www.nps.gov/rich/learn/historyculture/bdcbulletin.htm.

23. McClellan to Stanton, Savage Station, VA, June 28, 1862 (telegram), in Sears, *The Civil War Papers of George B. McClellan*, 322–23.

24. Haynes, *A History of the Second Regiment . . . in the War of the Rebellion*, 103–4.

25. Dame to Anna D. Berry, On Skedadle, June 29, 1862, Berry letter-book, NHHS.

26. 1893 *Boston Journal* interview.

27. Dame to Berry, On Skedadle, June 29, 1862, Berry letter-book, NHHS.

28. Abbott, "Harriet Dame"; 1893 *Boston Journal* interview.

29. Henry E. Parker, "An Account of Civil War Battles near Richmond, Virginia, in the Spring of 1862" (postwar), in Parker Papers, NHHS.

30. 1893 *Boston Journal* interview.

31. Dame to Berry, On Skedadle, June 29, 1862, Berry letter-book, NHHS.

32. Dame to Berry, On Skedadle, June 29, 1862, Berry letter-book, NHHS.

33. 1893 *Boston Journal* interview.

34. Haynes to Lane, On James River, July 2, 1862, in Haynes, *A Minor War History*, 58–59.

35. These were both Union victories in two ways: Union casualties were slighter, and Union forces prevented Lee's army from overrunning the retreat across the Peninsula.

36. Casualty figures fromNational Park Service Web sites, https://www.nps.gov/rich/learn/historyculture/mhbull.htm#:~:text=Slightly%20more%20than%205000%20

Confederates,in%20central%20or%20southern%20Virginia, https://www.nps.gov/rich/learn/historyculture/glendalebull.htm.

37. Col. Gilman Marston to Joseph Hibbert, acting adjutant general, Camp near Harrison's Landing, July 10. 1862, in *ORs*, ser. 13, chap. 23, The Peninsula Campaign, 132.

38. 1893 *Boston Journal* interview.

39. John S. Godfrey to Dame, Pasadena, CA, Mar. 4, 1896, Harriet P. Dame Papers, NHHS.

40. 1893 *Boston Journal* interview.

41. 1893 *Boston Journal* interview.

42. Haynes, *A History of the Second Regiment . . . in the War of the Rebellion*, 298.

43. Lt. John D. Cooper to brother, Camp at Harrison's Landing, James River, July 21, 1862, in *Independent Democrat*, Aug. 7, 1862.

44. Haynes, *History of the Second Regiment . . . Its Camps, Marches and Battles*, 89.

45. Anna D. Berry letter-book, NHHS.

46. Censuses of 1850 and 1860: Janice Brown e-mail (Berry genealogy), Mar. 31, 2020.

47. Huntington Porter Smith obituary, *Boston Globe*, Nov. 27, 1908.

48. George W. Gordon to Angeline Gordon, Camp 2d NH, Harrison's Landing, July 7 and 14, 1862, Gordon Papers, NHHS.

49. Haynes, *History of the Second Regiment . . . Its Camps, Marches and Battles*, 89.

50. Haynes to Lane, July 19, 1862, in Haynes, *A Minor War History*, 61.

51. Pvt. Charles E. Jewett to brother and sister, Harrison's Landing, July 14, 1863, Jewett Letters, UNH.

52. Abbott, "Harriet Dame"; Dame to Bryant, Pineland, Oct. 1, 1883.

53. Jonathan Letterman, *Medical Recollections of the Army of the Potomac* (New York: S. Appleton and Co., 1866), 5–10.

54. Franklin Pierce to Henry Parker, Concord, July 24, 1861, Parker Papers, NHHS.

55. Parker to Mary Parker, 2d. N. H. Reg't Near James River, and Near Harrison's Landing, VA, July 8 and 27, Aug. 1, 5, and 10, 1862, Parker Papers, NHHS.

56. Dame to Bryant, Pineland, Oct. 1, 1883.

57. Abbott, "Harriet Dame."

58. Abbott, "Harriet Dame."

59. Gordon to Angeline Gordon, in the Field Near Warrenton Junction, VA, Aug. 26, 1862, Gordon Papers, NHHS.

60. Haynes, *History of the Second Regiment . . . Its Camps, Marches and Battles*, 26.

61. Haynes to Lane, Camp Near Alexandria, VA, Sept. 6, 1862, in Haynes, *A Minor War History*, 66.

62. Haynes, *A History of the Second Regiment . . . in the War of the Rebellion*, 123–24.

63. Haynes, *A History of the Second Regiment . . . in the War of the Rebellion*, 123–24.

64. Report of Lt. Gen. Thomas J. Jackson, C. S. Army commanding Second Corps, of operations Aug. 15–Sept. 3, *ORs*, ser. 16, chap. 24, Operations in northern Virginia, West Virginia, and Maryland, 641–48.

65. The fight at Kettle Run was one of several Union engagements with the forces of Stonewall Jackson. Confederate troops captured a large supply of Union stores, burned the rest, and moved on to occupy an excellent defensive position on the Bull Run battlefield.

66. Haynes, *A History of the Second Regiment . . . in the War of the Rebellion*, 125–27.

67. Dame to Bryant, Pineland, Oct. 1, 1883.

68. Abbott, "Harriet Dame."

69. Dame to Bryant, Pineland, Oct. 1, 1883; 1893 *Boston Journal* interview.

70. Haynes, *A History of the Second Regiment . . . in the War of the Rebellion*, 127–28.

71. Sears, *Lincoln's Lieutenants*, 316.

72. John J. Hennessy, *Historical Report on the Troop Movements at the Second Battle of Manassas, August 28 through August 30, 1862* (Denver: US Dept. of the Interior, National Park Service, Denver Service Center, Northeast Team, 1985), 43.

73. Sears, *Lincoln's Lieutenants*, 211, 316–21. Even late in the day, Sears asserts, Pope was "fully delusional about the enemy."

74. Haynes, *A History of the Second Regiment . . . in the War of the Rebellion*, 128.

75. Hennessy, *Historical Report*, 169–70.

76. Sears, *Lincoln's Lieutenants*, 317.

77. Hennessy, *Historical Report*, 169–70.

78. Joseph W. A. Whitehorne, *The Battle of Manassas* (Washington, DC: Center of Military History, United States Army, 1990), 48–49.

79. Haynes to Cornelia Lane, Camp near Alexandria, Sept. 6, 1862, in Haynes, *A Minor War History*, 67–68; Haynes, *A History of the Second Regiment . . . in the War of the Rebellion*, 128–34.

80. John Hennessy, *Return to Bull Run: The Campaign and Battle of Second Manassas* (New York: Simon & Schuster, 1993), 250–53.

81. Haynes, *A History of the Second Regiment . . . in the War of the Rebellion*, 130–34. Morgrage, Smiley, and Littlefield deaths described in photo captions, 130, 131, 134.

82. Sgt. Hugh H. Richardson to Jewett's father, Camp near Alexandria, VA, Sept. 16, 1862, Jewett Letters, UNH.

83. John Foote Norton, *The History of Fitzwilliam, New Hampshire, from 1752–1887* (New York: Burr Printing House, 1888), 306–7.

84. Haynes, *Muster Out Roll of the Second New Hampshire in the War of the Rebellion* (Lakeport, NH: Private print of Martin A. Haynes, 1917), 23.

85. George W. Gordon to Angeline Gordon, Columbia Hospital, Washington, DC, Sept. 8, 1862, Gordon Papers, NHHS.

86. Haynes, *A History of the Second Regiment . . . in the War of the Rebellion*, 138–40.

87. Edward N. McConnell, "A Brief History of Company A 139th Regiment, Pennsylvania Volunteers," *Western Pennsylvania History Magazine* 44, no. 4 (Oct. 1972): 308.

88. BG Cuvier Grover to Capt. Joseph Dickenson (Hooker's assistant adjutant general), *ORs*, ser. 16, chap. 24, Operations in northern Virginia, West Virginia, and Maryland, 438.

89. Maj. J. D. Cooper to BG Natt Head (New Hampshire adjutant general), in the Field, Dec. 20, 1864, in Natt Head, *Report of the Adjutant-General of the State of New Hampshire for the Year Ending June 1, 1866*, 2 vols. (Concord, NH: George E. Jenks, State Printer, 1866), 151.

90. Dame to Louise V. Bryant, Pineland, Oct. 1, 1883.

91. M. A. Dillon to Pension Committee, Washington, DC, Mar. 11, 1884, in Dame pension account, *Reports of Committees of the United States Senate: First Session of the Forty-Eight Congress, 1883-'84* (Washington, DC: GPO, 1884), 2.

92. Carrie Deppen to George Ladd, Myerstown, PA, July 10, 1862, Gilder-Lehrman Institute of American History, New York.

93. Ladd to Deppen, Berkley Place, VA, Aug. 8, 1862; Lt. William, W. Ballard, Co. B, 2nd NH, to Susan Abbott, Camp near Fairfax Seminary, VA, Oct. 25, 1862; and Abbott to Deppen, all in Richard Long, *Dearest Carrie: The Civil War Romance of a Myerstown Girl and a New Hampshire Boy* (Morgantown, PA: Mastoff Press, 2004), 56–59.

94. *ORs*, ser. 1, vol. 1, pt. 2, Correspondence, Etc., Sept. 3–Nov. 14, 1862, 249–50.

95. US Surgeon General's Office, *The Medical and Surgical History of the War of the Rebellion* (Washington, DC: Government Printing Office, 1870), 1:124–25 and 262, including Richard H. Coolidge, medical examiner, to William Hammond, surgeon general, Washington, DC, Sept. 10, 1862.

96. Dame to Bryant, Pineland, Oct. 1, 1883.

97. Stephen Dow Beckham, "Lonely Outpost," *Oregon Historical Quarterly* 70, no. 3 (Sept. 1969): 233–57.

98. Dame to Bryant, Pineland, Oct. 1, 1883.

99. Dame to Bryant, Pineland, Oct. 1, 1883.

100. Abbott, "Harriet Dame."

101. Report of Maj. Gen. Samuel P. Heintzelman, US Army, Commanding Third Corps, Army of the Potomac, of Operations Aug. 14–Sept. 2, Hdqrs., Defenses of Washington South of the Potomac, Arlington, VA, Oct. 21, 1862, in *ORs*, ser. 16, chap. 24, Campaign in northern Virginia, 415.

102. Haynes, *A History of the Second Regiment . . . in the War of the Rebellion*, 135. Haynes reports that after entering the battle with 338 men of the original 1,000, the Second lost 16 killed, 87 wounded, and 29 missing. This left 206 men to report for duty.

7. "THE GREAT ARMY OF THE SICK"

1. Larkin Mason to Gov. Nathaniel Berry, Washington, DC, Nov. 26, 1862, Executive Papers Collection, New Hampshire State Archives. Mason was the principal agent appointed by the governor to see to the needs of New Hampshire soldiers in the field. As the war intensified, others would be appointed to similar roles.

2. Martin A. Haynes, *History of the Second Regiment New Hampshire Volunteers: Its Camps, Marches and Battles* (Manchester, NH: Charles F. Livingston, 1865), 113–14.

3. George W. Gordon to Angeline Gordon, Camp 2d NH, Centreville, Nov. 15, 1862, Gordon Papers, NHHS.

4. Martin A. Haynes, *A History of the Second Regiment, New Hampshire Volunteer Infantry, in the War of the Rebellion* (Lakeport, NH: Private print of Martin A. Haynes, 1896), 132.

5. Abner Durgin to My Dear Mother, Centerville, VA, Nov. 9, 1862, Durgin Family Papers, courtesy of Marcy Fuller.

6. Haynes, *A History of the Second Regiment . . . in the War of the Rebellion,* 144–45.

7. Mason to Gov. Berry, Nov. 26, 1862.

8. "Hon. Larkin D. Mason," *Granite Monthly* 34, no. 6 (June 1903): 455–56.

9. Mason to Gov. Berry, Nov. 26, 1862.

10. James M. McPherson, *Battle Cry of Freedom: The Civil War Era* (New York: Oxford Univ. Press, 1988), 570–71.

11. Haynes, *A History of the Second Regiment . . . in the War of the Rebellion,* 118–20; Haynes to Cornelia Lane, in Camp Opposite Fredericksburg, Tuesday morning, Dec. 16, 1862, in Martin A. Haynes, *A Minor War History Compiled from a Soldier Boy's Letters to "The Girl I Left Behind Me,"* 1861–1864 (Lakeport, NH: Private print of Martin A. Haynes, 1916), 82.

12. Casualty figures from American Battlefield Trust Web site.

13. Haynes to Cornelia Lane, in Camp Opposite Fredericksburg, Tuesday morning, Dec. 16, 1862, in Haynes, *A Minor War History,* 82.

14. Haynes to Cornelia Lane, in Camp Opposite Fredericksburg, Tuesday morning, Dec. 16, 1862, in Haynes, *A Minor War History,* 82. Haynes's letters to Lane from mid-December to late February chronicle camp rumors about a move.

15. Mike Pride, *Our War: Days and Events in the Fight for the Union* (Concord, NH: Monitor Publishing Co., 2012), 123–24.

16. Dame to Louise V. Bryant, Pineland, Oct. 1, 1883.

17. Dame to Louise V. Bryant, Pineland, Oct. 1, 1883.

18. Prejudice toward prospective women nurses took many forms. Typically, a surgeon warned a Maine woman that she would regret giving up the comforts of home for "the rough life at camp." Another surgeon told her she would not receive adequate pay. See Jane E. Schultz, *Women at the Front: Hospital Workers in Civil War America* (Chapel Hill: Univ. of North Carolina Press, 2004), 62–63.

19. "First Annual Report of the New Hampshire Soldiers' Aid Association," June 17, 1863, NHHS.

20. "The Great Army of the Sick: Military Hospitals in Washington," Washington, DC, Feb. 23, 1863, published in *New York Times,* Feb. 26; John Swinton to Walt Whitman, Times office, Wednesday night, two o'clock, Feb. 25, 1863, The Walt Whitman Archive, https://whitmanarchive.org/published/periodical/journalism/tei/per.00195.html, https://whitmanarchive.org/biography/correspondence/tei/loc.00593.html.

21. "First Annual Report of the New Hampshire Soldiers' Aid Association."

22. Dame to Bryant, Pineland, Oct. 1, 1883.

23. "First Annual Report of the New Hampshire Soldiers' Aid Association."

24. S. A. A. T. [Sarah Ann Ayer Twombly] to *Independent Democrat* (Alton, NH), Mar. 23, 1863, published Apr. 12.

25. Many women traveled to field hospitals to care for sick and wounded husbands, sons, and brothers. As Schultz notes, some stayed on after their loved ones died, finding that caring for a dead soldier's comrades was a "most fitting tribute" to him. Schultz, *Women at the Front,* 59–60.

26. Schultz, *Women at the Front,* 59–60.

27. "Miranda Tullock," *Granite Monthly* 4 (Dec. 1880): 110–11. Miranda Swain married Thomas Tulloch after the war, volunteered for many charities, and helped start a nursing school in Washington, DC.

28. Oliver Pillsbury to Gov. Nathanial Berry, Washington, DC, Feb. 28, 1863, Executive Papers Collection, NHSA.

29. "The Great Army of the Sick," *New York Times,* Feb. 26, 1863, The Walt Whitman Archive.

30. Harriet P. Dame to Miss Cornelia Leach in East Westmoreland, NH, sent from New Hampshire Soldiers' Aid Association, 517 Seventh St., Rooms 9 and 10, Third Story, Washington, DC, May 24, 1863, David Morin Civil War Collection.

31. Francis H. Buffam, *A Memorial of the Great Rebellion: Being a History of the Fourteenth Regiment, New Hampshire Volunteers, Covering Its Three Years of Service, with Original Sketches of Army Life, 1862–1865* (Boston: Franklin Press, Rand, Avery, and Co., 1882), 99. Camp Adirondack was in the Eckington area of Washington.

32. Estimates vary, but most say that illness caused two-thirds of soldier deaths during the Civil War.

33. Buffam, *A Memorial,* 322.

34. Dame to Leach, May 24, 1863, David Morin Civil War Collection, NHHS.

35. "Contributions to the N. H. Soldiers' Aid Association at Washington," J. D. Stevens to *Independent Democrat* (Washington, DC), July 27, 1863, published Aug. 16, 1863.

36. Asa W. Bartlett, *History of the Twelfth Regiment, New Hampshire Volunteers in the War of the Rebellion* (Concord, NH: Ira C. Evans, printer, 1897), 604.

37. Nathan A. Marzoli, "'Their Loss Was Necessarily Severe': The 12th New Hampshire at Chancellorsville," *Army History* no. 101 (Fall 2016): 22–23.

38. James D. Stevens, "Contributions to the N. H. Soldiers' Aid Association," *Independent Democrat,* Aug. 16, 1863.

39. "First Annual Report of the New Hampshire Soldiers' Aid Association."

40. Receipt for Foss's coffin and shipping instructions in Dame Papers, NHHS.

41. Dame to Bryant, Oct. 1, 1883.

42. David Arthur Brown, comp., *The History of Penacook, N.H., from Its First Settlement in 1734 up to 1900* (Concord, NH: Rumford Press, 1902), 184–85.

43. "First Annual Report of the New Hampshire Soldiers' Aid Association."

44. Nina Silber argues that these relief efforts created new bonds among women and

connected them to national political aims. Nina Silber, *Daughters of the Union: Northern Women Fight the Civil War* (Cambridge, MA: Harvard Univ. Press, 2011), 163–64.

45. Major Otis F. R.Waite, *A Claremont War History: April, 1861, to April, 1865* (Concord, NH: McFarland & Jenks, Printers, 1868), 291–92.

46. Stephen G. Abbott, *The First Regiment New Hampshire Volunteers in the Great Rebellion* (Keene, NH: Sentinel Printing Co., 1890), 260–62.

47. H. L. Robinson, *History of Pittsfield in the Great Rebellion* (Pittsfield, NH: H. L. Robinson, 1893), 182–83.

48. Swain to Mrs. R. L. French [of Pittsfield, NH], New Hampshire Soldiers' Aid Rooms, 517 7th Street, Washington, DC, July 27, 1864, in Robinson, *History of Pittsfield,* 181.

49. J. D. Stevens to Gov. Joseph Gilmore, Washington, DC, July 27, 1863, Executive Papers Collection, NHSA.

50. *The National Cyclopedia of American Biography* (New York: James T. White and Co., 1897), 5:299.

51. "First Annual Report of the New Hampshire Soldiers' Aid Association."

52. "First Annual Report of the New Hampshire Soldiers' Aid Association."

53. Amanda Akin to My Dear Sister Gulie, Armory Hospital, Washington, DC, May 14, 1863, in Amanda Akin Stearns, *The Lady Nurse in Ward E* (New York: The Baker and Taylor Co., 1909), 22–27.

54. "First Annual Report of the New Hampshire Soldiers' Aid Association."

55. Robert Corning diary, Mar. 4, 10, and May 11, 1863, Corning Papers, NHHS.

56. *Independent Democrat,* May 7 and 25, 1863.

57. Haynes, *A Minor War History,* 91.

58. Charles N. Kent, *History of the Seventeenth New Hampshire Volunteer Infantry, 1862–1863* (Concord, NH: Rumford Press, 1898), 50–54, 80, 86–88, 122, 152, 160.

59. Haynes, *A History of the Second Regiment . . . in the War of the Rebellion,* 157–61.

60. Alfred F. Whipple diary, June 10 [?] and 13, 1863, in Kent, *History of the Seventeenth,* 110.

61. Haynes to Cornelia Haynes, Taneytown, MD, June 30, 1863, in Haynes, *A Minor War History,* 104–7.

8. GHASTLY HARVEST

1. Joseph H. Foster, "A Visit to the Battlefield," intro. and ed. Michael J. Birkner and Richard Winslow, *Adams County (PA) History* 11, article 5 (2005): 41–42.

2. Allan Nevins, ed., *A Diary of Battle: The Personal Journals of Charles S. Wainwright, 1861–1865* (New York: Harcourt, Brace & World Inc., 1962), 254.

3. Sarah Broadhead diary, July 13, 1863, in Syd Lieberman, "Voices of Gettysburg," https://web.archive.org/web/20110901182240/http://voicesofgettysburg.com/sarah/.

4. Foster, "A Visit to the Battlefield," 42.

5. Foster, "A Visit to the Battlefield," 43.

6. Timothy J. Orr, "On Such Slender Threads Does the Fate of Nations Depend," Papers of the Gettysburg National Military Park Seminar, Apr. 8–9, 2006, Gettysburg, PA (published 2008), 121–22, 139, http://npshistory.com/series/symposia/gettysburg_seminars/11/essay5.pdf.

7. Foster, "A Visit to the Battlefield," 42–43.

8. Foster, "A Visit to the Battlefield," 43.

9. Bailey official report, HQ 2d NH 3d Brigade, 2d Division, 3d Army Corps, near Gettysburg, July 5, 1863, in Executive Papers Collection, NHSA.

10. Bailey official report.

11. Martin A. Haynes, *History of the Second Regiment New Hampshire Volunteers: Its Camps, Marches and Battles* (Manchester, NH: Charles F. Livingston, 1865), 131–36.

12. Haynes, *History of the Second Regiment ... Its Camps, Marches and Battles,* 139.

13. Haynes to Cornelia Haynes, Gettysburg, PA, July 4, 1863, in Haynes, *A Minor War History Compiled from a Soldier Boy's Letters to "The Girl I Left Behind Me," 1861–1864* (Lakeport, NH: Private print of Martin A. Haynes, 1916), 107–8.

14. Bailey official report.

15. Haynes to Cornelia Haynes, Gettysburg, PA, July 4, 1863, in Haynes, *A Minor War History,* 107–8.

16. Lt. John D. Cooper to Governor Gilmore, July 9, 1863, Executive Papers Collection, NHSA.

17. Casualty figures: Augustus D. Ayling, *Revised Register of the Soldiers and Sailors of New Hampshire in the War of the Rebellion* (Concord, NH: Ira C. Evans, 1895).

18. Charles N. Kent, *History of the Seventeenth New Hampshire Volunteer Infantry, 1862–1863* (Concord, NH: Rumford Press, 1898), 161.

19. Pvt. John Burrill to parents, July 13, 1863, in Karlton D. Smith, "'We Drop a Comrade's Tear': Colonel Edward Lyon Bailey and the Second New Hampshire Infantry at Gettysburg," Papers of the Ninth Annual Gettysburg National Military Park Seminar, Apr. 6–7, 2002, Gettysburg, PA, 2002, 115, http://npshistory.com/series/symposia/gettysburg_seminars/9/essay5.pdf/.

20. Albert Whipple diary, July 5, 1863, in Kent, *History of the Seventeenth New Hampshire Volunteer Infantry,* 111–12.

21. Haynes, *A History of the Second Regiment ... in the War of the Rebellion,* 180–85.

22. George W. Gordon to Angelina Gordon, July 4, 9, 14, 19, 1863, Gordon Papers, NHHS. The historian Elizabeth R. Varon suggests that the notion of Gettysburg as a "turning point" in the war is a retrospective judgment. Gordon's sobering assessment in the immediate aftermath of the battle supports this interpretation. Elizabeth R. Varon, *Armies of Deliverance: A New History of the Civil War* (New York: Oxford Univ. Press, 2019), 265.

23. Gregory A. Coco, *A Strange and Blighted Land: Gettysburg: The Aftermath of Battle* (Gettysburg: Thomas Publications, 1995), 188, 81, 307.

24. Broadhead diary, July 1–3, 7–13, in Syd Lieberman, *Voices of Gettysburg,* 188, 81, 307, https://web.archive.org/web/20110901182240/http://voicesofgettysburg.com/sarah/.

25. Daniel Skelly, *A Boy's Experiences during the Battle of Gettysburg* (N.p.: Printed privately, 1932), 21–22.

26. Mrs. Tillie (Pierce) Alleman, *At Gettysburg or What a Girl Saw and Heard of the Battle* (New York: W. Lake Borman, 1889), 74, 82.

27. Coco, *A Strange and Blighted Land*, 86.

28. "The Field of Battle Near Gettysburg," July 7, 1863, letter, *The Philadelphia Age*, reprinted in *Alexandria Gazette*, July 11, 1863.

29. "The Invasion of Pennsylvania," *Evening Star* (Washington, DC), June 16, 1863.

30. "The Situation," *New York Herald*, June 23. 1863. For travel difficulties, see Broadhead, diary, June 27, 1863, and Isaac W. Monfort to Gov. O. O. Morton, Washington, July 16, 1863, in *Daily Journal* (Evansville, IN), July 25.

31. Andrew B. Cross, "Battle of Gettysburg and the Christian Commission," in *United States Christian Commission: Second Report of Maryland* (Baltimore: Sherwood & Co., 1863), 13–14, 25.

32. *Philadelphia Public Ledger,* July 15, 1863, in Coco, *A Strange and Blighted Land,* 69.

33. "Rejoicing" and "Our Regiments," the latter including Larkin D. Mason to Gilmore, Philadelphia, July 10, 1861, *Independent Democrat,* July 16, 1863.

34. C. C. Jewett, Camp of 16th Mass. Vols., near Beverly Ford, VA, Aug. 22, 1863, in Samuel L. Abbot, MD, and James C. White, MD, eds., *The Boston Medical and Surgical Journal* 69 (1863): 101–3.

35. T. C. Grey to Sydney H. Gay, *New York Tribune*, Gettysburg, July 3, 1863, in Coco, *A Strange and Blighted Land*, 155; Gregory A. Coco, *A Vast Sea of Misery: A History and Guide to the Union and Confederate Field Hospitals at Gettysburg, July 1–November 20, 1863* (Gettysburg: Thomas Publications, 1996), 100–101.

36. Henry W. Bellows, president, US Sanitary Commission, "Nurse Gilson—A Recollection of Gettysburg," in *Chelsea (MA) Telegraph & Pioneer*, Mar. 5, 1864.

37. Haynes, *A History of the Second Regiment . . . in the War of the Rebellion,* 300.

38. Jewett, Camp of 16th Mass. Vols., Near Beverly Ford, VA, Aug. 22, 1863, in Abbot and White, eds., *Boston Medical and Surgical Journal* 69 (1863): 103.

39. Antietam quotation from Gilson letter of Sept. 19, 1862: Mrs. P. M. Clapp, "Helen L. Gilson: A Memorial," in *Old and New,* vol 5., January to June 1872 (Boston: Roberts Brothers, 1872), 458–59.

40. Nina Silber identifies Bellows as one of several prominent Union men who, through his leadership of the Sanitary Commission, helped connect women to the national agenda. Nina Silber, *Daughters of the Union: Northern Women Fight the Civil War* (Cambridge, MA: Harvard, Univ. Press, 2005), 176–77.

41. Bellows, "Nurse Gilson."

42. Coco, *A Strange and Blighted Land,* 162–65.

43. Richard W. Musgrove, *Autobiography of Richard W. Musgrove* (Bristol, NH: Mary D. Musgrove, 1921), 92–94.

44. Varon, *Armies of Deliverance,* 268.

45. Cross, "Battle of Gettysburg and the Christian Commission," 16.

46. "The Railroad Commissioner," *Boston Post*, Jan. 17, 1878.

47. Asa W. Bartlett, *History of the Twelfth Regiment, New Hampshire Volunteers in the War of the Rebellion* (Concord, NH: Ira C. Evans, printer, 1897), 481.

48. Henry Bellows, "The Field of Gettysburg," New York, letter dated July 14, 1863, in *Chicago Tribune*, July 20, 1863.

49. Georgeanna Woolsey to Francis Bacon, Fishkill, NY, Aug. 6, 1863, in Georgeanna Woolsey Bacon and Eliza Woolsey Howland, *My Heart Toward Home: Letters of a Family during the Civil War*, ed. Daniel John Hoisington (Roseville, MN: Edenborough Press, 2001), 313–14, and Georgeanna Woolsey Bacon, *Three Weeks at Gettysburg* (New York: Anson D. F. Randolph, 1863), 5, 9, 11, 13.

50. William Watson letters of July 9, 18, and 20, 1863, in Paul Fatout, ed., *Letters of a Civil War Surgeon* (Lafayette, IN: Purdue Univ. Press, 1996), 71–72.

51. C. C. Jewett, "After-Treatment of Amputations and Resections in the Third Corps Field Hospital after Gettysburg," *The Boston Medical and Surgical Journal* 70 (1864): 212–13.

52. Bellows, letter dated July 14, 1863, *Chicago Tribune*, July 20, 1863.

53. Mike Pride, *Our War: Days and Events in the Fight for the Union* (Concord, NH: Monitor Publishing Co., 2012), 154–59.

54. *Portsmouth (NH) Gazette*, July 16, 1863.

55. Oliver Pillsbury to Gov. Joseph Gilmore, Henniker, NH, July 16, 1863, Executive Paper Collection, NHSA.

56. Ebenezer Ross to Gilmore, Manchester, July 15, 1861, and Mayor T. T. Abbott to Gilmore, July 16, 1861, Executive Papers Collection.

57. Lt. Col. Joseph Abbott to Gilmore, HQs, 7th NH, Morris Island, SC, July 22, 1861, Executive Papers Collection.

58. Lloyd Ostendorf, "New Mary Todd Lincoln Photograph," *Illinois Historical Journal* 83, no. 2 (Summer 1990): 109–12.

59. Lincoln to Gilmore, Aug. 7, 1863, Lincoln Papers, LOC.

60. George Francis to Gilmore, South Sutton, NH, Aug. 3, 1863, Executive Papers Collection, NHSA. Daniel Francis returned to duty and served out his hitch.

61. Augusta D. Edgerly to Gilmore, Lancaster, NH, July 16, 1863, Executive Papers Collection, NHSA. Charles Edgerly was mustered out in Concord on Oct. 26, 1863.

62. T. T. Wheat to Gilmore, 2nd Corps Hospital Gettysburg, July 16, 1863, Executive Papers Collection.

63. A. M. Shaw to Gilmore, Gettysburg, July 13, 1863, Executive Papers Collection.

64. Oliver Wyatt to Gilmore, Gettysburg, July 11, 1863, Executive Papers Collection.

65. D. K. Foster to *New Hampshire Patriot* (Pittsfield, NH), Aug. 25, 1863, published Sept. 9, 1863.

66. Wyatt to Gilmore, Baltimore, July 15, 1863, Executive Papers Collection.

67. Mason to Gilmore, July 16, 1863, Gettysburg, PA, Executive Papers Collection.

68. S. C. Clark to Gilmore, July 20, Gettysburg, PA, Executive Papers Collection.

69. Jane Boswell Moore, "An Incident at Gettysburg," in *United States Christian Commission: Second Report of Maryland* (Baltimore: Sherwood & Co., 1863), 104–6.

70. Mason to Gilmore, July 25, 1863, and Robert Corson to Gilmore, July 21, 1863, Executive Papers Collection.

71. Joseph K. Barnes, dir., *The Medical and Surgical History of the War of the Rebellion (1861–65)*, vol. 2, *Surgical History* (Washington, DC: GPO, 1870), 476.

72. Barnes, *The Medical and Surgical History of the War of the Rebellion*, 2:83.

73. Maj. John D. Cooper to adjutant general of New Hampshire, Second Regiment, NH, In the Field, Dec. 20, 1864, in *Report of the Adjutant General of the State of New Hampshire for the Year Ending May 20, 1865* (Concord, NH: Amos Hadley, State Printer, 1865), 1:153.

74. Haynes, *A History of the Second Regiment . . . in the War of the Rebellion*, 172–75.

75. Barnes, dir., *The Medical and Surgical History of the War of the Rebellion*, 2:277.

76. George Waldo Browne, comp., *Manchester Historic Association Collections*, vol. 4, *1908–10* (Manchester, NH: Manchester Historic Association, 1910), 282–84. Barker spent eight weeks in Richmond's Libby Prison before his transfer to prisons in New Orleans and then Salisbury, NC. He was released as part of a prisoner exchange.

77. Ezra W. Abbott to Gilmore, Philadelphia, July 29, 1863, Executive Papers Collection, NHSA.

78. D. K. Foster to Isaac S. Carr, Camp Hospital, 3d Army Corps, 2d Division, near Gettysburg, July 19, 1863, and Asa O. Carr profile, in H. L. Robinson, *History of Pittsfield in the Great Rebellion* (Pittsfield, NH: H. L. Robinson, 1893), 183–85, 52–54.

79. Bartlett, *History of the Twelfth*, 125.

80. Bartlett, *History of the Twelfth*, 125.

81. Foster to *New Hampshire Patriot* (Pittsfield, NH), Aug. 25, 1863.

82. Larkin Mason to Gilmore, July 25 and 27, Executive Papers Collection.

83. Allie Ward, "Burying the Dead," *Gettysburg Compiler*, Aug. 12, 2012.

84. Joseph Greeley to Gilmore, Coleman's Eutaw House, Baltimore, July 24, 1863, Executive Papers Collection.

85. "N. H. Soldiers," *Independent Democrat*, Aug. 20, 1863.

86. Haynes, *A History of the Second Regiment . . . in the War of the Rebellion*, 183.

87. Pvt. Samuel H. Oliver to Ellen Vickery, Point Lookout, MD, Aug. 12, 1863, in National Park Service, "The Life of a Civil War Soldier" (teachers' guide), 52, https://www.nps.gov/gett/learn/education/classrooms/upload/Teacher-s-Guide-for-Trunks-3-2013-508.pdf. Vickery had married Ellen Prichard in Manchester on February 2, 1863, NARA pension files.

88. Haynes, *A History of the Second Regiment . . . in the War of the Rebellion*, 183.

89. Mason to Gilmore, Gettysburg, July 27 and 31, 1863, Executive Papers Collection.

90. Coco, *A Vast Sea of Misery*, 167–68.

91. Gregory A. Coco, "A Laborious and Vexatious Task," Gettysburg Seminar Papers.

92. Mason to Gilmore, July 31, 1863.

93. E. P. Vollum to Col. John M. Culver, Washington, DC, July 29, 1863, in Coco, "A Laborious and Vexatious Task."

94. Vollum to Culver, Washington, DC, July 29, 1863, in Coco, "A Laborious and Vexatious Task."

95. Sophronia E. Bucklin, *In Hospital and in Camp: A Woman's Record of Thrilling Incidents among the Wounded in the Late War* (Philadelphia: John E. Potter and Co., 1869), 142–44, 188.

96. Pvt. Jonathan Merrill to Belinda J. Russell, US General Hospital, Newton Univ., House 3, Ward 1, Baltimore, MD, July 4, 1864, www.horsesoldier.com/products/28593.

97. Lonnie R. Speer describes Andersonville as "nothing more than a concentration camp." During the nearly fourteen months it operated, 12,919 Union POWs died there. At one point 32,899 prisoners occupied a space designed for 10,000. By comparison, Point Lookout, the largest Union POW camp, opened seven months before Andersonville and had the most prisoner deaths of any Union camp: 3,584. Lonnie R. Speer, *Portals of Hell: Military Prisons of the Civil War* (Mechanicsburg, PA: Stackpole Press, 1997), 259, 329, 332.

98. 2nd NH roster in Ayling, *Revised Register.*

99. Haynes to Cornelia Haynes, Washington, DC, July 29, 1863, in Haynes, *A Minor War History*, 113.

100. General-in-Chief Henry Halleck to Maj. Gen. George G. Meade, Washington, DC, July 23, 1863, and Nehemiah Ordway to Gilmore, Washington, DC, July 24, 1861, Executive Papers Collection, NHSA; anon. 12th NH soldier, "Memorandum of the March of the 12th New Hampshire, June 11–July 31, 1863," NHHS; Speer, *Portals of Hell*, 152.

101. Anon. 12th NH soldier to *Independent Democrat*, Camp 12th Reg. NH Volunteers, Point Lookout, MD, Aug. 17, 1863, published Aug. 27, 1863.

102. Gilman Marston to Gilmore, telegram, Washington, DC, July 31, 1863, Executive Papers Collection, NHSA.

103. Haynes, *A History of the Second Regiment . . . in the War of the Rebellion*, 170, 183–85,

104. [E. H. D.] Dascomb to editor, *Daily American*, Manchester, near Falmouth, Jan. 30, 1863, published Feb. 4, 1863.

105. From "A Dying Volunteer," in *Selections from the Poetical Composition of E. Dascomb* (privately printed), Gettysburg National Military Park, in Savannah Rose, "Killed at Gettysburg: Edmund Dascomb, 2d N.H.," https://killedatgettysburg.org/edmund-dascomb-2nd-new-hampshire/.

9. BOUND FOR DIXIE

1. George Dame obituary, *New Hampshire Patriot*, Aug. 26, 1863. Poor sanitation caused both chronic diarrhea and dysentery. In her study of Civil War illnesses, Dr. Bonnie Brice Dorwart explains the difference between them. In addition to unsanitary habits and conditions, flies spread these diseases after picking up bacteria from decaying fecal matter or flesh. Chronic diarrhea caused watery stools, which could lead to shock or even death. Dysentery produced bloody stools. The number of cases in the Union Army each year regularly equaled well over half the number of troops. Bonnie Brice Dorwart, MD,

Death Is in the Breeze: Disease during the American Civil War (Fredericksburg, MD: The National Museum of Civil War Medicine, Inc, 2009), 35.

2. Frances M. Abbott, "Harriet Dame: Interesting Sketch of the Veteran Army Nurse," *People and Patriot* (Concord, NH), Sept. 20, 1892.

3. Mike Pride and Mark Travis, *My Brave Boys: To War with Colonel Cross and the Fifth New Hampshire* (Hanover, NH: Univ. Press of New England, 2001), 252.

4. Maj. O. A. Mack to Godfrey, Office of Acting Asst. Provost Marshal General, Concord, Aug. 14, 1863, and John Legro, Provost Dept., Rochester, NH, Oct. 20 and Nov. 9, 1863, all in David Morin Civil War Collection, NHHS.

5. Mike Pride, *Our War: Days and Events in the Fight for the Union* (Concord, NH: Monitor Publishing Co., 2012), 177.

6. Death statistics: Fifteenth and Sixteenth New Hampshire rosters, Augustus D. Ayling, *Revised Register of the Soldiers and Sailors of New Hampshire in the War of the Rebellion* (Concord, NH: Ira C. Evans, 1895).

7. Mason Tappan to Gov. Joseph Gilmore, Bradford, NH, Jan. 4, 1864, quoting a 4th NH soldier.

8. Dame to Louise V. Bryant, Pineland, Oct. 1, 1883.

9. Dame to Louise V. Bryant, Pineland, Oct. 1, 1883.

10. Barton diary, Dec. 5, 1863, Hilton Head, SC, in William E. Barton, *The Life of Clara Barton: Founder of the Red Cross* (Boston: Houghton Mifflin Co., 1922), 1:255–58.

11. Dame to Bryant, Pineland, Oct. 1, 1883.

12. Dame to Bryant, Pineland, Oct. 1, 1883.

13. An amphibious assault captured Port Royal on Nov. 7, 1861, with little bloodshed on either side.

14. Col. Elbridge J. Copp, *Reminiscences of the War of the Rebellion, 1861–1865* (Nashua, NH: Telegraph Publishing Co., 1911), 47, 74, 77.

15. Dame to Bryant, Pineland, Oct. 1, 1883.

16. Diary of Lt. James H. Linsley, 10th Connecticut Volunteers, Morris Island, Oct. 22 and 24, 1863, Smathers Library, Univ. of Florida, https://ufdc.ufl.edu/UF00096099/00004/8j.

17. Daniel Eldridge, *The Third New Hampshire and All About It* (Boston: Press of E. B. Stillings & Co., 1893), 405–6.

18. Leander Harris to Emmy Harris, Morris Island, Nov. 28, 1863, Harris Papers, UNH.

19. Abner Durgin to Caroline Durgin, Point Lookout, MD, Nov. 22, 1863, Durgin Family Papers, courtesy of Marcy Fuller.

20. Dame to Bryant, Pineland, Oct. 1, 1883.

21. Henry F. W. Little, *The Seventh Regiment New Hampshire Volunteers in the War of the Rebellion* (Concord, NH: I. C. Evans, Printer, 1896), 66–70.

22. About 20 percent of St. Augustine residents departed after the Union occupation. Stephen V. Ash, *When the Yankees Came: Conflict & Chaos in the Occupied South* (Chapel Hill: Univ. of North Carolina Press, 1995), 20.

23. Pride, *Our War*, 240.

24. Extracts from the reports of Surgeon William W. Brown, 7th New Hampshire Volunteers. St. Augustine, Florida, ending Sept. 30 and Dec. 31, 1862, in Joseph K. Barnes, dir., *The Medical and Surgical History of the War of the Rebellion (1861–65)* (Washington, DC: GPO, 1870), 1:81.

25. John T. Sprague, *The Origin, Progress, and Conclusion of the Florida War, 1848* (repr., Gainesville: Univ. of Florida Press, 1964), xii–xiv. The coalition of Indigenous people known to white America as Seminoles (their largest tribe) attempted to resist efforts to evict them from Florida for forty-two years, from 1816 to 1858. Sprague was involved in the latter part of the second war, 1835–42.

26. Dame to Bryant, Pineland, Oct. 1, 1883.

27. Dame to Bryant, Pineland, Oct. 1, 1883.

28. Stephen B. Oates, *A Woman of Valor: Clara Barton in the Civil War* (New York: Free Press, 1994), 171–75, 186–87, 195.

29. *Obituary Record of Graduates of Amherst College for the Academic Year Ending July 9, 1874* (Amherst, MA: Henry M. McCloud, Printer, 1874), 157. Orloff Mather Dorman, Marguerite Dorman's husband, had practiced law in St. Augustine and Jacksonville before the war and served with US forces in the so-called Seminole war of the 1840s. The couple chose to leave Florida when the state seceded in 1861.

30. Barton diary, Dec. 5, 1863, in Barton, *The Life of Clara Barton*, 255–58.

31. Barton diary, Dec. 5, 1863, in Barton, *The Life of Clara Barton*, 255–58.

32. Dame to Bryant, Pineland, Oct. 1, 1883.

33. Dame to Bryant, Pineland, Oct. 1, 1883.

34. Rep. Ossian Ray's comments, in *Congressional Record, Containing the Proceeding and Debates of the Forty-Eighth Congress, First Session* (Washington, DC: GPO., 1884), 15:5135.

35. Lonnie R. Speer, *Portals of Hell: Military Prisons of the Civil War* (Mechanicsburg, PA: Stackpole Books, 1997), 152–53.

36. Simon P. Fifield to William H. Mix, Point Lookout, MD, Jan. 21, 1864, David Morin Civil War Collection, NHHS.

37. "Chaplain" [Adams] to Messrs. Editors, Feb. 3, 1865, in *Independent Democrat*, Feb. 16, 1865.

38. Dame to Gilmore, Washington, DC, Dec. 26, 1863, Executive Papers Collection, NHSA.

10. COLD HARBOR

1. Richard W. Musgrove, *Autobiography of Richard W. Musgrove* (Bristol, NH: Musgrove, 1921), 123.

2. Musgrove, *Autobiography*, 123–24.

3. Dame to Gilmore, Washington, DC, Dec. 26, 1863, Executive Papers Collection, NHSA.

4. The association's changing mission is documented in the 1864 Executive Papers Collection.

5. Ron Chernow, *Grant* (New York: Penguin Press, 2017), 335–37, 356–58.

6. Mason to Gilmore, So. Tamworth, Jan. 9, 1864, Boston, Jan. 19, 1864, Executive Papers Collection.

7. Mason to Gilmore, Near Portsmouth, VA, Jan. 28, 1864, Executive Papers Collection.

8. Rogers Holden, ed., "A Civil War Chaplain's Story: John Wesley Adams 2nd N. H. Volunteers, 1863–1865," memoir in pamphlet (Wells, ME: Book Barn Press, 1995), introduction.

9. Chaplain John W. Adams, "Miss Harriet P. Dame," in Major Otis F. R. Waite, *New Hampshire in the Great Rebellion* (Claremont, NH: Tracy, Chase & Company, 1870), 126–27.

10. Holden, "A Civil War Chaplain's Story," 5–8.

11. Holden, "A Civil War Chaplain's Story," 10.

12. Haynes to Cornelia Haynes, Point Lookout, MD, Dec. 31, 1863, Jan. 29, 31, Feb. 7, and Mar. 25, 1864, in Martin A. Haynes, *A Minor War History Compiled from a Soldier Boy's Letters to "The Girl I Left Behind Me," 1861–1864* (Lakeport, NH: Private print of Martin A. Haynes, 1916), 143, 148–50, 156.

13. Haynes, *A Minor War History*, Mar. 25, 1863, 157.

14. George W. Gordon to Angeline Gordon, Point Lookout, MD, Dec. 2, 1863, Gordon Papers, NHHS.

15. For a thoughtful examination of deserter executions during the war, including their effect on those ordered to witness them, see Peter S. Carmichael, *The War for the Common Soldier: How Men Thought, Fought, and Survived the Civil War* (Chapel Hill: Univ. of North Carolina Press, 2018), 174–229.

16. Mike Pride, *Our War: Days and Events in the Fight for the Union* (Concord, NH: Monitor Publishing Co., 2012), 225–26.

17. Haynes to Cornelia Haynes, Yorktown, VA, Apr. 15 continuation of letter begun Apr. 13, in Haynes, *A Minor War History*, 162–63.

18. Martin A. Haynes, *History of the Second Regiment New Hampshire Volunteers: Its Camps, Marches and Battles* (Manchester, NH: Charles F. Livingston, 1865), 165.

19. Gordon to Angeline Gordon, Camp 2d NHV, near Bermuda Hundred, May 27, 1864, Gordon Papers, NHHS.

20. Larkin D. Mason to Gilmore, telegram, May 10, 1864, Executive Papers Collection, NHSA.

21. Dame to Bryant, Pineland, Oct. 1, 1883.

22. "Chaplain" to Editor, *Independent Democrat* (Williamsburg, VA), May 2, 1864, published May 12. Haynes, *A History of the Second Regiment . . . in the War of the Rebellion* (Lakeport, NH: Private print of Martin A. Haynes, 1896), 217–18.

23. Haynes, *A History of the Second Regiment . . . in the War of the Rebellion*, 217–18.

24. Haynes to Cornelia Haynes, Williamsburg, VA, Apr. 20 and May 4, 1864, and Camp Between Bermuda Hundred and Petersburg, VA, May 9, 1864, in Haynes, *A Minor War History*, 164–67.

25. Earl J. Hess, *Liberty, Virtue and Progress: Northerners and Their War for the Union* (New York: Fordham Univ. Press, 1997), 98–99.

26. Allen C. Guelzo, *Fateful Lightning: A New History of the Civil War and Reconstruction* (Oxford: Oxford Univ. Press, 2012), 233–37.

27. Samuel Duncan to Julia Jones, H'd Q'rs., 2nd Brig., 3d Divis., 18th Army Corps, City Point, VA, May 7, 1864, Duncan and Jones Letters, NHHS.

28. Dame to Bryant, Pineland, Oct. 1, 1883.

29. "The New Hampshire Second," *Concord Daily Monitor*, May 23, 1864, quoting Maj. John D. Cooper's May 17 letter.

30. Haynes to Cornelia Haynes, Headquarters, 2nd NHV., Point of Rocks, VA, May 18, 1864, in Haynes, *A Minor War History*, 168.

31. "The New Hampshire Second," *Monitor*, May 23, 1864.

32. Luther Locke to editor, Bermuda Hundreds, May 19, 1864, *Concord Daily Monitor*, May 25, 1864.

33. 2nd Lt. A. C. Holbrook to Gilmore, Chesapeake Hospital, Near Fort Monroe, VA, May 29, 1864, Executive Papers Collection, NHSA.

34. Chernow, *Grant*, 378–94.

35. Haynes to Cornelia Haynes, Headquarters of 2d New Hampshire, near Petersburg, VA, May 27, 1864, in Haynes, *A Minor War History*, 170–71.

36. Gordon to Angeline Gordon, near Bermuda Hundred, May 27, 1864, Gordon Papers, NHHS.

37. Haynes, *History of the Second Regiment . . . Its Camps, Marches and Battles*, 173–74.

38. Holden, "A Civil War Chaplain's Story," 19.

39. Chernow, *Grant*, 403.

40. Gordon to Angeline Gordon, Pamunkey River Va., May 30, 1864, Gordon Papers, NHHS.

41. Sophronia E. Bucklin, *In Hospital and in Camp: A Woman's Record of Thrilling Incidents among the Wounded in the Late War* (Philadelphia: John E. Potter and Co., 1869), 247, 249.

42. Report of Thomas A. McParlin, medical director of the Army of the Potomac, Medical Director's Office, Nov. 28, 1864 (army medical report for Jan. 14 through July 31, 1864), in US Surgeon General's Office, *The Medical and Surgical History of the War of the Rebellion* (Washington, DC: Government Printing Office, 1870), 2:160.

43. Haynes, *A History of the Second Regiment . . . in the War of the Rebellion*, 231.

44. Chernow, *Grant*, 405.

45. Asa W. Bartlett, *History of the Twelfth Regiment, New Hampshire Volunteers in the War of the Rebellion* (Concord, NH: Ira C. Evans, printer, 1897), 201–4.

46. Haynes, *History of the Second Regiment . . . Its Camps, Marches and Battles*, 174–76.

47. Holden, "The Story of a Civil War Chaplain," 20.

48. Haynes, *History of the Second Regiment . . . Its Camps, Marches and Battles*, 176.

49. Holden, "The Story of a Civil War Chaplain," 20.

50. H. B. Fowler to Angeline Gordon, Base Hospital, Point of Rocks, VA, Nov. 15, 1864, Gordon Papers, NHHS.

51. William H. H. Fernal to "My Dear Friend," Camp, 12th NH, in the Field, June 22, 1864, in 12th New Hampshire Volunteers papers, 1863–64, 1893, NHHS; Bartlett, *History of the Twelfth*, 211–12.

52. Bucklin, *In Hospital and in Camp*, 248–49; Ernest B. Furgurson, *Not War But Murder: Cold Harbor 1864* (New York: Alfred A. Knopf, 2000), 188.

53. Bartlett, *History of the Twelfth*, 207–8.

54. Holden, "The Story of a Civil War Chaplain," 22.

55. Bartlett, *History of the Twelfth*, 214.

56. McParlin report, in Joseph K. Barnes, dir., *The Medical and Surgical History of the War of the Rebellion (1861–65)*, vol. 2, *Surgical History* (Washington, DC: GPO, 1870), 161. The numbers and many descriptive phrases in this paragraph are based on McParlin's thorough, candid report.

57. Barnes, *Medical and Surgical History*, 161–65, including McParlin to Gen. George Gordon Meade, near Cool Arbor, VA, June 5, 1864, 161.

58. Barnes, *Medical and Surgical History*, 161–65, including McParlin to Gen. George Gordon Meade, near Cool Arbor, VA, June 5, 1864, 161.

59. Furgurson, *Not War*, 202, 205–6, 212–15.

60. Bartlett, *History of the Twelfth*, 209.

61. James M. McPherson, *Battle Cry of Freedom: The Civil War Era* (New York: Oxford Univ. Press, 1988), 735. McPherson attributes this quotation to Horace A. Porter, Grant's aide-de-camp and, in 1897, the author of *Campaigning with Grant*. Grant also briefly expressed his regrets for ordering the attack at Cold Harbor in his own memoirs.

62. Ezra W. Abbott to Gilmore, New Hampshire Aid Assn Rooms, Washington, DC, June 8, 1864, Executive Papers Collection, NHSA.

63. Ezra W. Abbott to Gilmore, New Hampshire Aid Assn Rooms, Washington, DC, June 8, 1864, Executive Papers Collection, NHSA.

64. Locke to Amos Hadley, *Concord Daily Monitor*, May 24, 1864.

65. For an excellent account of Vermont's wartime hospitals, see Nancy E. Boone and Michael Sherman, "Designed to Cure: Civil War Hospitals in Vermont," *Vermont History* 69 (Winter/Spring 2001): 173–200.

66. Locke to Gilmore, Bermuda Hundred, June 4, 1864, Medical Director's Office, US Army, Fortress Monroe, June 7, 1864, and on hospital boat, June 8, 1864, Executive Papers Collection, NHSA.

67. Ezra W. Abbott to Gilmore, White House Landing, June 14, 1864, Executive Papers Collection.

68. Bartlett, *History of the Twelfth*, 212.

69. Charles A. Hackett to Gilmore, Washington, DC, June 11, 1864, Executive Papers Collection.

70. Frances M. Abbott, "Harriet Dame: Interesting Sketch of the Veteran Army Nurse," *People and Patriot* (Concord, NH), Sept. 20, 1892.

71. Haynes, *A History of the Second Regiment . . . in the War of the Rebellion*, 177.

72. US Surgeon General's Office, *Medical and Surgical History*, 2:176–77.

73. Marston to Gilmore, Cold Harbor, June 11, 1864, Executive Papers Collection.

74. Waite, *The Great Rebellion*, 126.

75. Dame to Bryant, Pineland, Oct. 1, 1883.

11. POINT OF ROCKS

1. Dame to Bryant, Pineland, Oct. 1, 1883.

2. Rogers Holden, ed., "A Civil War Chaplain's Story: John Wesley Adams 2nd N. H. Volunteers, 1863–1865" (memoir in pamphlet) (Wells, ME: Book Barn Press, 1995), 23–24.

3. Dame to Bryant, Pineland, Oct. 1, 1883.

4. Adelaide W. Smith, *Reminiscences of an Army Nurse during the Civil War* (New York: Greaves Publishing Co., 1911), 80, 84.

5. These battles, known collectively as Grant's Overland campaign, involved almost nonstop fighting. After Lee's army attacked Grant's in the Virginia Wilderness on May 5, 1864, the armies fought for three days. They reengaged at Spotsylvania Court House (May 8–21) and the North Anna River (May 23–26). The Cold Harbor campaign began on May 31. Total casualty figures for May 5–June 24 vary widely, peaking at one hundred thousand.

6. James M. McPherson, *Battle Cry of Freedom: The Civil War Era* (New York: Oxford Univ. Press, 1988). 758–60.

7. Stephen B. Oates, *A Woman of Valor: Clara Barton in the Civil War* (New York: Free Press, 1994), 250–66, including quotation from letter to William Ferguson, July 1, 1864, 252.

8. Barton to My Most Esteemed and Dear Friend, Point of Rocks, VA, July 5, 1864, in William E. Barton, *The Life of Clara Barton: Founder of the Red Cross* (Boston: Houghton Mifflin Co., 1922), 1:283.

9. Ezra A. Abbott to Gilmore, in sight of the trenches, Petersburg, June 24, 1864, Executive Papers Collection, NHSA.

10. Abbott to Gilmore, Ninth Army Corps, in front of Petersburg, June 28 and June 30, 1864, Executive Papers Collection.

11. McPherson, *Battle Cry of Freedom*, 756.

12. Miranda Swain to Mrs. R. L. French, New Hampshire Soldiers' Aid Rooms, 517 7th St., Washington, DC, July 27, 1864, in H. L. Robinson, *History of Pittsfield in the Great Rebellion* (Pittsfield, NH: H. L. Robinson, 1893), 181–82.

13. Larkin Mason to Friend [Amos] Hadley [editor], undated, in *Independent Democrat*, July 21, 1864. Late in the nineteenth century, Augustus D. Ayling, New Hampshire's adjutant general, produced a careful account of all men who served in state military units during the war. By his count, in a state whose 1860 population was 326,073, 34,496 soldiers and sailors took up arms and 4,840 of them died. These included 1,934 killed in battle, 2,407 dead of disease, and 499 dead of other causes. Augustus D. Ayling, *Revised Register of the Soldiers and Sailors of New Hampshire in the War of the Rebellion* (Concord, NH: Ira C. Evans, 1895), 1123.

14. Dame to Bryant, Pineland, Oct. 1, 1883.

15. Robinson, *History of Pittsfield*, 185–86.

16. D. L. Day, *My Diary of Rambles with the 25th Mass. Infantry with Burnside's Coast Division; 18th Corps and the Army of the James* (Milford, MA: King and Billings Printers, Gazette Office, 1884), July 10, 20, 1864, diary entries, 140–42.

17. Day, *My Diary of Rambles*, Aug. 1, 1864, 143.

18. Day, *My Diary of Rambles*, July 20, Aug. 8, 1864, 141, 144.

19. R. S. S. Stubbs to editors, *Independent Democrat*, Base Hospital, 18th Army Corps, near Point of Rocks, VA, Aug. 22, 1864, published Sept. 1, 1864.

20. Stubbs to editors, *Independent Democrat*.

21. Dame to Bryant, Pineland, Oct. 1, 1883.

22. Granville P. Conn, *A History of the New Hampshire Surgeons in the War of Rebellion* (Concord, NH: New Hampshire Association of Military Surgeons, Ira Evans, Printer, 1906), 150.

23. Moses Greeley Parker, "Reminiscences of Personal Interviews with Lincoln," *Contributions of the Lowell Historical Society* (Lowell, MA: Butterfield Printing Co., 1913), 1:382–83.

24. Photograph and caption of Dame and Whisky in log hut, Martin A. Haynes, *A History of the Second Regiment . . . in the War of the Rebellion* (Lakeport, NH: Private print of Martin A. Haynes, 1896), 240.

25. Major Otis F. R. Waite, *New Hampshire in the Great Rebellion* (Claremont, NH: Tracy, Chase & Company, 1870), 126–27.

26. Haynes, *A History of the Second Regiment . . . in the War of the Rebellion*, 250–56.

27. John W. Adams, "My Experience as Army Chaplain (1863–1865)" (postwar speech), 25–26, http://www.westbrookhistoricalsociety.org/diaries/CHAPLAIN%20JOHN%20W%20Adams.pdf.

28. Wisconsin started a trend on Sept. 21, 1862, when its legislature voted to allow its soldiers in the field to cast absentee votes in presidential elections. In the late spring of 1864, New Hampshire became the seventeenth and final Union state to enfranchise its soldiers in the field before that year's election. See Oscar Osburn Winther, "The Soldier Vote in the Election of 1864," *New York History* 25, no. 4 (Oct. 1944): 441–42.

29. Haynes, *A History of the Second Regiment . . . in the War of the Rebellion*, 258.

30. McPherson, *Battle Cry of Freedom*, 770–73; 1864 election totals from https://www.270towin.com/1864_Election/interactive_map.

31. Conn, *A History of the New Hampshire Surgeons*, 49.

32. Dame to Bryant, Pineland, Oct. 1, 1883.

33. Sophronia E. Bucklin, *In Hospital and in Camp: A Woman's Record of Thrilling Incidents among the Wounded in the Late War* (Philadelphia: John E. Potter and Co., 1869), 5–8, 38–39. For Dix's qualifications for nurses, see Judith Giesberg, "Ms. Dix Comes to Washington," *New York Times*, Apr. 27, 2011, https://opinionator.blogs.nytimes.com/2011/04/27/ms-dix-comes-to-washington/.

34. Giesberg, "Ms. Dix Comes to Washington," 332–34.

35. Giesberg, "Ms. Dix Comes to Washington," 337–38, 341.

36. "The Privates' Tribute," *Boston Sunday Globe,* July 26, 1885. For the Sunday edition after the death of Ulysses S. Grant, *Globe* reporters interviewed scores of veterans in the newspaper's circulation area who had encountered Grant during the war. Private Jones was among them.

37. "Journal of the Proceedings of the Thirty-Fourth Annual Encampment of the Department of New Hampshire, Grand Army of the Republic" (Concord: Printed for the Department, 1901), 87.

38. Dame to Bryant, Pineland, Oct. 1, 1883.

39. Rev. E. F. Williams, "Report of the Commission's Work in the Army of the James from November 1864 to the Close of the War," in *United States Christian Commission of the Army and Navy for the Year 1865* (Philadelphia: United States Christian Commission, Mar. 1866), 109–10.

40. Rev. Burdett Hart, "Report of the Commission's Work in the Army of the James," *United States Christian Commission of the Army and Navy for the Year 1865* (Philadelphia: United States Christian Commission, Mar. 1866), 158–59.

41. Bucklin, *In Hospital,* 337, 343–46.

42. Allen C. Guelzo, *Fateful Lightning: A New History of the Civil War and Reconstruction* (Oxford: Oxford Univ. Press, 2012), 467–70.

43. Stanton to Lincoln, Mar. 25, 1865, Lincoln Papers, LOC.

44. Parker, "Reminiscences," 383–84.

45. George A. Bruce, *The Capture and Occupation of Richmond* (Private print of George A. Bruce, n.d.), 5–6.

46. Charlie Washburn to family, Richmond, Apr. 3, 1865, in Nelson Lankford, *Richmond Burning: The Last Days of the Confederate Capital* (New York: Penguin Books, 2002), 116, 157.

47. "Chaplain" [John W. Adams] to Messrs. Editors, Headquarters, 2d NHV, Richmond, VA, Apr. 5, 1865, in *Independent Democrat,* Apr. 12.

48. Haynes, *A History of the Second Regiment . . . in the War of the Rebellion,* 265.

49. Dame to Berry, letter fragment, Bladensburg, probably Oct. 28, 1861, in Berry letter-book, NHHS.

50. Lizzie Corning diary, Apr. 10, 1865, Corning Papers, NHHS.

51. "Rejoicing in Concord," *Independent Democrat,* Apr. 13, 1865.

52. Janice Brown, *Cow Hampshire: New Hampshire's History Blog,* Apr. 4, 2015, http://www.cowhampshireblog.com/2015/04/14/concord-new-hampshires-connection-to-abraham-lincolns-assassination/.

53. Michael W. Kauffman, *American Brutus: John Wilkes Booth and the Lincoln Conspiracies* (New York: Random House, 2004), 47, 78–79.

54. T. Lamar Caudle to Bertram O'Nassis Sheldon, Laurel, MD, July 25, 1983, in Lincoln Financial Corp., "The Assassination of Abraham Lincoln: Physicians," a collection of newspaper stories and letters about Lincoln's medical care, https://archive.org/details/assassinationofaphylinc/page/n1/mode/2up?q=abbot. Among others, Abbott's reports appeared in "The Dying Scenes," *Philadelphia Telegraph,* and "EXTRA: The Death of the President," *Evening Star* (Washington, DC), both Apr. 15, 1865.

55. Caudle to Sheldon, Laurel, MD, July 25, 1983.

56. Helena Papaioannou and Daniel W. Stowell, "Dr. Charles A. Leale's Report on the Assassination of Abraham Lincoln," *Journal of the Abraham Lincoln Association* 24, no. 1 (Winter 2013): 40–53.

57. Lizzie Corning diary, Apr. 15–16, 1865, Corning Papers, NHHS.

58. Chaplain Adams to Messrs. Editors, Headquarters, Second NH Volunteers, Manchester, VA, Apr. 29, 1865, in *Independent Democrat,* May 11, 1865.

59. Bucklin, *In Hospital,* 368, 372.

60. Report of Rev. George N. Marden, *United States Christian Commission for the Army and Navy* (fourth annual report, Feb. 1866), 142–43.

61. Mary A. Gardner Holland, *Our Army Nurses: Interesting Sketches, Addresses, and Photographs of Nearly One Hundred of the Noble Women Who Served in Hospitals and on Battlefields during Our Civil War* (Boston: B. Williams & Co, 1895), 155.

62. Dame to Bryant, Pineland, Oct. 1, 1883.

63. Asa W. Bartlett, *History of the Twelfth Regiment, New Hampshire Volunteers in the War of the Rebellion* (Concord, NH: Ira C. Evans, printer, 1897), 482, 688.

64. Larkin D. Mason to Gov. Frederick Smyth, Washington, DC, May 17, 1865, Executive Papers Collection, NHSA.

65. "Harriet Dame," in Waite, *New Hampshire,* 127; the means of reaching Richmond from Point of Rocks was described in Bucklin, *In Hospital,* 376.

12. TILL DEATH DID THEM PART

1. Chaplain John W. Adams to Messrs. Editors, Richmond, June 15, 1865, in *Independent Democrat,* June 22.

2. Adams's account: Major Otis F. R. Waite, *New Hampshire in the Great Rebellion* (Claremont, NH: Tracy, Chase & Company, 1870), 127–28.

3. Waite, *New Hampshire in the Great Rebellion,* 128.

4. Martin A. Haynes, *A History of the Second Regiment, New Hampshire Volunteer Infantry, in the War of the Rebellion* (Lakeport, NH: Private print of Martin A. Haynes, 1896), 266.

5. Adams's account: Waite, *New Hampshire in the Great Rebellion,* 127.

6. Bonnie Brice Dorwart, MD, *Death Is in the Breeze: Disease during the American Civil War* (Fredericksburg, MD: The National Museum of Civil War Medicine, Inc, 2009), 35.

7. Dame to Bryant, Pineland, Oct. 1, 1883.

8. Haynes, *A History of the Second Regiment . . . in the War of the Rebellion,* 267.

9. Adams to Messrs. Editors, Richmond, VA, June 15, 1865, in *Independent Democrat,* June 22, 1865.

10. J. W. Adams, HQ 2nd NH, Sub District, Northern Neck, District North East Virginia, Warsaw, C.H., VA, to *Independent Democrat,* Aug. 2, 1865, published Aug 17, 1865.

11. Adams to *Independent Democrat,* Aug. 2, 1865.

12. In Allen Guelzo's account, President Andrew Johnson's opinions matched those of the white Southerners encountered by Adams. Johnson opposed political equality for

formerly enslaved people and preferred that they be sent back to Africa. See Allen C. Guelzo, *Fateful Lightning: A New History of the Civil War and Reconstruction* (Oxford: Oxford Univ. Press, 2012), 247–48.

13. Adams to *Independent Democrat,* Aug. 2, 1865.

14. Stephen V. Ash, *When the Yankees Came: Conflict & Chaos in the Occupied South* (Chapel Hill: Univ. of North Carolina Press, 1995), 232–34.

15. Elizabeth R. Varon, *Armies of Deliverance: A New History of the Civil War* (Oxford: Oxford Univ. Press, 2019), 428.

16. Adams to Messrs. Editors, Headquarters, 2d N. H. Vols, Warsaw, VA, Oct. 31, 1865, in *Independent Democrat,* Nov. 11.

17. Haynes, *A History of the Second Regiment . . . in the War of the Rebellion,* 267.

18. Haynes, *A History of the Second Regiment . . . in the War of the Rebellion,* 268.

19. Frances M. Abbott, "Harriet Dame: Interesting Sketch of the Veteran Army Nurse," *People and Patriot* (Concord, NH) Sept. 20, 1892.

20. Horace Nutter Colbath, ed., *The Barnstead Reunion, N.H., August 30, 1882* (Concord, NH: Ira C. Evans, Printer, 1882), 100.

21. A. L. Leach et al., *The Travers Region, Historical and Descriptive, with Illustrations and Scenery and Biographical Sketches of Some of Its Prominent Men and Pioneers* (Chicago: H. R. Page & Co., 1884), 39–40, 239, 242.

22. J. A. Prescott to Gen. J. N. Patterson, Washington, DC, June 2, 1866, in Harriet Dame Papers, NHHS.

23. "Secretary William E. Chandler," in John B. Clarke, *Sketches of Successful New Hampshire Men* (Manchester, NH: John B. Clarke, 1882), 256.

24. "Famous Army Nurse," *Perrysburg (OH) Journal,* Mar. 28, 1900 (from *New York Sun*).

25. "Joint Resolution in Favor of Harriet Dame," in *Laws of the State of New Hampshire, Passed June Session, 1867* (Manchester, NH: John B. Clarke, State Printer, 1867), 248.

26. Abbott, "Harriet Dame."

27. *Official Register of the United States, Containing a List of Officers and Employees in the Civil, Military, and Naval Service on the 30th of June, 1879,* compiled and printed under the direction of the Office of the Secretary of the Interior (Washington, DC: GPO, 1879), 1:28.

28. "Veterans' Re-Union," *Farmer's Cabinet* (Amherst, NH), Oct. 20, 1875.

29. "Hospital Heroines of the Civil War," *Washington Times,* May 24, 1903.

30. The best contemporary account of the Garfield assassination and medical treatment is Candice Millard's *Destiny of the Republic: A Tale of Madness, Medicine and the Murder of a President* (New York: Knopf Doubleday, 2011).

31. "The Union Veterans Corps Fair," *Evening Star,* Feb. 28, 1882.

32. *Congressional Record, Containing the Proceeding and Debates of the Forty-Eighth Congress, First Session* (Washington, DC: GPO, 1884), 15:5135.

33. Dame to Bryant, Pineland, Oct. 1, 1883.

34. Dame to Bryant, Pineland, Oct. 1, 1883.

35. *Congressional Record,* 15:5135.

36. Time line: "New Hampshire Veterans Association History"; "About Women," *Columbian and Democrat* (Bloomsburg, PA), Sept. 10, 1886; Haynes, *A History of the Second Regiment . . . in the War of the Rebellion*, 326.

37. Haynes, *A History of the Second Regiment . . . in the War of the Rebellion*, 326.

38. Haynes, *A History of the Second Regiment . . . in the War of the Rebellion*, 335.

39. Note on card with Dame photographs in Military Order of the Loyal Legion of the United States (MOLLUS) photo albums at US Army Heritage and Education Center, Carlisle Barracks, PA, dateline Washington, DC, Jan. 4, 1886.

40. "The Two Heroines," *Londonderry (VT) Sifter*, June 9, 1887.

41. "The 10-Cent Fund," *National Tribune*, Mar. 5, 1885.

42. "Society News," *Sunday Herald* (Washington, DC), Oct. 11, 1885.

43. "City News Paragraphs," *Washington Critic*, June 15, 1887.

44. Harriet P. Dame to Dr. Christopher P. Elliot [Dorothea Dix's Unitarian pastor], Washington, DC, Aug. 16, 1887, MS Am 1838, Box 18, 804, Dorothea Lynde Dix, Dix Papers, Houghton Library, Harvard Univ.

45. Thomas J. Brown, *Dorothea Dix: New England Reformer* (Cambridge, MA: Harvard Univ. Press, 1998), 341–44.

46. Dame to My Dear Good Friend [Dorothea Dix], Washington, DC, Apr. 5, 1886, MS Am 1838, Box 4, 179, Dix Papers, Houghton Library, Harvard Univ.

47. The late historian Stuart McConnell wrote that after a moribund period in the 1870s, the Grand Army recovered, grew swiftly, and pushed hard to expand pension eligibility and increase payments for various classes of veterans. *Glorious Contentment: The Grand Army of the Republic* (Chapel Hill: Univ. of North Carolina Press, 1992), 143–53.

48. Hannah Metheny, "'For a Woman': The Fight for Pensions for Civil War Army Nurses" (undergraduate honors thesis, College of William and Mary [Scholar Commons], June 2013), 2–35; Katelynn Ruth Vance, "'They Set Themselves to Undermine the Whole Thing': Gender and Authority in the Work of Union Female Nurses," (master's thesis, Univ. of New Hampshire, Durham, Spring 2017), https://scholars.unh.edu/cgi/viewcontent.cgi?article=1923&context=thesis.

49. "Arch Unveiled," *Boston Globe*, July 5, 1892.

50. "The Most Frightful Calamity," *Wheeling (WV) Intelligencer*, June 10, 1893.

51. "Relief Measure," *Evening Star*, June 10, 1893, and subsequent investigation coverage; Anna Snyder, "The Curse of Ford's Theatre?," https://www.fords.org/blog/post/stories-from-the-archives-the-curse-of-ford-s-theatre/.

52. "The Potomac Relief Corps," *National Tribune*, Apr. 4, 1889; "Women and the G.A.R.," *Evening Star*, Mar. 22, 1892.

53. *Waterbury (CT) Democrat*, Jan. 25, 1896.

54. *Evening Star*, Nov. 4, 1893. Several online inflation calculators consulted for 2021 property value.

55. "A Proposed New Episcopal Parish on the Heights North of the City," *Evening Star*, June 15, 1889, and *Star*, June 20, 1902.

56. Herbert B. Titus affidavit [copy] re Warren pension, undated, Warren to Gen. Joab Patterson, 919 A St., N. W. Washington, DC, Mar. 4, 1896; and Dame to Patterson, Treasury Dept., Washington, DC, June 30, 1881, all in Dame Papers, NHHS.

57. Time line: Barton Papers, LOC, https://www.loc.gov/collections/clara-barton-papers/articles-and-essays/timeline/. Also see https://www.clarabartonmuseum.org/mso/.

58. *Evening Star,* Feb. 4, 1895; *Arizona Republican,* Feb. 23, 1895.

59. Granville P. Conn, *A History of the New Hampshire Surgeons in the War of Rebellion* (Concord: New Hampshire Association of Military Surgeons, Ira Evans, Printer, 1906), 26.

60. *Waterbury Democrat,* Jan. 25, 1896.

61. *Evening Star,* Feb. 12, 1896; and *Chicago Tribune,* Feb. 13, 1896.

62. Dame to Joab Patterson, Nov. 17 and 29, 1897, in Dame Papers, NHHS.

63. *Boston Globe,* Aug. 26, 1896.

64. Mrs. Corporal Tanner, "In Memory of Miss Harriet P. Dame," *Western Veteran* (Topeka, KS), Aug. 22, 1900.

65. "Miss Dame Dead," *Concord Evening Monitor,* Apr. 24, 1900.

66. Charles R. Corning diary, Apr. 25, 1900, in Corning Papers, NHHS.

67. "Her Labors Over," and "At Miss Dame's Funeral," *Concord Evening Monitor,* Apr. 28, 1900.

68. "Woman's Military Funeral," *Sunday Herald* (Boston), Apr. 29, 1900.

69. *Concord Evening Monitor,* Apr. 28, 1900.

70. "Journal of the Proceedings of the Thirty-Fourth Annual Encampment of the Department of New Hampshire, Grand Army of the Republic" (Concord, NH: Printed for the Department, 1901), 87.

71. Corning diary, Apr. 28, 1900, in Corning Papers, NHHS.

72. *Boston Globe,* Aug. 3, 1901; *Washington Bee,* Nov. 30, 1901.

73. *Boston Journal,* Aug. 28, 1901; "Journal of the Proceedings of the Thirty-Fourth Annual Encampment," 63.

74. "Journal of the Proceedings of the Thirty-Fourth Annual Encampment," 52–54.

75. Haynes, *A History of the Second Regiment . . . in the War of the Rebellion,* 297.

76. "Journal of the Proceedings of the Thirty-Fourth Annual Encampment," 53.

77. "Journal of the Proceedings of the Thirty-Fourth Annual Encampment," 55–57.

78. 2010 inventory: New Hampshire Division of Historical Resources, https://concordnh.gov/DocumentCenter/View/1134/Dame-School-Inv-form?bidId=.

79. Martin A. Haynes, *Muster Out Roll of the Second New Hampshire in the War of the Rebellion* (Lakeport, NH: Private print of Martin A. Haynes, 1917), 52.

80. *Laws of the State of New Hampshire, Passed January Session, 1901* (Manchester, NH: Arthur E. Clarke, Public Printer, 1901), 629.

81. "Honors to Miss Dame," *Evening Star,* Jan. 4, 1893.

82. Marianne Berger Woods, "C. L. Ransom in Cleveland: A Woman at Work," https://academic.csuohio.edu/tah/regional_arts/Cleveland_as_a_Center/p19clransom.pdf.

83. With thanks to Terry Pfaff, chief operating officer of the New Hampshire General Court (Legislature), for confirming that Dame's portrait was indeed the first of a woman to be hung in the State House.

84. 1893 *Boston Journal* interview, in Berry letter-book, NHHS.

Selected Bibliography

ABBREVIATIONS

LOC—Library of Congress
GNMP—Gettysburg National Military Park (archives)
MNBP—Manassas Battlefield Park
NHHS—New Hampshire Historical Society
NHSA—New Hampshire State Archives
ORs—*Official Records of the War of the Rebellion*
UNH—Milne Special Collections, Univ. of New Hampshire Library

ARCHIVES

Adams, Enoch G. Adams Papers, UNH
Barton, Clara. Barton Papers, LOC
Berry, Anna D. Berry letter-book, "A Woman in the War: 1862: The Story of Miss Dame, Nurse of the Second New Hampshire Regiment," NHHS
Broadhead, Sarah. Broadhead diary, Syd Lieberman, "Voices of Gettysburg," https://web.archive.org/web/20110901182240/http://voicesofgettysburg.com/sarah/
Corning, Charles Robert. Corning Papers, NHHS
Dame, Harriet P. Dame Papers, NHHS
David Morin Civil War Collection (letters and documents written by and pertaining to many New Hampshire soldiers), NHHS
Dix, Dorothea Lynde. Dix Papers, Houghton Library, Harvard Univ.
Drown, Leonard. Drown Family Papers, NHHS
Duncan, Samuel A., and Julia Jones. Samuel A. Duncan and Julia Jones Letters, NHHS

Durgin Family Papers, courtesy of Marcy Fuller

Executive Papers Collection, NHSA

Godfrey, John S. Godfrey Papers, NHHS

Gordon, George W. Gordon Papers, NHHS

Harris, Leander. Harris Letters, 1852–1912, UNH

Jewett, Charles E. Jewett Letters, 1858–64, UNH

Leaver, Thomas B. Leaver letter-book, compiled by his brother Henry Leaver, NHHS

Lincoln, Abraham. Lincoln Papers, LOC

Linsley, James H. Diary of Lt. James H. Linsley, 10th Connecticut Volunteers, 1863, Smathers Library, Univ. of Florida, https://ufdc.ufl.edu/UF00096099/00004/8j

Low, Sarah. Low Letters and diary, NHHS

Parker, Henry. Parker Papers, NHHS, http://freepages.rootsweb.com/~henryeparker/genealogy/war_letters_files/1862/HEP32.htm

Patterson, Joab. Patterson Papers, UNH

Thompson, Ai B. Thompson Letters (copies), MNBP

12th New Hampshire Volunteers. Papers, 1863–64, 1893, NHHS

Walt Whitman Archive, https://whitmanarchive.org/

Wilbur, Julia. Wilbur transcribed 1865 diary, Haverford College Quaker and Special Collections, https://www.alexandriava.gov/uploadedFiles/historic/info/civilwar/JuliaWilburDiary1865.pdf

BOOKS

Abbot, Samuel L., MD, and James C. White, MD, eds. *The Boston Medical and Surgical Journal* 69 and 70 (1863 and 1864).

Abbott, Stephen G. *The First Regiment New Hampshire Volunteers in the Great Rebellion.* Keene, NH: Sentinel Printing Co., 1890.

Alleman, Mrs. Tillie (Pierce). *At Gettysburg or What a Girl Saw and Heard of the Battle.* New York: W. Lake Borland, 1889.

Ash, Stephen V. *When the Yankees Came: Conflict & Chaos in the Occupied South.* Chapel Hill: Univ. of North Carolina Press, 1995.

Ayling, Augustus D. *Revised Register of the Soldiers and Sailors of New Hampshire in the War of the Rebellion.* Concord, NH: Ira C. Evans, 1895.

Bacon, Georgeanna Woolsey. *Three Weeks at Gettysburg.* New York: Anson D. F. Randolph, 1863.

Bacon, Georgeanna Woolsey, and Eliza Woolsey Howland. *My Heart toward Home: Letters of a Family during the Civil War.* Edited by Daniel John Hoisington. Roseville, MN: Edenborough Press, 2001.

Baker, Jean H. *The Politics of Continuity: Maryland Political Parties from 1858 to 1870.* Baltimore: John Hopkins Univ. Press, 1973.

Barnes, Joseph K., dir. *The Medical and Surgical History of the War of the Rebellion (1861–65)*. Vol. 2, *Surgical History*. Washington, DC: GPO, 1870.

Bartlett, Asa W. *History of the Twelfth Regiment, New Hampshire Volunteers in the War of the Rebellion*. Concord, NH: Ira C. Evans, printer, 1897.

Barton, William E. *The Life of Clara Barton: Founder of the Red Cross*. Vol. 1. Boston: Houghton Mifflin Co., 1922.

Bouton, Nathaniel. *The History of Concord: From Its First Grant in 1725, to the Organization of the City Government in 1853, with a History of the Ancient Penacooks: The Whole Interspersed with Numerous Interesting Incidents and Anecdotes, Down to the Present Period, 1855, Embellished with Maps, with Portraits of Distinguished Citizens, and Views of Ancient and Modern Residences*. Concord, NH: B. W. Sanborn, 1856.

Brown, David Arthur, comp. *The History of Penacook, N.H., from Its First Settlement in 1734 up to 1900*. Concord, NH: Rumford Press, 1902.

Brown, Thomas J. *Dorothea Dix: New England Reformer*. Cambridge, MA: Harvard Univ. Press, 1998.

Browne, George Waldo, comp. *Manchester Historic Association Collections*. Vol. 4, *1908–1910*. Manchester, NH: Manchester Historic Association, 1910.

Bruce, George A. *The Capture and Occupation of Richmond*. N.p.: Private print of George A. Bruce, n.d. https://babel.hathitrust.org/cgi/pt?id=mdp.39015069330556&view=1up&seq=10&skin=2021

Brumgardt, John R., ed. *Civil War Nurse: The Diary and Letters of Hannah Ropes*. Knoxville: Univ. of Tennessee Press, 1980.

Bucklin, Sophronia E. *In Hospital and in Camp: A Woman's Record of Thrilling Incidents among the Wounded in the Late War*. Philadelphia: John E. Potter and Co., 1869.

Buffam, Francis H. *A Memorial of the Great Rebellion: Being a History of the Fourteenth Regiment, New Hampshire Volunteers, Covering Its Three Years of Service, with Original Sketches of Army Life, 1862–1865*. Boston: Franklin Press, Rand, Avery, and Co., 1882.

Carmichael, Peter S. *The War for the Common Soldier: How Men Thought, Fought, and Survived the Civil War*. Chapel Hill: Univ. of North Carolina Press, 2018.

[Chandler, William E.] *The Statue of John P. Hale Erected in Front of the Capitol and Presented to the State of New Hampshire by William E. Chandler*. Concord, NH: Republican Press Association, 1892.

Charlton, Edwin A. *New Hampshire as It Is*. Claremont, NH: Tracy & Co., 1856.

Chernow, Ron. *Grant*. New York: Penguin Books, 2017.

Clarke, John B., ed. *Sketches of Successful New Hampshire Men*. Manchester, NH: John B. Clarke, 1882.

Coco, Gregory A. *A Strange and Blighted Land: Gettysburg: The Aftermath of Battle*. Gettysburg: Thomas Publications, 1995.

———. *A Vast Sea of Misery: A History and Guide to the Union and Confederate Field Hospitals at Gettysburg, July 1–November 20, 1863* Gettysburg: Thomas Publications, 1996.

Congressional Record, Containing the Proceeding and Debates of the Forty-Eighth Congress,

First Session. Vol. 15. Washington, DC: GPO, 1884.

Conn, Granville P. *A History of the New Hampshire Surgeons in the War of Rebellion.* Concord: New Hampshire Association of Military Surgeons, Ira Evans, Printer, 1906.

Copp, Col. Eldridge J. *Reminiscences of the War of the Rebellion, 1861–1865.* Nashua NH: Telegraph Publishing Co., 1911.

Cudworth, Warren H. *History of the First Regiment (Massachusetts Infantry).* Boston: Walker, Fuller & Co., 1866.

Davis, William C. *Battle at Bull Run: A History of the First Campaign of the Civil War.* Baton Rouge: Louisiana State Univ. Press, 1977.

Day, D. L. *My Diary of Rambles with the 25th Mass. Infantry with Burnside's Coast Division; 18th Corps and the Army of the James.* Milford, MA: King and Billings Printers, Gazette Office, 1884.

Dorwart, Bonnie Brice, MD. *Death Is in the Breeze: Disease during the American Civil War.* Fredericksburg, MD: The National Museum of Civil War Medicine, Inc, 2009.

Douglass, Frederick. *The Life and Times of Frederick Douglass: From 1817–1882, Written by Himself; with an Introduction by the Right Hon. John Bright.* London: Christian Age Office, 1892. First published 1882.

Dubbs, Carol Kettenburg. *Defend This Old Town: Williamsburg during the Civil War.* Baton Rouge: Louisiana State Univ. Press, 2002.

Eldridge, Daniel. *The Third New Hampshire and All About It.* Boston: Press of E. B. Stillings & Co., 1893.

Encyclopedia of Massachusetts: Biographical-Genealogical. Chicago: The American Historical Society, 1910.

Fatout, Paul, ed. *Letters of a Civil War Surgeon.* West Lafayette, IN: Purdue Univ. Press, 1996.

Fox, William F. *Regimental Losses in the American Civil War, 1861–1865: A Treatise on the Extent and Nature of the Mortuary Losses in the Union Regiments, with Full and Exhaustive Statistics Compiled from the Official Records on File in the State Military Bureaus and at Washington.* Albany, NY: Albany Publishing Co., 1889.

Furgurson, Ernest B. *Not War But Murder: Cold Harbor 1864.* New York: Alfred A. Knopf, 2000.

Guelzo, Allen C. *Fateful Lightning: A New History of the Civil War and Reconstruction.* Oxford: Oxford Univ. Press, 2012.

Haynes, Martin A. *History of the Second Regiment New Hampshire Volunteers: Its Camps, Marches and Battles.* Manchester, NH: Charles F. Livingston, 1865.

———. *A History of the Second Regiment, New Hampshire Volunteer Infantry, in the War of the Rebellion.* Lakeport, NH: Private print of Martin A. Haynes, 1896.

———. *A Minor War History Compiled from a Soldier Boy's Letters to "The Girl I Left Behind Me," 1861–1864.* Lakeport, NH: Private print of Martin A. Haynes, 1916.

———. *Muster Out Roll of the Second New Hampshire in the War of the Rebellion.* Lakeport, NH: Private print of Martin A. Haynes, 1917.

Head, Natt. *Report of the Adjutant-General of the State of New Hampshire for the Year Ending June 1, 1866.* 2 vols. Concord, NH: George E. Jenks, State Printer, 1866.

Hennessy, John J. *Historical Report on the Troop Movements at the Second Battle of Manassas, August 28 through August 30, 1862.* Denver: US Dept. of the Interior, National Park Service, Denver Service Center, Northeast Team, 1985.

————. *Return to Bull Run: The Campaign and Battle of Second Manassas.* New York: Simon & Schuster, 1993.

Hess, Earl J. *Liberty, Virtue and Progress: Northerners and Their War for the Union.* New York: Fordham Univ. Press, 1997.

Holland, Mary A. Gardner. *Our Army Nurses: Interesting Sketches, Addresses, and Photographs of Nearly One Hundred of the Noble Women Who Served in Hospitals and on Battlefields during Our Civil War.* Boston: B. Williams & Co, 1895.

Hutchinson, Gustavas B. *A Narrative of the Formation and Services of the Eleventh Massachusetts Volunteers, from April 15, 1861, to July 14, 1865.* Boston: A. Mudge & Sons, 1893.

Jewett, Jeremiah Peabody. *History of Barnstead from Its First Settlement in 1727 to 1872.* Lowell, MA: Marden & Rowell (Printers), 1872.

Kauffman, Michael W. *American Brutus: John Wilkes Booth and the Lincoln Conspiracies.* New York: Random House, 2004.

Kent, Charles N. *History of the Seventeenth New Hampshire Volunteer Infantry, 1862–1863.* Concord, NH: Rumford Press, 1898.

Lankford, Nelson. *Richmond Burning: The Last Days of the Confederate Capital.* New York: Penguin Books, 2002.

Laws of the State of New Hampshire, Passed January Session, 1901. Manchester: Arthur E. Clarke, Public Printer, 1901.

Laws of the State of New Hampshire, Passed June Session, 1867. Manchester: John B. Clarke, State Printer, 1867.

Leach, A. L., et al. *The Travers Region, Historical and Descriptive, with Illustrations and Scenery and Biographical Sketches of Some of Its Prominent Men and Pioneers.* Chicago: H. R. Page & Co., 1884.

Letterman, Jonathan, MD. *Medical Recollections of the Army of the Potomac.* New York: S. Appleton and Co., 1866.

Little, Henry F. W. *The Seventh Regiment New Hampshire Volunteers in the War of the Rebellion.* Concord, NH: Seventh New Hampshire Veteran Association, I. C. Evans, Printer, 1896.

Long, Richard. *Dearest Carrie: The Civil War Romance of a Myerstown Girl and a New Hampshire Boy.* Morgantown, PA: Mastoff Press, 2004.

Lyford, James O., ed. *History of Concord, New Hampshire, from the Original Grant in Seventeen Hundred and Twenty-Five to the Opening of the Twentieth Century.* 2 vols. Concord, NH: Rumford Press, 1903.

McFarland, Henry. *Sixty Years in Concord and Elsewhere: Personal Recollections of Henry McFarland.* Concord, NH: Rumford Press, 1899.

McPherson, James M. *Battle Cry of Freedom: The Civil War Era.* Oxford: Oxford Univ. Press, 1988.

Merrill, R. Irving. *Merrill & Son's Concord City Directory for 1860–61, and Every Kind of Desirable Information for Citizens and Strangers.* Concord, NH: Rufus Merrill & Son, 1860.

Millard, Candice. *Destiny of the Republic: A Tale of Madness, Medicine and the Murder of a President*. New York: Knopf Doubleday, 2012.

Mitchell, Reid. *The Vacant Chair: The Northern Soldier Leaves Home*. New York: Oxford Univ. Press, 1993.

Morrison, Leonard Allison. *The History of Windham in New Hampshire (Rockingham County), 1719–1883*. Boston: Couples, Upham, & Co., 1883.

Musgrove, Richard W. *Autobiography of Richard W. Musgrove*. Bristol, NH: Mary D. Musgrove, 1921.

The National Cyclopedia of American Biography. Vol. 5. New York: James T. White and Co., 1897.

Nevins, Allan, ed. *A Diary of Battle: The Personal Journals of Charles S. Wainwright, 1861–1865*. New York: Harcourt, Brace & World Inc., 1962.

Norton, John Foote. *The History of Fitzwilliam, New Hampshire, from 1752–1887*. New York: Burr Printing House, 1888.

Oates, Stephen B. *A Woman of Valor: Clara Barton in the Civil War*. New York: Free Press, 1994.

Obituary Record of Graduates of Amherst College for the Academic Year Ending July 9, 1874. Amherst, MA: Henry M. McCloud, Printer, 1874.

Official Register of the United States, Containing a List of Officers and Employees in the Civil, Military, and Naval Service on the 30th of June, 1879. Vol. 1. Compiled and printed under the direction of the Office of the Secretary of the Interior. Washington, DC: GPO, 1879.

Old and New. January to June 1872. Vol. 5. Boston: Roberts Brothers, 1872.

Page, Elwin L. *Abraham Lincoln in New Hampshire*. Introduced and updated by Mike Pride. Concord, NH: Monitor Publishing Co., 2009. First published 1929.

Pride, Mike. *Our War: Days and Events in the Fight for the Union*. Concord, NH: Monitor Publishing Co., 2012.

Pride, Mike, and Mark Travis. *My Brave Boys: To War with Colonel Cross and the Fifth New Hampshire*. Hanover, NH: Univ. Press of New England, 2001.

Reports of Committees of the United States Senate: First Session of the Forty-Eighth Congress, 1883–'84. Washington, DC: GPO, 1884.

Robinson, H. L. *History of Pittsfield in the Great Rebellion*. Pittsfield, NH: H. L. Robinson, 1893.

Schell, Mary L., ed. *The Love Life of Brig. Gen. Henry M. Naglee, Consisting of a Correspondence of Love, War, and Politics*. New York: Hilton & Co., 1867.

Schultz, Jane E. *Women at the Front: Hospital Workers in Civil War America*. Chapel Hill: Univ. of North Carolina Press, 2004.

Sears, Stephen W. *The Civil War Papers of George B McClellan: Selected Papers, 1860–65*. New York: DaCapo Press, 1992.

———. *Lincoln's Lieutenants: The High Command of the Army of the Potomac*. Boston: Houghton Mifflin Harcourt, 2017.

Skelly, Daniel A. *A Boy's Experiences during the Battle of Gettysburg*. N.p.: Printed privately, 1932.

Smith, Adelaide W. *Reminiscences of an Army Nurse during the Civil War.* New York: Greaves Publishing Co., 1911.

Speer, Lonnie R. *Portals of Hell: Military Prisons of the Civil War.* Mechanicsburg, PA: Stackpole Books, 1997.

Sprague, John T. *The Origin, Progress, and Conclusion of the Florida War, 1848.* Reprint, Gainesville: Univ. of Florida Press, 1964.

Stearns, Amanda Akin. *The Lady Nurse of Ward E.* New York: The Baker and Taylor Co., 1909.

United States Christian Commission of the Army and Navy for the Year 1865. Fourth annual report. Philadelphia: US Christian Commission, Mar. 1866.

United States Christian Commission: Second Report of Maryland. Baltimore: Sherwood & Co., 1863.

US State Department. *The Statutes at Large of the United States of America from December, 1883, to March, 1885.* Vol. 33, 48th session of Congress. Washington, DC: GPO, 1885.

US Surgeon General's Office. *The Medical and Surgical History of the War of the Rebellion.* 2 vols., 6 parts. Washington, DC: Government Printing Office, 1870–88.

Varon, Elizabeth R. *Armies of Deliverance: A New History of the Civil War.* New York: Oxford Univ. Press, 2019.

Waite, Major Otis F. R. *A Claremont War History: April, 1861, to April, 1865.* Concord, NH: McFarland & Jenks, Printers, 1868.

———. *New Hampshire in the Great Rebellion.* Claremont, NH: Tracy, Chase & Company, 1870.

Watson, David. *The Concord City Directory, Containing the Names, Residences and Business of the Residents in the Compact Part of the City, with a Map of the City Engraved Expressly for This Work.* Concord, NH: Steam Press of McFarland and Jenks, 1864.

Whitehorne, Joseph W. S. *The Battle of Manassas.* Washington, DC: Center of Military History, United States Army, 1990.

Yacovone, Donald, ed. *A Voice of Thunder: A Black Soldier's Civil War.* Urbana: Univ. of Illinois Press, 1998.

ARTICLES, THESES, AND REPORTS

Abbott, Frances M. "Harriet Dame: Interesting Sketch of the Veteran Army Nurse," *People and Patriot* (Concord, NH), Sept. 20, 1892.

Adams, John W. "My Experience as Army Chaplain (1863–1865)." Postwar speech. http://www.westbrookhistoricalsociety.org/diaries/CHAPLAIN%20JOHN%20W%20Adams.pdf.

Beckham, Stephen Dow. "Lonely Outpost: The Army's Fort Umpqua." *Oregon Historical Quarterly* 70, no. 3 (Sept. 1969): 233–57.

Boone, Nancy E., and Michael Sherman. "Designed to Cure: Civil War Hospitals in Vermont." *Vermont History* 69 (Winter/Spring 2001): 173–200.

Brown, Janice. *Cow Hampshire: New Hampshire's History Blog.* https://www.cowhampshire blog.com/.

Coco, Gregory A. "A Laborious and Vexatious Task," Gettysburg Seminar Papers. http://npshistory.com/series/symposia/gettysburg_seminars/6/essay9.htm#55.

Foster, Joseph H. "A Visit to the Battlefield." Introduced and edited by Michael J. Birkner and Richard E. Winslow. *Adams County (PA) History* 11, no. 5 (2005): 35–44.

Godfrey, Mary Olive. "Strafford's First City—Dover by the Cocheco," *Granite Monthly* 28, no. 4 (Apr. 1900): 193–242.

Hodgman, Burns P. "St. Paul's Episcopal Church: One Hundred Fiftieth Anniversary Observed—Historical Address." *Granite Monthly* 49, no. 1 (Jan. 1917).

Holden, Rogers, ed. "A Civil War Chaplain's Story: John Wesley Adams 2nd N. H. Volunteers, 1863–1865" (memoir in pamphlet). Wells, ME: Book Barn Press, 1995.

"Journal of the Proceedings of the Forty-Eighth Convention of the Protestant Episcopal Church." Concord, NH: Press of Asa McFarland, 1848.

"Journal of the Proceedings of the Forty-Seventh Convention of the Protestant Episcopal Church." Manchester, NH: Manchester American Office, 1847.

"Journal of the Proceedings of the Thirty-Fourth Annual Encampment of the Department of New Hampshire, Grand Army of the Republic." Concord, NH: Printed for the Department, 1901.

Lincoln Financial Corporation. "The Assassination of Abraham Lincoln (Physicians): Excerpts from Newspapers and Other Sources." Lincoln Financial Corp., undated. https://archive.org/details/assassinationofaphylinc/page/n1/mode/2up?q=abbott

Malesky, Robert. "The Enslaved Families Who Worked This Land." *Bygone Brookland: Tales from a Storied DC Neighborhood* blog. http://bygonebrookland.com/local-lore-the-enslaved.html.

———. "The Sculptor and the Slave." *Bygone Brookland: Tales from a Storied DC Neighborhood* blog. ,http://bygonebrookland.com/local-lore-the-sculptor-and.html.

Marzoli, Nathan A. "'Their Loss Was Necessarily Severe': The 12th New Hampshire at Chancellorsville." *Army History* no. 101 (Fall 2016): 6–29.

McConnell, Edward N. "A Brief History of Company A 139th Regiment, Pennsylvania Volunteers." *Western Pennsylvania History Magazine* 44, no. 4 (Oct. 1972): 307–18.

Metheny, Hannah. "'For a Woman': The Fight for Pensions for Civil War Army Nurses." Undergraduate honors thesis, College of William and Mary (Scholar Commons), June 2013.

National Park Service. "The Life of a Civil War Soldier" (teachers' guide). Gettysburg National Military Park, 2008. https://www.nps.gov/gett/learn/education/classrooms/upload/Teacher-s-Guide-for-Trunks-3-2013-508.pdf.

"New Hampshire Veterans Association History." http://weirsbeach.com/reasons-to-visit/history/veterans/nh-va-history/.

Orr, Timothy J. "On Such Slender Threads Does the Fate of Nations Depend: The Second United States Sharpshooters Defend the Union Left." Papers of the Gettysburg National Military Park Seminar, Apr. 8–9, 2006, Gettysburg, PA (published 2008), 121–22, 139. http://npshistory.com/series/symposia/gettysburg_seminars/11/essay5.pdf.

Ostendorf, Lloyd. "New Mary Todd Lincoln Photograph: A Tour of the White Mountains in Summer, 1863." *Illinois Historical Journal* 83, no. 2 (Summer 1990): 109–12.

Papaioannou, Helena, and Daniel E. Stowell. "Dr. Charles A. Leale's Report on the Assassination of Abraham Lincoln." *Journal of the Abraham Lincoln Association* 24, no. 1 (Winter 2013): 40–53.

Parker, Moses Greeley, MD. "Reminiscences of Personal Interviews with Lincoln." *Contributions of the Lowell Historical Society*, 1:382–87. Lowell, MA: Butterfield Printing Co., 1913.

Rafuse, Ethan S. "'The Spirit Which You Have Aided to Infuse': A. Lincoln, Little Mac, Fighting Joe, and the Question of Accountability in Union Command Relations," *Journal of the Abraham Lincoln Association* 38, no. 2 (Summer 2017), https://quod. lib.umich.edu/cgi/p/pod/dod-idx/spirit-which-you-have-aided-to-infuse-a-lincoln-little-mac.pdf?c=jala;idno=2629860.0038.203;format=pdf.

Rose, Savannah. "Killed at Gettysburg: Edmund Dascomb, 2d N.H." https://killedatgettysburg.org/edmund-dascomb-2nd-new-hampshire/.

Smith, Karlton D. "'We Drop a Comrade's Tear': Colonel Edward Lyon Bailey and the Second New Hampshire Infantry at Gettysburg." In *Papers of the Ninth Annual Gettysburg National Military Park Seminar*, Apr. 6–7, 2002, Gettysburg, PA, 2002, 101–21.

Snyder, Anna. "The Curse of Ford's Theatre?" https://www.fords.org/blog/post/stories-from-the-archives-the-curse-of-ford-s-theatre/.

"The Thirty-Seventh Annual Report of the American Home Missionary Society." New York: John A. Gray & Green, Printers, 1863.

Union School District. *Annual Reports of the Schools in the City of Concord*. Concord, NH: Frank J. Batchelder, 1886.

Vance, Katelynn Ruth. "'They Set Themselves to Undermine the Whole Thing': Gender and Authority in the Work of Union Female Nurses." Master's thesis, Univ. of New Hampshire, Durham, Spring 2017. https://scholars.unh.edu/cgi/viewcontent.cgi?article=1923&context=thesis.

Ward, Allie. "Burying the Dead." *Gettysburg Compiler*, Aug. 12, 2012. https://gettysburg-compiler.org/2012/08/02/burying-the-dead-by-allie-ward-54463/#more-8.

Winther, Oscar Osburn. "The Soldier Vote in the Election of 1864" *New York History* 25, no. 4 (Oct. 1944): 440–58.

Woods, Marianne Berger. "C. L. Ransom in Cleveland: A Woman at Work." https://academic.csuohio.edu/tah/regional_arts/Cleveland_as_a_Center/p19clransom.pdf.

NEWSPAPERS

Alexandria (VA) Gazette
Arizona Republican
Boston Globe
Boston Journal

Boston Post
Boston Sunday Globe
Chelsea (MA) Telegraph & Pioneer
Chicago Tribune
Columbian and Democrat (Bloomsburg, PA)
Concord (NH) Daily Monitor
Concord Evening Monitor
Coos Republican (Lancaster, NH)
Daily American (Manchester, NH)
Daily Journal (Evansville, IN)
Dover (NH) Gazette
Evening Star (Washington, DC)
Evening Telegraph (Philadelphia)
Farmer's Cabinet (Amherst, NH)
Independent Democrat (Concord, NH)
Londonderry (VT) Sifter
Manchester (NH) Daily Mirror
National Tribune (Washington, DC)
New Hampshire Patriot (Concord)
New Hampshire People and Patriot (Concord)
New Hampshire Sentinel (Keene)
New Hampshire Statesman (Concord)
New York Herald
New York Sun
Perrysburg (OH) Journal
Philadelphia Age
Portsmouth (NH) Gazette
Public Ledger (Philadelphia)
Springfield (MA) Republican
Sunday Herald (Boston)
Sunday Herald (Washington, DC)
Washington Bee
Washington Critic
Washington Post
Washington Times
Waterbury (CT) Democrat
Western Veteran (Topeka, KS)

Index